P9-AOS-678

COMMERCIAL RELATIONS BETWEEN RUSSIA AND EUROPE 1400 to 1800

INDIANA UNIVERSITY PUBLICATIONS
RUSSIAN AND EAST EUROPEAN SERIES
Volume 33

COMMERCIAL RELATIONS BETWEEN RUSSIA AND EUROPE 1400 to 1800

Collected Essays

by

WALTHER KIRCHNER

Published by

INDIANA UNIVERSITY • BLOOMINGTON

Russian and East European Series
Russian and East European Institute
Indiana University
Volume 33

All orders should be addressed to the
Indiana University Press
10th and Morton Streets
Bloomington, Indiana

Library of Congress Catalog Card Number: 66-64236
Printed in the United States of America

PREFACE

The author has had two major reasons for submitting anew, in book form and with a comprehensive introduction, the following essays previously published in a great variety of historical journals in three different languages. More than half of these journals are used chiefly by specialists in a given field, yet, as the theme indicates, the articles address themselves to a very broad group of historians—to European, Russian, and economic historians alike—who may not be able to peruse regularly so varied a group of periodicals. It may therefore be useful to make the essays more easily accessible.

With the current fashionable emphasis on ideologies, parties, social movements and theories, the call for "concrete" studies should not go unheard. The economic data of international relations must be integrated into our mode of thinking and become part of the basis for our judgment of political, social, military, and even ecclesiastical history. They must be made to form an indispensible factor in international relations, in which the study of ideology, diplomacy and law does not suffice as a basis. Without them we are pursuing chimeras. We should not leave the study of the economic data in history, especially as far as Russian-Western relations are concerned, to those who start from a preconceived model or frame of reference.

A difficult decision has been whether or not to revise the articles in the light of the research of a number of eminent scholars who have published their findings since the appearance of my articles. The results of their research, while contributing essential facts and new interpretations, have, however, not necessitated a revision of the papers here presented. Nevertheless, something of a compromise has been made insofar as a few additions have been made in the notes for the purpose of calling attention to interesting new books on some of the subjects and discussing critical, new, or challenging interpretations. Since my book addresses itself as much to historians specializing in European and American history as to specialists in the Russian field, care has been taken to cite whenever possible works in Western languages. Sources and monographs available exclusively in Russian have been referred to only when unavoidable. In this connection recent Russian publications have been given preference.

As to the translation of those articles here published which originally were written in German or French, the translation, made by the author himself, has been rendered freely for the sake of clarity of style and correctness of meaning.

The author wishes to thank the editors of the various journals (listed on the first page of each chapter) for permitting the reprinting, or translation into English, of his original articles. He is greatly obliged to Professor Robert W. Campbell, Director of the Russian and East European Institute of Indiana University, for the inclusion of his book in the Institute's series; he appreciates the editorial and bibliographical assistance given by Mrs. Lou Ann Brower; and he would like to express his particular gratitude to Professor Fritz T. Epstein, whose care and scholarship have been most helpful in every way.

It would have been a pleasure to thank those who have helped the author in his studies during the twenty years since the appearance of the first of the articles here reprinted. The Institute for Advanced Study in Princeton, where I was a member in 1955 and 1956, and the American Philosophical Society, which gave me a grant in 1956, should be named in particular. But alas, there are too many—colleagues, librarians, politicians, administrators, assistants, and others—to whom I owe a large debt of gratitude for aid and advice—sometimes given knowingly, sometimes inadvertently, sometimes personally and sometimes through the printed word and in ever so many ways. A grateful remembrance of all of them as a sign of my thankfulness I can and do offer.

TABLE OF CONTENTS

The following articles have been translated from German or French. The original titles were the following:

I: "Über den russischen Aussenhandel zu Beginn der Neuzeit"

III: "Die Bedeutung Narwas im 16. Jahrhundert; ein Beitrag zum Studium der Beziehungen zwischen Russland und Europa"

V: "Le commencement des relations économiques entre la France et la Russie (1550-1650)"

VII: "Relations économiques entre la France et la Russie au 18e siècle"

Iceland
Trondjhem
Bergen
Åbo
Birka
Stockholm
Reval
Ösel
Gothland
Riga
Mitau
Helsingör
Copenhagen
Belt
Sound
Schleswig
Cork
Hull
Amsterdam
The Hague
Rostock
Danzig
Königsberg
Hamburg
Lübeck
Stettin
London
Utrecht
Vistula
Bruges
Goslar
Berlin
Calais
Antwerp
Warsaw
Leipzig
Dieppe
Cologne
Jena
Breslau
Rouen
Marburg
Sedan
Mainz
Frankfurt
Paris
Verdun
Prague
Cracow
Nuremberg
Orleans
Rhine
Ratisbon
Nantes
Augsburg
La Rochelle
Basel
Zurich
Vienna
Bern
Aarau
Geneva
Bordeaux
Lyon
Venice
Genoa
Danube
Montpellier
Marseille
Florence
Livorno
Lisbon
Rome
Cadiz
0
200
400
600
MILES

Vardo
Pechenga
White Sea
Archangel
St. Nicholas
Dvina
Perm
Ekaterinburg
Viborg
Volkhov
Cronstadt
Narva
Novgorod
Dorp
Pskov
Nizhni-Novgorod
Kazan
Suzdal
Moscow
Orenburg
Dünaburg
Polotsk
Vitebsk
Düna
Smolensk
Saratov
Volga
Don
Dnieper
Astrakhan
Tana
Ochakov
Odessa
Cherson
Chabag
Crimea
Feodosia
(Caffa)
Tiflis
Black Sea
Byzantium
Pera

COMMERCIAL RELATIONS BETWEEN RUSSIA AND EUROPE 1400 to 1800

Introduction

SOME REMARKS ON THE COURSE OF RUSSIAN-WESTERN TRADE RELATIONS

The beginnings of Russian-Western commercial relations came late and their development was slow.[1] Sources are scarce, and recent historians have been inclined to draw too far-reaching conclusions from the few documents we possess and to exaggerate the importance of early Russian-Western trade. Geographical and economic data of the ninth and tenth centuries A. D. indicate that commercial connections must have been very limited. Distance explains much of their initial weakness. Swamps and forests constituted serious obstacles, and warring tribes imperiled the traveling merchant. Transportation was difficult even on the main trade artery—that which led from Kiev via Prague or the Danube to Ratisbon, Mainz, Verdun and other Western centers. Few, and only small rivers run in an east-westwardly direction, and the Danube itself turns south long before reaching Kievan territory.

Of no less importance was the fact that productive capacities in Kievan Rus, as in Frankish lands, were limited. Both sides possessed a measure of technical proficiency, and needs for a large-scale exchange of manufactured goods did not exist. Neither side depended upon what the other had to offer. The East furnished some furs, wax, honey, flax, silver utensils; the West, some spices, dyes, cloth, wine, metals, and church vessels. Luxury items, slaves, and weapons seem to have played the major role. The luxury items came, of course, largely from the Orient and touched both Russia and the Western world chiefly in transit, destined as they often were by the Eastern Islamic parts of the world for the Mohammedan possessions in Spain and northern Africa. Slaves likewise constituted an Eastern export, while weapons traveled chiefly in an opposite direction. All goods traded on the overland route had to be of substantial value and comparatively easy to transport in order to warrant the expenses of the long trip. Much of the commerce was in the hands of Arabic and Jewish rather than Slavic or Frankish merchants.

The sea constituted at the time a secondary link. Kiev was situated far from either the Black or the Baltic Sea, and river transportation with its needs for portages was strenuous and expensive. To be sure, some trade occurred on the three available sea lanes, the Arctic, the Baltic, and the Black Sea routes. They connected, on the one side, the northern provinces of Kievan Rus and the not yet Christianized lands of northern Europe, and, on the other, the southern provinces and Byzantium with its possessions. Though these connections were to become important later, from the ninth through the eleventh centuries they constituted but a weak link with what has been here termed "the West." For the Arctic route around the North Cape served only local needs. The Baltic route connected Novgorod in the east with Birka in the center and with Schleswig (Hedeby) in the west. From Hedeby, eastern goods for Western Europe were shipped across Holstein and were reloaded on boats upon reaching the North Sea. However, the types of ships which then existed were not adequate for the transport of substantial quantities of goods over dangerous sea routes. Only after a new type of ship, the cog, had been fully developed between 1000 and 1200 could the merchants manage a regular, complete navigation from the North Sea through Skagerrak, Kattegat and the Sound to the Baltic Sea. Only then could they institute those close ties between Russia and the West which marked the Late Middle Ages.

As to the Black Sea-Mediterranean route, Byzantium controlled the connecting Straits of the Bosporus and Dardanelles. Though we have some news about occasional traders from the Rus in southern Europe, in Italy or Spain, contacts with the West by this route were extremely rare. Meetings did occur in Constantinople or Pera; nevertheless, the Byzantine barrier remained substantially effective until the thirteenth century.

The actual extent of trade in those times is unknown. Sources do not suffice for even an approximate estimate. Historians have tried to use as a guide the reports about dues levied at various points on the main Danube route. But these records give little information, and the scanty surviving ones, being unclear, have invited too much speculation. Unfortunately, they do not even make it possible for us to distinguish, without doubt, between that part of the trade which connected the Frankish or Holy Roman Empire with Western Slavs and Magyars and that which served points farther east—and especially Kievan Rus.[2]

Historians have tended to draw too sweeping conclusions also from two or three monetary transactions which were carried out between the cloister of St. Emmeran in Ratisbon and Kiev. They have seen in them signs of a "mature" trade. But since the transactions were connected with marriage settlements and church activities, their value as a guide for trade activities should not be overestimated.[3] To be sure, considerable hoards of money of Frisian, Ottonian, Anglo-Saxon and other Western origin have been unearthed in Russia. They date chiefly from the period 1000 to 1090. But some authorities have come to question, at least to a certain extent, speculations and conclusions as to type and scope of trade transactions on the basis of finds of coins. They argue that some hoards represent war booty; that others indicate the love of treasure or ornament rather than the fact of commercial activity; and that the very fact of the burying of the coins demonstrates that they did not serve the assumed purpose of means of payment, which would promote trade. Unless it can reliably be established, so these critics insist, that they were buried only after having fulfilled their original purpose for a substantial space of time, no final conclusions should be drawn from them. Yet, when taken in conjunction with other archaeological and documentary hints which we possess, the presence and spread of as many Western coins as have been found in Russia can be accepted as a fair indicator of commercial relations.[4]

From the available evidence at our disposal we can only deduce that trade between Kievan Rus and the West existed, but that it was weak. Commercial contacts and influences were limited. It is not correct to speak, as has been done, of very "lively" connections comparable to those existing between Western kingdoms.

With the decline of Kiev in the twelfth century and the rise of the new "Russia" in the upper Volga region, distances to the West increase and the scene shifts. Overland connections become more complicated and are gradually replaced by overseas connections. With this change, the way was paved for a sizable increase of commercial contacts. They were promoted by the economic development of the West. Urbanization proceeded, new production centers arose, the entire economy was invigorated. Needs for exports and imports grew, and the Russia of Smolensk, Pskov, Novgorod, and Suzdal-Moscow offered in both respects numerous opportunities. The fact that from 1240 on most of the country was under Tartar domination played a minor role in this development. Soviet historians, as well as some of the earlier Russian scholars and their Western followers, have inclined to accentuate the impact of the so-called Tartar "yoke." Their investigations are of great value in assessing the actual role of the Tartars. But Tartar domination was of little importance as far as commercial connections with the West were concerned. Before the Tartars ever came these connections had weakened, owing chiefly to the removal of the Russian center from Kiev to the Volga area in the twelfth century. It is then that a new age in Russian-Western relations had dawned. The Tartar occupation, on the other hand, had little effect on them. In the thirteenth and following centuries, just when the Tartars ruled in Russia, the curve of Russian-Western trade climbs steadily.

Expansion of trade took place both in the Baltic and in the Black Sea areas. This expansion was but one aspect of a much wider, much more comprehensive evolution of Western Civilization and cannot be separated from other great movements of the age. We witness in the twelfth and thirteenth centuries the undertakings of the Church Militant, its crusades and missions; the new economic ventures of the Western entrepreneur; the acquisition of cultivable land by peasants, feudal lords, and Church in thinly populated Eastern regions; and we see also the energy engendered and displayed by medieval Europe at its height in the areas of science, letters, and arts. All these trends combined to strengthen the interest of the West in the East and to bring forth, together with other spiritual and material accomplishments, the movement later to be labelled the "Urge to the East." Trade relations between Russia and the West benefited from it.

In the Black Sea region trade relations were invigorated by the Western conquest of Constantinople in 1204 during the Fourth Crusade. The door was thereby opened for Genoese and Venetian merchants to sail also into the Black Sea and establish factories in Kaffa and Tana. Their few overland connections through Danubian lands fell more and more into disuse, serving but little after the West-Russian principalities, such as Galicia and Chernigov, had seceded or been incorporated into the Hungarian, Lithuanian or Polish commonwealth. But Kaffa and Tana flourished, and the Tartar overlords actually promoted rather than hindered the connections which merchants from Moscow built up with the Italians there.[5]

In the Baltic area the entire region comprising the Baltic and North Seas, from Novgorod, Riga, Åbo, and Danzig to Lübeck, Bruges, London, and Bergen came to form a trading unit. Here the Hanseatic League served as pathmaker. The importance of the League for Russian-Western trade overshadowed by far that of the Italian merchants. Soviet historians overstate the case when they present the role of Moscow and its commercial interests in trade with the West via the Black Sea as comparable with the role of Novgorod with its Hanseatic links.[6] The Italian merchants who came to the Black Sea ports were interested primarily in trade with the Tartars; and if in the course of the fourteenth century some of them travelled up the Don or Volga and through the steppes to Moscow, or if Russian merchants visited Tana and Kaffa, the sources do not prove that large-scale business on the order of that of the Hanseats in Novgorod could be conducted by them.

A number of special factors which reflect on the path of the Russian-Western trade relations in the most important Baltic region stand out during these three centuries (coinciding approximately with the time of Tartar rule in Eastern Europe). First, the age is characterized by the almost monopolistic position which the Hanseatic merchants held. By way of Lübeck and Bruges, their commercial activities linked up also with those of southern Europe. Only Sweden with her grandduchy of Finland and the various countries bordering on Russia contributed notable additional links between Russia and the West. Late in the fourteenth, or early in the fifteenth century the Dutch began to play a role. But even smuggling, which was extensive, was largely carried on—except for the frontier populations in Karelia or Livonia and the surreptitious traders among the coastal inhabitants on the Baltic littoral—by the Hanseats themselves. It was Hanseats who traveled into the interior of Russia to Polotsk, Smolensk, Moscow and as far as Nishni Novgorod. Wherever possible they interposed themselves as intermediaries, directing traffic via Lübeck. They extended their hold on East-West trade by regulating, with the help of their fleet, the flow of goods; they instituted boycotts or promoted free trade.[7] Sometimes they supported the policies of the popes, who tried to exercise an influence on the Russian Church through economic pressure, and occasionally they cooperated with the Swedes.[8] As time went on the two Hanseatic cities of Riga and Reval, much to the dismay of other Hanseats, began to interpose themselves as special links between East and West and sought to enforce the rule that all trade "von Gast zu Gast" be prohibited.

A second factor of special importance was the lack of an active foreign-carrying trade on the side of the Russians.[9] To be sure, we occasionally hear of a Russian ship visiting a foreign port, and in most trade agreements reciprocity was insisted upon by the Russians. But though they reserved the right to ventures abroad, including the right to establish factories or staple places, the Russian merchants made little use of it. Their goods traveled almost entirely in Hanseatic bottoms and seldom for Russian account. Essentially, they were satisfied with maintaining settlements in various cities in border lands where they could meet foreign merchants, as in Riga, Reval, Dorpat, or even Åbo. Otherwise, they let the Western overseas trader come to Novgorod, or also to Polotsk, Smolensk and a few other towns of their own where they could, under agreements carefully worked out, exercise a measure of control over him. Not commercial necessity but some kind of political shrewdness seems to have made them insist on the right to reciprocity. At least this right affirmed the principle of equality. Moreover, it could possibly serve at some appropriate future moment as a bartering point. Thus the active trade with all its social, political and cultural implications remained in the hands of the West as represented chiefly by the Hanseatic merchants. No Russian navy and merchant marine was developed; no establishment of consequence was founded abroad. (See Chapter I.)

Third, contrary to sometimes prevailing views, the exchange of goods between Russia and the West did not mean an exchange of the raw materials of the East against the manufactured goods of the West. Both sides provided mainly natural products—the West: salt, herring, wine, metals, horses, and grains; the East: furs, skins, honey, flax, hemp, and wax. The chief manufactured goods were, on the Eastern side, leather and some Oriental luxury articles; on the Western, cloth from Flanders, England and Germany. The cloth trade was of great and steadily increasing significance. Some silver was shipped too. The importers on both sides re-exported a considerable part of the goods they bought.

Fourth, Russia was not "colonially exploited," as has some time been assumed. Investigations of recent years on the basis of a few surviving fourteenth century account books indicate that prices, considering costs of transportation, did not differ fundamentally in Novgorod from those of Bruges. The trade partners were essentially equal in standing and in their level of commercial maturity.[10] Credit transactions occurred regularly, even though they were, as a rule, officially prohibited to the members of the Hanseatic League. An unequal barter system such as we connect with the concept of colonial exploitation was not practiced.

Lastly, even in the age of the flourishing of Russian-Western trade in Hanseatic times, the Western merchants were not at home in their Russian surroundings. An infinite number of difficulties beset them in their dealings with Russian traders, and, as will be shown in Chapter XII, this situation has persisted down into the most recent past.

If we consider the Tartar period (1240-1480) as a whole,

we find that commercial relations between Russia and the West, although sometimes disturbed by wars, boycotts, legal strife and ill will, were in general peaceful and very extensive. They were carried on in a way that over centuries turned out to be satisfactory and fruitful for both sides. Seldom overshadowed by politics, they generally went on regardless of political and military strife. The stability of the borders which we witness through centuries greatly promoted stability of trade relations. By 1240 Western Civilization had essentially made its farthest eastward advance. The West was not to get beyond the borders then established, nor did the Russians penetrate westward.

The situation began to change in the second half of the fifteenth century. Static ways made room for dynamic developments. The general peace which, notwithstanding local difficulties, had prevailed was broken. An aggressive expansionist policy of the Muscovite state began, coinciding with a similar movement of West European nations (whose main force was, however, no longer directed at eastern lands but at western seaways). Novgorod fell to Moscow between 1472 and 1494; it ceased to exist as the great trading center of East-West commerce. Livonia was invaded by Muscovite armies at the turn of the century and the old, mutually advantageous connections in Riga and Reval were interrupted. Politics gained the upper hand where commerce had reigned before.

The sixteenth century confirmed this trend. The Hanse now lost for good the position of dominance which she had held during the Middle Ages, even though she retained an important and, for its members, lucrative place for another century and more. The position of Riga and Reval was shaken. After having succeeded for a time in concentrating in their own hands a major part of the West-East business, the two towns were faced in 1558 with a catastrophic invasion of Livonia by Ivan IV. It led to the collapse of the state of the Livonian Order and soon thereafter to the loss of independence by both Riga and Reval.

They had to accept new masters—Poland and Sweden respectively. In 1570 Novgorod was once more ravaged by the Muscovites, and it never recovered. As a result trade began to seek new paths.

One of the new contacts, important in a special way, was made between Russia and Denmark. In 1493, Ivan III concluded a treaty, which may have failed in its immediate purpose of promoting commerce since Denmark could offer but few of the commodities needed by Russia,[11] but did pave the way for broader Russian trade connections with Western countries. For Russia depended on Denmark because the Danish kings were in control of the Sound, which all traffic from the North Sea to the Baltic and vice versa had to use.[12] Ever since the second part of the fifteenth century they had enforced the levying of dues there. Although the dues were low enough not to impede commerce seriously, a threat to the freedom of Russian-Western trade beyond the Baltic existed. It sufficed to make amicable relations with Denmark a necessity for the Russians.

Another contact—one of far greater portent—was made between Russia and England. In 1553 English seamen reopened for traffic the old Arctic route past the North Cape. The true significance of this event is still often misrepresented.[13] It did not lie, at least during the sixteenth century, in that the Arctic route could substitute for the Baltic artery of that the English could take the place of Hanseats or Dutch. For a long time traffic in the north remained minimal compared to that by way of the Sound and the Baltic. But what the northern passage did achieve was that ships could reach Russia independently of the Baltic powers and that Russians could send freely diplomats, agents and traders to Western countries. This liberated Russia from dependence upon the good will of neighbors. With access to Russia open by way of the White Sea, control in the Baltic area lost much of its sting. No longer was it useful for any port, league of towns or kingdom to exclude others from Baltic harbors or to interfere with their Russian connections. Another passage to Russia was open—even though King Frederick II of Denmark also succeeded at times in collecting dues for this passage, which led through waters lying between his Norwegian kingdom and Iceland.[14] Besides English ships soon Dutch also began to use it, and in the 1570's French ships, too, found their way to the White Sea. (See Chapter V.)

We therewith enter a period of keen Western rivalry in Russian-Western trade. It was welcome to the tsar, who was its main beneficiary. He gladly encouraged German and Dutch, French and other merchants, along with the members of the English Muscovy Company, to visit his realms. He even suffered, or actually promoted, contacts with illegal English competitors of the Muscovy Company, although the Company besieged him to acknowledge its own exclusive rights to all Russian trade.

The possibility of extending Russian-Western trade opportunities to many countries was greatly enhanced by an event that occurred within five years of the opening of the northern route: the conquest of Narva by the Russians. The seizure of the town meant that finally the Russians had also gained a port on the Baltic which gave all nations direct access to the Russian market. To be sure, Narva's development, like that of the Arctic ports, was slow and, moreover, restricted by the inadequacies of its harbor. The town could never take the place of either Riga or Reval. But as with the north, it was future expectations which the merchants connected with its acquisition by Russia rather than reality that counted. And even when Russia lost the town in 1581 to the Swedes, the old monopolistic conditions prevailing formerly in the two large Livonian ports were not re-established. (See Chapter III.)

In the face of the greatly increased communication facilities in the north and the Baltic, the collapse of direct Russian-

Western trade via the Black Sea was not of decisive importance. After the conquest of Constantinopole by the Turks, the Italians were forced to give up their factories in the Crimea and at the mouth of the Don. Not for three centuries could substantial East-West connections by the southern route be rebuilt. The Italians sought to make up for their losses by overland ventures. Like the great upper-German merchant houses from Augsburg and Nuremberg, and like those of Leipzig, so Italian entrepreneurs undertook trips across the Empire and Poland-Lithuania to Moscow. Owing to expenses and political and religious difficulties, the turnover on this route remained, however, very limited.[15]

Simultaneously with the reorientation of trade routes in the middle of the sixteenth century came changes in the types of the commodities traded by East and West. The Europe of the Renaissance, Reformation, and Age of Discovery had needs different from those of earlier times. The secularization of the Western world led to rapid technological advances. As a result, an interest in other than the formerly traded commodities was evoked. Metals came to play a more important role, both for agricultural and for military purposes. Bronze for cannons was imported by Russians in increasing quantity. It became more readily available when, especially in the Netherlands, many church bells were broken during the times of the Anabaptist, inconoclastic storms. Luxury goods found a more ready market in Muscovy, and cloth assumed a yet greater role than ever before. English cloth substituted increasingly for Flemish and Rhenish materials. Interest increased also in colonial goods, which the West had in growing supply. Salt imports, on the other hand, were less needed owing to Russian production, and herring likewise diminished in importance.

The West, too, changed its buying habits. It showed less interest in Russia's foremost export product: furs. The Reformation, both Protestant and Catholic, had brought about a growing puritanical spirit, owing to which the demand for everything that could serve as adornment and ostentatious consumption was reduced. Falling prices for fur evinced the change in the situation, which was clearly demonstrated in 1595 when Tsar Feodor sent large quantities of fur to Prague as a subsidy for the emperor in his wars against the Turks. When they arrived, the market was glutted and little was offered for them by the fur dealers. Russia's wax export was likewise affected by the Reformation—fewer candles were burned after many churches had become Protestant and many cloisters were secularized. Oriental luxury goods and spices failed to make up for the losses; the hopes which Western and Russian merchants had attached to their sale via Russia were not fulfilled. On the other hand, naval stores of all kinds gained in importance. Urgently sought by the seafaring nations bordering on the Atlantic for their new colonial enterprises, they kept the trade balance active for the East. This contributed, in turn, to the fact that active participation by the Russians in shipping and overseas enterprises remained extremely restricted.

Lastly, growing Western imigration into Russia affected East-West trade. Western technicians, busy in many fields, who were disappointed at home were attracted to Russia. Together with native craftsmen they furthered the introduction of new methods, particularly in the fields of armament and construction. As a result, different materials and goods came into demand. Doctors arrived and medicines of various kinds were imported.

The period between the middle of the fifteenth and the beginning of the seventeenth century thus brought considerable changes in the patterns of Russian-Western commerce. Yet it was only with the consolidation of the Russian state after the Times of Trouble (1605-1613) that a new age began. In the preceding period the foundations on which Russian-Western commerce had rested had in essence remained medieval in character. (See Chapter VI.) Only with the middle and second part of the seventeenth century and with the eighteenth can we trace the first elements of a modern economy. Initially, the modern tendencies expressed themselves perhaps more in theory than in practice. Yet we find (1) an adaptation of the goods exchanged between East and West to the needs of an age in transition to industrial life; (2) a transformation of the medieval tradeways into a communication system which, after the first permanent successes of Russia's "urge to the sea" and her acquisition of ports had been achieved, could serve the country more adequately than before; and (3) a growing assimilation of business methods to German, Dutch and English ways resulting from the "Westernization" of Russia.

On the other hand, in a number of respects Russian-Western trade up to the end of the eighteenth century bore traits rather alien to the habits of the West. Finance and methods of payment for trade transactions in Russia did not adjust to the practices of the West; ideas of competition, of laissez faire were repressed; and mercantilistic attitudes prevailed at a time when in the Western world physiocrats and free traders came to dominate. A middle class with an influence corresponding to that of Russia's progressive European trade partners did not emerge.[16]

These developments have to be viewed against the demographic background of vast population increases on all sides. Russia, for instance, appears to have had stagnant population figures from 1500 to 1700. Between 1700 and 1800 they tripled. Europe's populations had begun to grow rapidly even earlier. This background explains many of the forces leading to industrialization and to that transformation of agricultural production to which trade patterns had to adjust.

As to the types of commodities which East and West exchanged, the beginning industrial age, and particularly the fact that it started in the West at a time when Russia was still untouched by it, led to a greater differentiation. While Russia continued to supply chiefly raw materials and agricultural products, the West increasingly exported manufactured goods. In a sense the formerly existing equality was somewhat upset. By 1800, iron, which started to be in urgent demand especially in England, had become Russia's most coveted export item. Russian iron works shipped more of it to Western countries than did Swedish producers, who had long been in front.[17] Furthermore, grain exports increased. Intensive rather than extensive agriculture, especially in newly acquired territories, made this possible for Russia, and an industrializing Western society was eager to import grain. Attempts were also made to sell tobacco, which was planted in the Ukraine. Of the traditional Russian export goods, however, including fur, only naval stores and potash continued to play an important role.

In the meantime the West with its vast colonial resources built up a trade with Russia in a large variety of colonial products. Tea was at first imported into Russia not via Siberia, but through Western intermediaries. Holland and England furnished coffee, and England sent Virginia and Maryland tobacco which was far superior in quality to that of the Ukraine. Spices were likewise shipped in considerable quantities by the colonial powers of the West. Some changes occurred with the sales of weapons. In medieval times Russia had been considered as the schismatic enemy to whom arms should not be delivered; in the course of the eighteenth century, however, Russia became a member of the system of a European balance of power and was therefore sought as an ally by one European nation or another. Consequently, providing her with arms became a normal procedure. Russia bought also in increasing quantities tools, dyes, soap, paper and other industrial products of the West. Wine held its own as a lucrative trade object; cloth, however, diminished its share in the total turnover.

With regard to trade routes, the Baltic retained its lead,[18] but Narva's and also Reval's important roles came to an end and Riga had to take second place to St. Petersburg, which was founded in 1709. Peter the Great made special provisions to channel commerce to his new capital. As early as the middle of the eighteenth century the turnover in St. Petersburg was more than three times that of Riga. The northern route to Archangel flourished throughout the second half of the seventeenth century and remained important for most of the eighteenth. Thereafter, it lost proportionately in value. Instead, foreshadowing an entirely new situation, the reopening of the Black Sea route at the end of the eighteenth century made additional contacts possible. With the incorporation of the Ukraine and the conquest of the Crimea, both Russia and various Western countries could begin to realize their long-held plans for avoiding the uncomfortable Baltic route with its Danish dues, English privileges and Dutch financial controls. They started to use instead the route through the Straits of Constantinopole and across the Black Sea. Spain and France, Italy and Austria seized the opportunity. They extended their contacts with Russia to her newly acquired southern territories, and the English themselves endeavored to gain a share of the Black Sea trade. Results were at first somewhat disappointing for all. Hans Halm has given a vivid picture of conditions in the port of Cherson, chief outlet before the founding of Odessa in 1796.[19] But eventually, the situation improved, and in the nineteenth century the original expectations were fulfilled.

The third issue—that of opening Russia to Western ways and therewith to a broad-scale activity of Western entrepreneurs who established their own offices and agencies there—was probably the most important for Russian-Western trade. Already in previous centuries, especially since the time of Ivan III, a number of Westerners had departed for Russia. Craftsmen, soldiers and merchants had taken up residence in Moscow and other towns in order to serve the tsar. But the merchants who arrived in the eighteenth century were children of another age. They came not to serve the tsar, but as independent entrepreneurs. They created new demands, especially for luxuries, through the needs they had and through the undertakings they started and the example they set for the privileged and wealthy classes of Russia with whom they primarily came in contact. The export trade of both sides benefited from their activities. As early as the seventeenth century, there prospered the Dutch-German-Danish Marselis family which, so ably described by Erik Amburger,[20] offers but one example of the effect which the Western merchant exercised upon the Russian economy after the medieval spirit still permeating Ivan the Terrible's Muscovy had given way and new attitudes came to dominate.

Thousands of other immigrants followed, congregating no longer predominantly in the famous German suburb of Moscow, the _nemetskaia sloboda_, but weaving a broad net of Western enterprises all over Russia. Travels to Russia by businessmen also became a normal function. By 1800, many Western commercial establishments had been founded in Russia, and artisans, notwithstanding bitter opposition of their home governments, had found employment or opened their shops. Various nations maintained consulates in St. Petersburg and some also in Moscow, Riga and elsewhere. Russia had founded consulates abroad, in France and England, Germany and Spain. Russian businessmen, too, went abroad, even though their ventures were not very successful. They often traveled on foreign ships, and when they sailed on their own they found Dutch and Spaniards, English and French doing their utmost, behind a screen of friendliness, to frustrate them in their enterprises.

The various aforementioned factors, indicating a measure of modernization, reacted favorably on Russian-Western commerce. To them must be opposed a number of negative factors. First of all, in matters of finance, Russian conditions showed little advance over preceding centuries. While trade accounts among Dutch, English, Swedes and Germans were increasingly settled by bills of exchange, with Amsterdam and Hamburg acting as chief clearing houses and bankers, the modes of payment for Russian-Western commerce remained, deep into the eighteenth century, largely as they had been in earlier times.[21] The Russians did not have a banking system which allowed them to follow the example of the West. They did not enjoy equal credit, since they possessed neither a governmental organization and administration of finance nor an efficiently working judicial system which guaranteed adequate protection to foreign creditors. Their bookkeeping methods had fallen behind those of Western Europe.[22] Modern controls as they then existed in Spain, Sweden, England, Holland and in German states were lacking. Arbitrariness, bribery and smuggling flourished. The writings of Western merchants dealing or wanting to deal with Russia are full of complaints about these impediments. Particularly bad were conditions in the Russian customs offices, and their official statistics are of questionable value for the researcher who wants to form a picture of Russian-Western trade. The reports on exports and imports, for instance, which are available for St. Petersburg, Archangel, Riga and other ports of entry into Russia conceal rather than disclose the real extent of Russian-Western trade. A French consul in St. Petersburg estimated that in the 1730's at times 95 per cent of the imports escaped the prescribed dues.

A similar disadvantage for the development of Russian-Western commerce in the late seventeenth century and throughout the eighteenth resulted from the insistence of Russian statesmen on mercantilist principles. From the beginning of the seventeenth century on we find in the writings of political and economic thinkers in the West appeals for the liberalization of trade. The more mercantilism progressed in practice, the stronger became the voices of the advocates of free trade, especially in France and England. Toward the end of the eighteenth century laissez-faire principles had become widely accepted. Little of such a development can be traced for seventeenth- and eighteenth-century Russia.[23] In Moscow and in St. Petersburg the government was firmly resolved to follow mercantilist principles[24] or, as Bertrand Gille expressed it,[25] to hold to the theory of "étatisme." Despite occasional steps toward liberalization of trade, the policy which was pursued in Russia was that of state direction, centralization, and protecttionism. By no means only for fiscal reasons (which, to be sure, were related to the endeavor to encourage and strengthen Russian industry) or for the sake of revenue, but also in line with economic theory, tariffs remained high. Indeed, they were often so high and prohibitive that only the prevailing amount of smuggling and corruption could make possible an import and export business. Mercantilism expressed itself also in currency manipulations which served to accumulate bullion but hindered production and trade. Silver and copper coins deteriorated. Their export was prohibited; instead, the government insisted that Western merchants bring in valuable Western currency, especially rigsdaler, for paying customs dues, and this affected Russia's commerce adversely. Mercantilistic thought, and particularly the desire to export more than to import, dominated all trade negotiations with other countries.[26] Such a policy served the English and the Dutch, who purchased more in Russia than they sold because they reexported much of what they bought. But it hurt the other nations, for receiving so much Russian goods through English or Dutch mediation, they could not sufficiently increase their own imports from Russia to make possible large exports.

Russia's mercantilistic policies did not extend, however, to navigation and navigation acts. Even in Peter's and Catherine's times no sizable merchant fleet was created by Russia. The carrying trade remained in the hands of the West, with England and Holland leading and Germans, French, Swedes, and Spaniards maintaining smaller shares. Interestingly, the Russian government even negotiated an agreement in 1667 with an Armenian merchant company. This company gained not only the right to bring their skills to Novgorod, Smolensk and Archangel, but also that to export their goods beyond these places to Western countries under the condition that they would return to their homes by way of Russia.[27] Nor did Russia's mertilistic aims extend to questions of balance of payment. While the Russian government energetically and successfully pursued the goal of an active trade balance, it neglected the balance of payment. Large funds were expended for representative duties —financing trips abroad for court and landed nobility and their large entourages, training scientists at German and other universities, purchasing art treasures, paying pensions to foreign scholars and writers, and securing luxury goods far beyond the limits other countries under similar circumstances were accustomed to do. In order to live up to these obligations Russia floated loans abroad, availing herself in particular of the facilities offered in Amsterdam by houses such as that of Hope and Company. High interest rates had to be paid for the loans and repayments had to be punctual, which again burdened Russian-Western trade.

Under such state direction, a middle class such as existed in the West could not develop. This more than anything else handicapped the development of Russian-Western commerce. Notwithstanding measures to raise the status of the merchant class taken by Peter the Great and Catherine II, a large group of independent merchants did not come into being. Indeed, the tsars themselves, as well as the nobility, continued to use their political power to channel profitable business through their own hands. They monopolized lucrative connections, maintained for themselves the rights for the exploitation of mines and other raw material sources (including a large part of the agricultural production), and avoided the type of competition which accounted for the growth of Western business. Most of the export and import business thus remained dependent upon a class of people unwilling, and possibly devoid of the ability, to create a favorable basis for Russian-Western trade connections, and Russia remained a market with conditions alien to Western entrepreneurs. Commerce continued to suffer from this situation.

In summary, it may therefore be said that by 1800 a radical change in Russian-Western trade patterns had been achieved. With the incorporation of Poland even the land routes had become free. Russia's struggle for direct connections with the West had been won, and both sides profited. The monopolies of Western trading companies or nations had virtually disappeared; trade treaties, as a rule granting "preferred nation status" to the countries concerned, had been concluded; and to the extent to which freedom of the seas existed, ships of all lands could reach Russian ports: Archangel in the north, St. Petersburg, Riga and other ports on the Baltic, or Cherson and others on the Black Sea. Yet, the differences between the economic and social development in Russia and the evolution of the West had, if anything, increased. Russian-Western trade still exhibited aspects which set it apart from the trade carried on between the nations of the West.

What had not been achieved in the Age of the Enlightenment became now a task for the nineteenth century. Its beginnings were, however, not propitious. Wars may either speed up or delay developments: the Napoleonic wars delayed those changes in the structure of the Russian economy which might have given new impulses to Russian-Western trade relations. A few adjustments were made during the crisis, but they did not bring a permanent gain, and the liberalizing tendencies of Emperor Alexander I and some of his entourage found expression on paper rather than in practice. Only in the 1820's and 1830's, in the times of Mordvinov's and Kankrin's administration of finance, were steps undertaken which helped to modernize trade patterns. Yet even then state, tsar and nobility continued to retain a large share in business, and entrepreneurship in foreign trade made but little progress. A desperate financial situation forced the country to favor exports over imports, to control and to monopolize. Nor did profound social changes, which would have benefited the merchant class, seem desirable —even to men like Kankrin. For, those who exercised the power in the Russian state were invariably convinced that changes would endanger the entire structure on which the state rested.

Eventually the revolutionary movements of the 1840's, the Crimean War, and ultimately the emancipation of the serfs did put an end to the existing system and opened the way for the integration of Russia into the capitalistic frame of Western Europe. Within this frame Russian-Western trade also came to function, and the Russian market responded to the habits of the world market. Business cycles came to affect the tsarist empire as they affected Western nations,[28] and price fluctuations, especially in grain, corresponded to those in the West. Isolation with its advantages and disadvantages had to be abandoned. This tendency was strengthened by the introduction in Russia of the same modern money and currency policies to which the West was accustomed. Banks on the European model and their financial policies came to exercise a determining influence also in Russia. Joint stock companies were founded.[29]

Despite such integration, significant differences still remained and had an adverse effect on commercial relations between Russia and the West. Etatisme in Russia in the sense in which it had been practiced in the eighteenth century no longer prevailed, but as an underlying factor it did not disappear. It worked itself out in numerous prohibitions for foreign merchants, who were, for instance, restricted in their right to travel or who were allowed to sell their goods only in certain regions. It included laws preventing the Western trader from carrying on his business on a basis of equality with the native importer and exporter, or it affected the Jew, not only of Russian nationality but at times also of other countries, who was barred from conducting trade activities under the same conditions as Christians, and especially the Orthodox. It made it difficult for Russian merchants to move as freely within their own country and abroad as Westerners were accustomed to move. It also expressed itself in the tariff policy of the government. The demand for freedom of trade had become strong also in Russia. In Napoleonic times circumstances had made it difficult for it to be heeded. But also after the end of the French wars, mercantilistic trends strengthened by fiscal problems persisted. The tariff of 1822 was extremely high, and in addition, long lists of goods altogether prohibited were published. This choked the development of Russian-Western trade, except for smuggling. In 1841 the tariff was modified and the list of prohibited goods reduced; by 1856 to 1861 further reductions brought Russian tariff policies more in line with those of Western Europe. But from 1870 on, a tendency toward protectionism gained again the upper hand. State direction increased. As a result—again reminiscent of mercantilist endeavors—the trade deficits of the earlier part of the century, which a freer flow of goods had brought, were turned in the later part of the century once more into surpluses.

An additional impediment for Russian-Western trade consisted in the difficulty for the Western merchant of finding enough goods to buy from Russia. His chief interest was confined to grain and other agricultural products and a few special raw materials, such as oil or platinum. To be sure, in the later part of the nineteenth century the industrialization of Russia offered opportunities for a quick expansion of trade.[30] But in the first five or even six decades of the century this was less the case. It is difficult to gain a clear picture of this period because with the growing complexities of international trade the figures shown in the official statistics can be misleading. They give essentially only the data for bilateral transactions, but often triangular and more intricate relationships dominated. A New England merchant of the 1820's would, for instance, rather than limiting himself to selling cloth or even tobacco or cotton in Russia and exchanging it for nails or oil or metals, export his products to Cuba, buy sugar there and sail with it to St. Petersburg, sell it and buy hemp or quills for writing pens, ship these to England, and return from there with British wares. In view of the dynamics of the industrial age as opposed to the Middle Ages, his undertakings would, however, constantly change with the rapid decline of demand for one product and the rise of demand for another. When the steel pen was invented, quills suddenly ceased to be salable; when sugar beets were introduced in Russia for large-scale cultivation in the 1830's, the Cuban business would abruptly become unlucrative. The fortunes of individual businessmen would fluctuate and Russian trade would continue to offer unusual risks to the Western merchants.

Some of the manufacturers sought a way out by establishing factories in Russia. The German dye works, the Bayer factory, is but one example of an industrial plant which as early as 1863 founded a branch in Moscow. Other manufacturers everywhere had done, or did likewise, with the necessary concomitant effect not only on trade figures but also on the old issue of emigration. For the establishment of Western manufactures again necessitated the transfer of competent technicians to Russia. Trade, finance and emigration thereby assumed once more implications which reached beyond the realm of economics.

Is under such circumstances the suggestion possible that, in view of continued structural differences in the economy, state organization and mentality of the West and of Russia—differences which also mark the twentieth century—the flow of trade between the two areas was bound to be limited and a true supplementation of each other's needs was not to be expected? A great deal of additional research would be needed to answer the question. No comprehensive general presentation of Russian-Western commerce exists as yet, nor of Russian trade with individual states, such as the United States, Germany, England, Sweden or France. Neither the statistical material nor business data have been collected and adequately edited and analyzed nor has the influence of business on politics been traced. The subsequent studies, however, show that material is available which can provide insights into the problem and answers to it. The long, valuable and vital trade relationship of the Germans and Russians in Hanseatic times, the further growth of trade between Dutch, Germans and English with the Russians in the early modern period before the so-called "Westernization" of Russia at the turn of the eighteenth century, and also the development of Russian-Western connections in the nineteenth century prove that even though we cannot speak of a full integration and supplementation of the two trading areas, connections at almost all stages since Kievan times were necessary, possible and vigorous. In the late eighteenth and in the nineteenth centuries the backwardness of the Russian economy has made it appear as if new relationships were to be based on the respective production and needs of an industrialized West and on Russia providing agricultural products and raw materials. But the twentieth century with its irresistible drive toward industrialization everywhere has changed the path and has opened different perspectives for all Russian-Western trade relations.

It is within this framework of problems and considerations that the following essays belong. None aspires at proposing anything "definitive." They all are written with the thought that they may stimulate further investigation which, by impressing us with the need for integration of dominant economic interests into the otherwise bodyless general relations, will give us deeper insights into the history of Russia and the West.

Chapter I

ON RUSSIA'S FOREIGN TRADE IN EARLY MODERN TIMES*

A rather insignificant incident, which occurred in 1567 in the Danish Sound, reflects important international connections, and these, in turn, throw light on the economic relations between Russia and the West. In the first week of October of that year some fur traders on a "Russian ship," carrying merchandise from Russia and on its way from the Baltic Sea to the West, were invited by the Danish Admiral, Peter Huitfeld, to a drinking party in Helsingör. When they returned in their rowboat to their ship, it was no longer there. As it subsequently turned out, Huitfeld himself had had the ship seized and later sent to Danzig, where he disposed of it as well as the merchandise it carried.

The incident was reported to King Frederick II. Shocked by the outrageous violation of the important treaty of trade and alliance which existed between Denmark and Russia[1] and which stipulated unhindered passage to Antwerp for all Russian merchants whom the tsar dispatched there,[2] Frederick, in unprecedented haste, ordered the arrest of the admiral.[3] Huitfeld succeeded, however, in escaping abroad, and only two years later, under pressure exercised by the king, an agreement was signed in Copenhagen by which the tsar received compensation for what had been stolen.[4]

---

* Reprinted with permission from _Vierteljahrschrift für Sozial- und Wirtschaftsgeschichte_, Vol. 42, 1955.

Regrettably, the news about the incident is so meager that we do not know anything precise about the nationality of the ship and its captain, or about the port of destination and the type of its freight. Nor do we know who the owners of the merchandise were.[5] The sources which are published at the end of this present essay give us only very incomplete information. Russian materials are not available, and the registers of the Sound Dues fail us entirely. This is the more unfortunate, as we would have had here a unique opportunity for gaining some concrete knowledge about the fundamental problem of Russia's active foreign trade during the decisive sixteenth century.

In some respects we possess a clearer picture of Russia's foreign trade enterprises in earlier centuries than of those which were carried on in that very period when Russia consciously and energetically attempted to promote relations with the West. Trade connections had existed in the ninth and tenth centuries between Kiev and Ratisbon. Yet conclusions as to the extent of the trade, such as Francis (František) Dvornik has drawn when speaking of a "brisk intercourse,"[6] need a firmer foundation than the few sources still in existence permit. At the time of Kiev-Ratisbon relations Russia sent ships also to Sweden and possibly (according to Heydt) into the Mediterranean.[7] In places such as Thessalonica they exchanged their wares against those which traders from France and Spain brought there. But the question remains, who precisely was meant by these "Russians." There were merchants in Thessalonica who were not Russians but belonged to nations trading with Russia, such as the Frankish traders. They visited there on their return journey from the East. But there were probably also Northmen, Varangians, Jews and Arabs. They all composed a major part of the over-all "Russian" contingent. Jews, for instance, in part dominated the slave trade, which was also carried on with Mohammedan Spain by way of Ratisbon. Franks were prominent in the trade with swords (and also blades for swords which, interestingly, were imported as semi-manufactured goods into Kievan Rus).[8] Lest arms strengthen the war potential of the Slavs, their export was, however, officially prohibited from time to time, beginning in as early a period as that of Charlemagne.[9] Varangians probably handled principally the trade in furs, and they were also engaged in building merchant ships and other boats. But Russians, properly speaking, seem to have focused their attention chiefly on internal rather than on foreign trade. They were interested in river traffic rather than in navigating the high seas, as we may deduce from what we know of their ship-building activities. They specialized in uncovered boats, which were provided with comparatively weak masts. When later, around 1030, they undertook to invade Livonia, it was the levying of tribute, and not the conquest of a sea coast and the establishment of a port for foreign trade, that constituted their objective. At the place where they established the castle of Juriev, only later and under German domination, the important trading center of Dorpat developed. Trade was left by the Russians to guests from abroad.

An increase in active Russian export trade occurred in the course of the twelfth century. Sources which we possess indicate that "Russian merchants" visited Denmark, Gotland, Baltic harbors such as Schleswig and even inland towns such as Hildesheim. The First Novgorod Chronicle reports under the years 1130 and 1142 that Novgorod boats sailed on the Baltic.[10] The often cited privilege which granted the Russians the right to trade in Lübeck and accorded them exemption from dues there can, however, serve in our attempt to evaluate the extent of Russian foreign enterprises within narrow limits only.[11] For sources do not exist which show that the Russians ever made use of the rights they acquired. Indeed, we find again and again in the course of the centuries that the Russians formally insisted upon and gained certain trade privileges without actually exploiting them. For instance, the German-Russian treaties of 1229, 1259 and 1268 specifically stipulated reciprocity for all trade; only that of 1268 contained a restriction which referred to the obligation on the Russian side to use German boats as carriers.[12] Even then, we hear nothing of Russian moves to avail themselves of the opportunities. A considerable Russian merchant colony abroad is ascertainable for Riga, where credit was extended to them, where they possessed houses and where they could acquire citizenship. Had they, however, pursued the aim of carrying on an active foreign trade overseas, the port could have been more than just a meeting place; perhaps it could have been altogether theirs.

An inclination to take avowed intentions for deeds and to deduce from agreed-upon rights that they were automatically practiced seems to have been the main reason why, for instance, the Russian historian M. Slaviansky assumes that Novgorod merchants sailed regularly every year to the West and that this was so normal an undertaking that the chronicler did not even find the trips worth mentioning.[13] Not so long ago, another scholar, the Belgian Alexandre Eck, stated in his excellent monograph on the Russian Middle Ages that despite the lack of a Russian merchant fleet, Novgorod merchants of the thirteenth and fourteenth centuries sailed to the West, where they exchanged their goods for those of the West.[14] It is very likely that at one time or another they also considered the founding of a society of overseas merchants, and it is true that treaties permitting them unhindered travel were concluded. Concrete cases of overseas visits, however, are only rarely ascertainable. We learn that in 1327 a certain Timoske "Ruthenus" arrived in Lübeck;[15] that between 1370 and 1387, and especially in 1371, Russians visited Stockholm; and that toward the end of the century some of them came to Danzig. A. I. Nikitsky mentions that possibly they still traveled at that time beyond Danzig to Lübeck and Gothland, even though since the twelfth century these voyages were no longer made in ships of their own but in foreign boats. Yet we also possess indications which can serve as evidence to the opposite, namely that no trips abroad were undertaken. Thus, we find reports from Danzig dating from around 1470 which state that; to be sure, Russians from olden times on had visited this town, but that nothing was known about their having traveled beyond Danzig to Lübeck. Likewise, it is only at the very end of the fourteenth century that we hear of rumors reporting the "renewed" appearance of Russians on the seas.[16]

In considering the underlying factors for the situation as it has developed, it may be argued that while perhaps the Russians were by no means unable to carry on an active trade overseas, they were in fact not interested in it. Why should they expose themselves to the dangers of the sea, to the threat of pirates, to exploitation by Western merchants, to insults from the side of Non-Orthodox, to the abuses by other nations and the deceit of foreign inn-keepers, drivers, cheats and swindlers[17] if their trade balance was active; why, if by having all exchange of the goods carried on within their own confines they could retain the opportunity to supervise the foreign merchants as well as the quality of their merchandise and their entire business conduct? It is true that as a result of edicts restricting or prohibiting commerce, issued by German emperors, Roman popes, Swedish kings, and Hanseatic councilmen, they occasionally could be exposed to interruptions of trade. But in view of the great number of entrance gates to Russia—by way of Karelia, Viborg, Novgorod, Narva, Dorpat, the Duena river, across the Lithuanian border, or via Black Sea ports—and in view of the equally numerous opportunities for smuggling goods, the danger that embargoes might lead to disastrous consequences was not too great. Moreover, the Russians enjoyed the advantage that they could use the foreign merchants staying in Novgorod and the goods stored there as a pawn. This possibility could not fail to have an effect as a deterrent against inconsiderate actions by foreign trade-partners. Also, modern expansionist dreams, or the Faustian urge which persistently seeks new goals, may have been alien to the Russian man of the Middle Ages. Altogether the concepts of the later mercantilistic and technological age, as well as the atmosphere within which these were to develop, may not be applicable to medieval Russia.

Changes in trade patterns occurred in Russia during the fifteenth and sixteenth centuries, but new investigations are needed in order to ascertain their extent. On the basis of existing sources and without the publication of additional materials such as Russian account books (if available at all), it would be premature to propose definitive conclusions. It does seem certain, though, that the Russians at that time began to show an increasing interest in an overseas trade of their own. Whenever obstacles were put in their way, perhaps by the Germans, they resorted to quick countermeasures. From time to time they used reprisals and prohibited, for instance, all travel of Hanseatic merchants beyond Polotsk into the interior of Russia.

We know that goods for Russian account were shipped abroad in 1423 and 1455. German-Russian negotiations of the years 1426 and 1436 prove that Russians sailed on the sea. For at that time the Russians demanded that the Hanseats extend protection to them against competitors and pirates—a protection which the merchants, of course, could not extend, even if they had been willing to accord it. For they themselves were suffering from the same dangers. Russians also resumed foreign travel overland, entering into direct contact with Breslau and Venice. Their ambassadors, who left for Italy in 1438 in order to attend the Church Council called for the reunification of the Catholics and the Orthodox, took along goods which they and the merchants accompanying them on their mission marketed on the way. What they gained from this activity served not only for their own sustenance and for that of their attendants—as usual, they had not received other funds from the Moscow grandduke—but also provided profits. Some of these went into the prince's treasury, some into the pockets of the ambassadors themselves and of the merchants. Business was also later carried on by other Russian missions abroad. In 1472 Ivan the Great's ambassadors to Rome were accompanied by a Russian merchant whose name is known to us; and we are also familiar with the names of those who in 1572 followed the Russian embassy to Spain.[18]

Likewise, Russian merchants sailed overseas. To be sure, the famous trip of Afanasii Nikitin to India represents an exception,[19] but we have evidence of a number of voyages across the Baltic Sea to Livonian ports and to Danzig. Possibly Russians proceeded to Lübeck also.[20] According to Herberstein, some merchants sailed to the North Cape toward the end of the century, while others, after passing the Cape, reached Bergen in Norway. But whenever Russian merchants got abroad, they found themselves at a disadvantage—at least they were only too often not sufficiently acquainted with the prices which were paid on the Western markets. For the Novgorod business had possessed features of its own. It had made possible the formation of prices which only in part were dependent upon the ups and downs of prices on the Western markets, being sometimes considerably higher, sometimes lower than in other regions. Our knowledge of this issue is, however, still insufficient. We have some indications concerning price formation in Novgorod,[21] yet a comprehensive study remains the task of the future. In view of the business morale, or lack of a business morale, in the fifteenth and sixteenth centuries, and in view of the falsifications and trickeries with regard to measures, weights, quality of goods and currencies which were customary, it would be necessary to extend price research also to these factors. Only if we include them in our price studies and account for them, can we gain a reliable picture. Actually, one task which Ivan III generally put to his ambassadors consisted in investigating the level of prices in Europe and reporting to him about it.

Russians abroad were also at a disadvantage in that the Europeans did not welcome them as guests. Their bad manners, their dirtiness, their drunkenness and arrogance, and their brutality against their subordinates gave them a bad reputation. These qualities contributed to their meeting occasionally with adverse experiences, which we hear about in Sweden, Denmark, England and Italy.[22]

We thus find that at the beginning of the modern age the Russians did not yet possess much experience, and that they were received with little good will abroad. They had fared well with their traditional method of concluding their foreign business deals in their own border towns, especially in Novgorod, Pskov, Polotsk, Smolensk and Kaffa. Events at the time of their destruction of the Hanseatic factory in Novgorod had demonstrated that foreign countries were powerless in the face of Russian action. They also suggested that it might be advisable for the Russians to continue in the same ways to which they had been accustomed. Yet, in the course of the sixteenth century, at least two occasions arose which seemed to make changes attractive; and both these occasions occurred in connection with Denmark.

Ever since the early part of the century when new economic forces had come to the fore, upper-German merchant houses and especially that of the Fugger had shown an increasing interest in the Russian trade.[23] Thinking of their support, the Danish King Christian II therefore resolved early in the century to modernize Denmark's economic policies and to promote more up-to-date concepts and methods than those with which his Danish and Holstein nobility with their agrarian preoccupations were accustomed. In this context, he turned his attention to Russia, which could play a significant role. King Hans, his predecessor, had already laid a basis for closer ties with Russia by concluding a treaty with her. Christian II followed up Hans's policy and in 1517 accorded the Russians in Copenhagen all the rights which, reciprocally, the Danes had been given in Ivangorod.[24] This afforded the Russians a chance for escaping the monopolistic power which the Hanse and the Dutch at the time possessed. Under the protection of Denmark as the dominating power in the Sound, the Russians could now envisage the systematic organization of an active foreign trade of their own.

Immediately, the Russians tried to avail themselves of the possibilities. According to Arild Huitfeld's history, Russian ships arrived in Copenhagen in 1517.[25] That Russians sailed overseas is confirmed also by Berckmann's Chronicle of Stralsund. The most interesting report is, however, that of Reimar Kock in his Chronicle of Lübeck.[26] To be sure, we do not know what sources Kock used when writing his story or where his knowledge came from. At least the writer of this essay has failed, despite various efforts, to find the original data on which Kock bases his account. Kock relates that in 1517 the Russians sent a ship with good merchandise to Denmark. But the Danes had nothing to offer on their side but horses, pigs, sheep and meat, tallow, skins of cows and goats —in brief, nothing other than what the Russians themselves possessed; and at that, they did not even have enough of these commodities to make up in value for the goods which the Russians had brought on their ship. Thus nothing was left but to return. They thereupon spread the news that the Danish king had nothing else to offer but oats, herring and horses. When the Fuggers heard of this, Kock continues, they gave up all plans for trade and kept the money which they had intended to loan to the Danes. For they feared that Christian II would put it to no better use than covering the expenses of his wars against Sweden.[27]

Even though this report cannot be verified, it allows us to

draw a few conclusions. In the first place, we may deduce from it, and from the various other news, that in the second decade of the sixteenth century the Russians took practical steps for building up an active foreign trade. In the second place, we have reason to believe that their efforts were undertaken in conjunction with Denmark, which alone at the time possessed an international trade treaty with Russia. Third, it becomes clear that after a short while the Russians once more gave up their attempts. Perhaps we find an explanation for this latter fact when we consider that in essence the Russians were motivated by a desire to secure freedom of the seas. This freedom would give the merchants of other nations unhindered access to the Russian country and would simultaneously lead to a desirable sharp competition among the foreign suppliers. This, in turn, seemed more attractive than carrying on an active foreign trade of their own. Except for the tsar himself, the entrepreneurs in Russia did not have enough capital for undertaking risks such as would have been necessary. The tsar alone possessed the position, the means and the concerns of a large-scale merchant and trader. Only later in the century did the family of the Stroganovs also gain a place which enabled it to equip and send out overseas expeditions. It may furthermore be considered that the Russians did not possess what today in America is being called "know-how." And lastly, we may defend the view that at the beginning of the sixteenth century the Russians were still not serious in their desire to establish large-scale foreign contacts abroad.

Nevertheless, a more extensive Russian foreign trade might have developed, had at least Russia's most important partner, Denmark, possessed the capital, the entrepreneurs, and the "know-how." But the attempts which were made in 1517 sufficiently demonstrated Denmark's weakness.

Subsequent periods brought no change. New efforts were made three years later, climaxing in Christian II's resolution to establish a major "Merchants Trading Company."[28] The founding of such a Company had been envisaged as early as the middle of the fifteenth century by King Christoph the Bavarian. His successor, Christian I, had contemplated a similar establishment. But it was only Christian II who sized up correctly the need for capital and who actually undertook to secure it. He approached the Fuggers as well as the Occos of Amsterdam. Moreover, it was he who, for the sake of better supervision, moved the administration of the Sound Dues from Helsingör to Copenhagen. Of course, with all his plans, he pursued not only trade aims but also internal political objectives. Yet, he used the occasion to address invitations to the various foreign nations, asking them to come to his realms and to use his land as an intermediary for all East-West trade. The most interesting aspect of this offer, as far as Russian foreign connections are concerned, consists in the fact that a certain Paolo Centurione, who at the time was in Russian service, was attracted by it. He promptly tried to obtain both from the tsar and from the Danish king a monopoly for acting as the agent for Russo-Western trade. His offer is interesting also insofar as it contains many of the false promises, especially with regard to the reunion of the Orthodox and the Catholic churches, which later Russian agents were to make in order to render more palatable to the West the appearance of Russia on European markets. It is significant in this context that Christian II in issuing a privilege for Centurione calls him not a Russian but a Genoese and that, cautiously, he mentions Russia no more than once, and at that, in a most inconspicuous place.[29] The whole plan was, however, not very attractive to the trading nations and came to naught before Christian II's reign ended in catastrophe in 1523.

During the following half-century we seldom find Russian merchants in Western countries. They come to Riga; occasionally they appear, as we learn from debates at the Hanse diet of 1525, in Breslau (which they reach by traveling via Cracow);

or they travel as far as Antwerp. They accompany the few missions dispatched from Moscow to Germany, Italy and Spain; and in the North, they sail in their small boats from the Pechenga monastery to Vardøhus to make purchases or sales of fish and oil.[30] But only during the 1560's—in the same period when the initially mentioned incident occurred—is a second major attempt at trading directly in the West undertaken.

Again it was the development of new trade routes (this time achieved not by upper-German merchants but by the English, who in 1553 had opened the Northern route and who ever since had tried to establish a permanent trade link there) which called Muscovy's attention to the opportunities which an active foreign trade might bring. As early as 1557, when Tsar Ivan IV had concluded a peace treaty with Sweden, he had specifically demanded that his agents could travel unhindered to the West. At that time the primary aim which he envisaged had been visits to the markets of Antwerp.[31] But as it turned out, it was ultimately Denmark, and no other region, which because of her domination of the Sound offered the best prospects in the tsar's opinion. He therefore concluded with her the treaty of 1562. This treaty gave the Russians the right to establish factories or staples on Gotland and in Copenhagen.[32] It seems that this time Russia was resolved to put into practice what she had gained by way of privileges, so that the treaty had to be taken seriously. Consequently, the Danish King Frederick II promptly began to look for a suitable house on Gotland for the Russians. In 1563 he acquired a factory that seemed to be adequate, and apparently the Russians occasionally used it. At least one of them is recorded in the sources, since he had his money stolen there. It may, however, be mentioned here, in anticipation of later developments, that in 1577 the king offered the house for sale. By that time it had not only decayed, it had also become superfluous as far as Russian trade was concerned.[33]

As to their rights in Copenhagen, we have no news whatsoever that the Russians seriously occupied themselves at any time with the establishment of a factory there, despite the treaty having provided for it. All we hear is that early in the sixties they were playing with the idea of building a merchant fleet and that they hired a number of foreign artisans for this purpose.[34] We also learn—from Hakluyt—that several Russian merchants received, through the mediation of the Russian envoy Ossip Napea, permission from the tsar to ship goods to England. However, nothing came of this transaction, since the English refused to agree to it. The undertakings initiated by Russia thus did not get very far. Yet some Russian merchants did appear in Western countries. The Dutchman Simon van Salingen reports that even earlier than 1566 men from Russia, sent by the tsar to make purchases in Antwerp, had arrived there. He knew Russia well; later he was to lead, in the name of Christian IV, negotiations between the tsar and Denmark regarding a settlement of northern frontier disputes between Russia and Norway. In March 1566, two Russian merchants, Peter Pavlovich and Dmitri Kondratievich, reached Amsterdam; they came in order to do business on their own accounts.[35] In April 1567, Ivan sent other merchants to Amsterdam; their names were Ivan Afanasiev and Timofei Smivalov. In the same year a number of Russian merchants—a certain Tverdikov among them—came to England in order to barter furs for jewels and robes. Tverdikov had previously visited the Netherlands. From the attack which Huitfeld made on the Russian ship in the Sound toward the end of the year, we can deduce that additional visits abroad were made. This is confirmed by the formal request which the tsar made on April 24, asking for permission for the transit of his merchandise through the Sound. Altogether, we may assume that even though little about their travels is reported in the sources, the Russians did not give up their efforts to at least maintain the connections which they had started, or possibly to increase them by new direct links. This is certainly true for the period up to 1577, that is up to the time when Ivan's invasion of Livonia took a turn for the worse, or perhaps even up to 1581, when Narva fell to the Swedes. We know that in 1577 Russians sold furs and skins in Dordrecht in Holland, for a report has been preserved that at the time they were cheated out of their money.[36] We also know that in 1576 a Russian apparently brought his wares in his own ship by way of Trondjhem to Greenland,[37] and that in 1577 Oliver Brunel sold merchandise in Holland for the account of the Stroganovs. It is possible that the Stroganovs had commissioned him, in addition, with the task of having a ship built for them there, even though more credence should perhaps be attached to the report that his task consisted less in this than in hiring sailors to serve on two other ships which the Stroganovs had themselves built at the mouth of the Dvina river. These ships were to be used for voyages of discovery along the northern coast of Siberia. The same Brunel was also charged to purchase goods for the Stroganovs in Holland. Most of the agents used foreign bottoms for their travels and transports; it was only on the northern route that the Russians seem to have disposed of seafaring vessels of their own.

On the other hand, in considering Russian efforts to establish an active foreign trade, it should be remembered that as early as 1569 Ivan wrote deridingly to Elizabeth, queen of England, that his subjects could find ample nourishment at home so that they did not need to travel abroad to earn their living.[38] This proud statement is hardly convincing though. It would be closer to the truth to state that in the sixteenth century Russia found herself on a level of economic development in relation to the Western powers which made impossible the successful initiation of an active foreign trade. But whatever the underlying causes, the fact remains that Ivan's economic plans collapsed together with his political aims. Their fate was sealed through the failure of his Livonian undertakings. This failure sufficed to reduce Russia's foreign connections to a status such as had existed one hundred years earlier.

Subsequently treaties were again made which included empty stipulations regarding reciprocity. Such a treaty was concluded with Sweden in 1585—it provided the right of the Russian merchants to visit Stockholm. But nothing came of it. As the documents preserved in the town archives of Stockholm prove, no Russian colony existed there before the second decade of the seventeenth century. Perhaps jealousy on the part of Sweden was responsible for the failure to establish it earlier, yet more important other tasks captured Russia's primary attention, and nothing was done by her to create a basis for exploiting the opportunity. Even in Reval, where the Russians had owned a church in the fifteenth century,[39] we find that Russian traders became fewer and fewer.

Equal and reciprocal rights were also stipulated in the Treaty of Teusin of 1595. But at that time experiences which Russian envoys and merchants had had at about the same time elsewhere—in Bohemia—must have acted as a deterrent and have hindered carrying out the stipulations. Loaded with valuable furs, Russians had reached Prague. As soon as they had arrived, however, the prices for their wares had fallen—by 90 per cent, as some historians figure, or by 75, as others estimate. The fact that the purchase price was to serve the purpose of subventioning the German emperor in his campaign against the Turks and not that of securing a profit for the Russians themselves may have consoled them, yet the fact remains that here again an attempt at trading abroad had brought frustration.[40]

Despite various apparently promising starts, Russia thus proved to be, at the beginning of the modern age, still at a stage where she could demand equality with others but could not achieve it. Nor did the situation change under the short and unhappy administrations of Boris Godunov and Dimitri, both of them men well educated, modern and open to Western thought. Indeed, throughout the seventeenth and eighteenth centuries and even up to now, active participation of Russia in Western trade has remained comparatively weak. Should the cause for this weakness lie in a cultural flow which descends the farther it extends eastward? Certainly such a suggestion does not offer a satisfactory answer. For one cannot overlook the fact that in the course of time Russia too has long reached, and passed, the same level of economic and political development which, in line with the demands of mercantilistic thought, had once awakened in Europe the most vigorous trading and exporting efforts. The cause for the special position of Russia, which the conditions here described mirror for past centuries, must therefore lie elsewhere. Perhaps it lies in the fact that at all times Russia's development followed a pattern of its own. Each phase of her evolution reflects a special character—a character which marks also all other aspects of her entire history.

DANISH MSS. CONCERNING THE HUITFELD INCIDENT

In Rigsarkivet, Copenhagen:

1. Ca. 1520, Danske Kancl. Indlaeg til Reg. & Tegnelser: Application of Paolo Centurione to the Danish king.

2. Ca. 1520. Danske Kancl. Indlaeg til Reg. & Tegnelser; Privilege of Christian II to Paolo Centurione.

3. April 24, 1567, Tsar Ivan IV to King Frederick II; printed in: Iu. N. Shcherbachev, Russkie akty Kopengagenskago gosud. arkhiva, St. Pbg., 1897 (Russkaia Istorich. Biblioteka, v. 16), p. 58.

4. October 6, 1567. Ind. Breve til Danske Kanc. Peder Oxe to King Frederick II.

5. October 31, 1567. Tegnelse paa alle Landene, de

annis 1566-68, No. IX. Acta publica 1566-1571. A. Fol. 416 b. p. 211. Cf. Cancl. Brevbøger. Frederick II to Peder Oxe.

6. November 18, 1567. Cancl. Brevbøger: Frederick II confirms his order to Oxe regarding the arrest of Huitfeld.

7. May 11, 1568. Ausländisch. Registrant, 1567-1658. Fol. 413: Frederick II to Tsar Ivan IV.

8. September 6, 1568. (Copy in connection with No. 9).

9. September 6, 1568. Indkomne Breve til Danske Kancelli: Declaration of Peder Huitfeld.

In the Royal Library of Copenhagen:

10. May 10, 1569. Register paa alle Landene No. 9, de Annis 1566-1567 (1571). Fol. 241. p. 261: Undertaking of Peder Huitfeld to refund to the grandduke all that he has taken from the Russians on their ship in the Sound. At the City Hall of Copenhagen.

Chapter II

RUSSIA AND EUROPE IN THE AGE OF THE REFORMATION*

The topic "Russia and Europe" has been treated again and again and continues to constitute one of the most important problems down to our own days. Many books written on this topic are speculative and philosophical in nature and are largely based on generalizations. While they are full of ideas and stimulating to scholar and layman alike, they demonstrate crucial shortcomings for lack of a solid foundation resting on historical facts. We are, therefore, hardly ready for as sweeping conclusions regarding the relationship of Russia and the West as have been drawn, and it is the purpose of this paper to present a summary of the available and meaningful evidence and to propose a few tentative conclusions. These may serve to show why, at a time when people traveled widely in all directions, when commodities and practices were continually exchanged between East and West, when inventions such as the latest cannons or newly appearing diseases encountered no barrier at the frontiers of Poland,[1] the ideas which were to shake the foundations of Western Christianity found no entrance into territory east of this boundary line.[2]

The beginning of the Reformation found Russia in no wise a stranger in the European community. Not only did contacts exist, but at the time of the death of Ivan the Great in 1505,

---

* Reprinted with permission from <u>Archiv für Reformationsgeschichte</u>, XLIII, (1953).

they were already of a permanent nature. The road was opened for direct diplomatic East-West relations when the Moscow granddukes, after shaking off Tatar rule, acquired sovereignty. And they became unavoidable when, by the very act of the "gathering of the lands" under Ivan III, the buffer regions between East and West disappeared and Russia became an immediate neighbor of Europe.[3]

Necessarily, the most significant links—aside from those with neighbors like Finland, Livonia, Lithuania and Poland, where frontier issues had for a long time necessitated a certain intercourse—had been established between Russia and the two leading powers in Western Christendom, the emperor and the pope. As to the Empire, ever since 1486, when the German Nicholas Poppel had chanced upon the Muscovite realms, a constant though inconsequential stream of negotiations and negotiators had flowed back and forth. Plans for military and marriage alliances, for a common campaign against the Turks and for common action in Hungarian and Polish questions formed the chief points of negotiations and occasionally involved high policies, referring to most of Europe. In addition, Russian needs for architects and cannon-makers, or the private wishes of the German emperor (such as the purchase of falcons from the Muscovite grandduke) and other minor issues were brought up as occasion demanded.

Diplomatic intercourse with the pope had begun even earlier than that with the emperor. Negotiations about Ivan III's marriage to the Palaeologue Princess Sophy, started by two Venetian brothers and carried on by an Italian resident in Russia named Giovanni Battista Volpe, dated back to 1469. These negotiations were intended by the pope to lead to a rapprochement of the Eastern and Western churches. But this was not brought about; instead, intercourse with the papacy was essentially confined to the same questions which occupied the Empire, namely a common campaign against Turkey and peace issues between Russia and Poland. To these were added questions concerning increase of trade, but since the pope had little to offer in this field, Venice was drawn into the negotiations by Rome. Various Russian missions stopped over in Venice on their way to Rome and tried to engage the doges to send their envoys to Moscow, to trade directly with her, and to dispatch Italian artisans to help build the new tsarist empire.

By the beginning of the sixteenth century Russia had also entered into relations with a number of other European powers. Negotiations had been started in 1482 with Hungary. With Sweden no fewer than five treaties were concluded between 1482 and 1505. And a most significant relationship began with Denmark when in 1493 a treaty was concluded which provided for freedom of trade, safety of envoys, and equality of extradition procedures. It was the first West European alliance of Russia. It even led to plans for a Russo-Danish marriage alliance—the first serious plan of this sort since the time of Vladimir the Wise.

Because of lack of understanding on the part of Ivan, the expansion of diplomatic contacts had not been paralleled by a proportionate one in the commercial sphere. In 1478 and 1494 Ivan committed, as even Karamzin admits,[4] the fundamental error of destroying the great Hanseatic factory in Novgorod, the commercial gateway to Russia—a mistake which could in no way be made up by the founding of the fortress and port of Ivangorod opposite Livonian Narva. It is true that considerations of power politics by a state growing into a world power could not but triumph at that stage over intrinsically more important economic considerations; but the damage was done, and if a modern Soviet historian like Wipper tries to construe far-sighted motives for East-West connections on the part of Ivan III,[5] he only furnishes proof for the need for more factual and historically acceptable investigations.

Diplomacy, trade and the needs of the awakening Empire

had automatically brought about the establishment of the most important, the most creative link between East and West: the contact and influence of men. Russians now went abroad on diplomatic missions, visiting the pope in Italy, the emperor in Germany, and occasionally also other Western rulers. But the main traffic was in the opposite direction. Merchants from Germany and Poland had already come earlier, to be sure, to the grandduke's capital to purchase furs, yet it is only around 1480 that we can reliably trace a greater number of individually identifiable persons. There were medical men like the Italian Arnoldo, who attended Ivan himself, and a number of German or Jewish doctors; artists like the architect Rodolfo Fioraventi, also from Italy; Pietro Antonio Solari—generally described as "from Milan," but he came from the Tessin[6]—who, together with Marco Ruffo, erected parts of the Kremlin towers, walls and gates and built the Granovitaia Palace inside; Aleviso, another palace builder; stone-cutters like Bernardino de Borgomainero; two Germans who, together with two Russians, found the first silver mines near Pechora; a metal-founder, a smith, money-coiners, masons, cannon-makers from Italy, Germany and Lithuania; travelers; and Greek courtiers who had come with Sophia and had known the splendor of Naples, Florence, Rome.

Through these channels a certain exchange of ideas took place. Catholic Europe benefitted only little from it. Neither were there comprehensive travel reports written about Russia before Herberstein's famous account, nor was inspiration drawn from Eastern Art or the Eastern church. As to the gains of Russia, some Catholic writings and likewise a few classical works were translated into Slavonic around 1500.[7] For the first time a complete Russian version of the entire Bible, based on the Vulgate, was accomplished. Discussions of theological character took place, such as those of the Papal Legate Antonio with the Moscow metropolitan in 1472. And some attitudes, in line with western developments were accepted, affecting the Church through the emergence of a sect that became known under the name of Judaizers. The Judaizers promoted rationalistic thinking, opposed monasticism, icon adoration, as well as other Orthodox traditions, and translated some Jewish and Arab sources. Their ideas and the treatment they met show significant foreign influences. Although the Orthodox Church was generally not possessed of a missionary spirit leading to such extremes as persecution, inquisition and burning at the stake, exactly such methods were employed in the case of this sect. They were advocated by the Novgorod Archbishop Gennadii, who specifically appealed to the Spanish model for his rationale.[8]

Finally, the occasional adoption of parts of the Burgundian court ceremonial may be mentioned, mainly in relation to Austrian ambassadors; yet, in diplomatic intercourse the Russian language retained its claim over the Latin.

Such was approximately the extent of Russian-Western contact that prevailed at the start of the sixteenth century. This century, to be sure, brought an increase in East-West activity and a broadening of the perspectives, but here again cautious judgments may be called for. Present-day textbooks are inclined to present the sixteenth century as the period in which eastern and western histories begin to fuse into European history. This is true, however, for a few areas only, and it remains the task of a new investigation to state clearly which areas were concerned. For an understanding of this illuminates the whole relationship of East and West down to our own days.

The diplomatic sphere is not among the true links, notwithstanding the extensive and excellent treatises that have been written about it by men like Hans Uebersberger,[9] Father Pierling[10] and others. Uebersberger has dealt extensively with the Empire. We witness there that, except for the years 1558 to 1578 when the Russians made war on the empire's vassal state Livonia, the two issues of paramount interest to emperor and tsar continued to concern the possibility of a common struggle against the Moslem enemy and coordinated action in Polish affairs. However, a common Turkish campaign could not be organized, although at least once, in 1595, Russia paid subsidies to the Habsburgs. As for Poland, because of the Habsburg desire to protect Catholic brethern, cooperation never went much beyond favoring common candidates for the Polish throne.

With regard to Rome, the same issues—an all-Christian crusade against Turkey and a settlement of the Russian troubles with Poland—formed the chief objects of most of the negotiations. A third important topic has been comprehensively presented by Pierling, namely the reunion of the two Christian churches. This question, uppermost in the mind of the Holy See since the time of the Council of Florence, was handicapped by insincerity on both sides, ignorance prevailing in Rome regarding Russia, interruptions in negotiations owing to Polish opposition and fears, and finally, toward the end of the sixteenth century, by the establishment of a patriarchate in Moscow. Eventually Rome had to be content with more modest plans, such as the establishment of a Catholic church in Moscow, the introduction of some Jesuits, and the gradual increase of the prestige of the popes.

In evaluating the relationship of Russia with the Empire and the papacy in the age of the Reformation, it thus becomes evident that these relations lacked substance and missed political reality. As has been suggested on the basis of contemporary opinion, they may have served the tsar's pride rather than a practical purpose.[11] Seen from the East, the aims of the West were chimerical. Pope and emperor, unable to come to a meaningful agreement with the East, served only as tools to enhance Russia's prestige by recognizing the Moscow grandduke as tsar and as treaty partner, and to secure her a European position which corresponded to the ambitions of the shrewd eastern monarchs.

The links which were established with France or with the Order of the Teutonic Knights were not more substantial. Neither Russian interests in Francis I at the time of the election of Charles V, or later in the massacre of St. Bartholomew, nor French schemes for alliances or wars with Russia in the times of Henry II and Henry III were of practical consequence. And likewise, Russian relations with the Teutonic Knights concerned major European policies in which serious engagements did not result, even though at one time, in 1519, Russia also paid subsidies to the Order.[12]

The situation is, however, different when we come to Russian connections with the European powers of the North—with Sweden, Denmark and England. Here we deal with areas of broad significance. For the sixteenth century brought the fulfillment of Moscow's age-old aim of winning access to the open sea, both in the far North and in the Baltic area, and of establishing thereby direct contact with northern Europe. The route around the North Cape was opened in 1553, and in the Baltic area Novgorod's place was taken over by Narva after its conquest in 1558. Russia thus became partially independent of the good or ill will of her neighbors, men and messages could be sent to and from the West, foreign workers and agents could be invited without fear of arrest by jealous neighbors (as had happened in the well-known Schlitte case in 1549), and with her wealth in commodities needed by Europe, Russia could play a key role even in the distribution of political power elsewhere. Promptly arrangements which did not consist of grandiose but vague plans, but whose execution was within the realm of the possible and which were practical and of mutual benefit, were made with the seafaring nations of the North.

Denmark concluded in 1562 perhaps the most notable treaty. Its most important feature was that it showed complete reciprocity and bore out the fact that by then Russia had entered the North European community as a full partner.[13] The agreements with Sweden reflected similar trends,[14] and so did those with the North-German Hanseatic towns, which remained an important, often underestimated factor in Russian-European relations throughout the sixteenth century.[15]

Denmark, Sweden and the German Hanseatic towns found a growing competitor in the Dutch, who entered the field of Russian-European relations independently during the sixteenth century. After the capture of Narva by Ivan the Terrible their trade became one of the most important links between East and West.[16]

England was the last of the northern powers to enter into relations with Russia, but she soon rivaled in importance the older trading nations. No weighty state treaty was needed with her, nor were large-scale political negotiations carried on as with emperor and pope. Instead, beginning in 1564 we find a profitable and substantial practical intercourse. Dispensing with formalities, both sides arranged matters of trade, commodities, duties and monopolies, thus establishing a practical connection that became the real link between East and West,[17] and was soon extended to other than English partners.

Through these growing connections Europe became acquainted with eastern ways and dependent upon the influx of commodities from the East. A striking feature of this development is that the essential western connections of Russia lay almost exclusively with Protestant countries, and it was from these that the majority of foreigners were drawn who visited Russia for the sake of trade or for taking service there. During the first half of the sixteenth century those who came were mainly Germans and Scandinavians, later also English, Scots and Dutch. They established themselves in various towns from

Kholmogori on the White Sea to Astrakhan on the Caspian and in turn contributed to the growth of these towns. They brought western goods, including luxury objects, to Russia. They introduced new usages, created new wants, and thereby changed manners, customs, modes and objectives of production. They founded industries, particularly iron works, and introduced mercantilistic principles. European currencies appeared, German guilders, Danish rosenobles, English crowns, Venetian, Lithuanian and others. Actually, as a result of the enlarged trade connections, we can trace during the sixteenth century the first evidences of Russia being drawn into the system of business and trade cycles that have beset the Western world in the capitalistic era.[18]

While acknowledging the over-all effect of these important positive links between Russia and Europe, we must also remain aware of their limitations. Manifold essential features of Russian life were unaffected. As Kluchevsky put it, "for Orthodox Great Rus the Catholic and Protestant Wests were too alien, too suspect, in their faiths, methods, and customs to be safely imitated."[19] Russia continued to follow her own patterns, and in doing so she was, then as now, in some ways backward, in others ahead of, and in many respects simply different from Europe. She did witness, to be sure, the emergence of serfdom despite a growing money economy and despite its rapid decline in the West, and she did produce the pomiestie type of landlord and the miestnichestvo, or system of ranks; but she also created, earlier than the West, a civil service bureaucracy and developed popular representation and dumas unlike German, English, or French diets, parliaments, or states generals. Most important, she already saw in the sixteenth century the achievement of absolutism based on obligatory service to the tsar in exchange for his grace. And if we do find changes similar to those occurring simultaneously in Europe, as in questions of secularization of church-owned lands, we must beware lest we construe connections without due and acceptable evidence of actual causal relationships. There are many parallel developments depending upon stages of civilization and upon human nature, but independent of direct influences.

Turning from the world of political action to the areas of thought and individual achievement, we find, as in the general political field, some positive and many negative features of Russian-European relations. In the age of the Reformation, the West was still under the spell of the Renaissance. Some of its elements were transplanted into Eastern soil. We find in architecture some characteristic traits, which were brought there by the masters who had been called by Ivan the Great and which were imitated as the Muscovites became accustomed to them. Palaces were built embodying features of Italian castles. Cornices and large windows were imitated, iron construction and brick came into use, a better way of manufacturing and burning limestone was adopted, and some decorative principles exemplified in the West found acceptance.

In painting, too, Western influences can be traced which, according to I. Grabar,[20] had traveled via Byzantium and affected the iconography, for instance, of the Virgin. Perhaps also a growing amount of freedom of style and more dramatic expression can be demonstrated. There were, indeed, traces of European models, introduction of some symbolic presentations, and a certain realism even in human anatomy, at least in the paintings of western Russian artists. Foreigners could be found who made portraits. The art of the woodcut with the help of the printing press, following the German masters, was brought to the East around 1564 and showed representation of scenes closer to ordinary life than did the icons.

These innovations were of no small importance. They bear out the fact that intercourse between East and West was lively and that the East was receptive of Western manners and capable of integrating them. Yet it is necessary to consider the level with which we deal. For what has been described concerns outward features rather than essence, details of building and techniques of drawing and painting rather than spirit. It is in the one sphere that we can trace the results of the intercourse, and in the other that conscientious investigation fails to demonstrate effects. If the Renaissance stood for worldliness, sixteenth-century Russia rejected it; if it represented naturalism, nature continued to be proscribed in the East; if it extolled individualism, its glorification of man was disclaimed. The essence of humanism gained no hold. So important a figure as Maxim the Greek, who had studied and worked in Florence, Bologna, Padua, Milan and Venice, revolted against its "cult of antiquity, its naturalism and immorality."[21] And if he accepted its methods of philosophical criticism and some of its rules derived from the classics, and helped in the introduction of printing establishments, he exemplified the same emphasis on form rather than content which we had already mentioned with respect to architecture and painting.

The Reformation, like the Renaissance, being a product of the West's inner driving spirit, was in the same sense bound to be of little effect in Russia. The disputations of Ivan the Terrible with the Bohemian brother Johann Rokita in 1570, with the Livonian Lutheran pastor Bockhorn in 1577, or with his English doctor still later, led nowhere, and what we find of Reformation or heretical ideas in Russia was of an indigenous nature and owed little to the West. If there had been hopes for a rapprochement of Orthodoxy and the youthful Lutheran Church on the basis of their parallel rejection of papal authority and their kindred appeal to earliest Christian sources and traditions, such common grounds still proved to be too narrow. Maxim the Greek, once an admirer of Savonarola, had already rejected Luther's undogmatic, individualistic interpretation of man's relationship to God. No lasting Lutheran church was erected in Russia until Godunov permitted just one to the foreigners in the Moscow suburb. What influences can be found are East-Westward, consisting of a deeper understanding of the Eastern church by the West through its "rediscovery" by Protestant thinkers such as David Chyträus.

Nor did Catholicism, despite the pope's endeavors and important papal missions, fare any better. Russia also remained a stranger to scholastic tradition, to Thomism, and even to the mild reforming tendencies of Erasmus. A few Catholic books entered Russia, both directly and circuitously via Byzantium, and were distributed secretly; and in 1582 another religious disputation, this time with the Catholic nuntio Possevino, was held. But not even in the Moscow suburb was a Catholic church permitted.

The development of literature and music shows a similar direction. We witness an occasional interest, as with Fedor Ivanovich Karpov, who studied astrology and tried to translate Ovid, or with Kurbsky and a few others. The printing press was introduced about 1560. But it served within the narrow limits of religious publications only, and of the spirit of even the early Italian Renaissance writers or the sixteenth-century scientists nothing was felt in the East. In music, the situation was still more unpropitious, for Russia did not possess a notation for polyphony, nor was there any beginning, as in the West, of the chromatic style. The earliest scores date possibly from the beginning of the seventeenth century, and even they are somewhat obscure.

Special care and precise investigation are necessary in the area of science and artisanship. Too often we read about the desire of the tsars for European scientists and artisans. Such general statements are misleading. What the tsars did seek was an improvement of armaments, and their efforts to secure foreign help concerned chiefly the art of war. Miners were sought to get the raw material for a modern army, cannon-makers and engineers were requested, and arquebusiers were introduced. European methods of making guns, of fortifying towns, of planting mines and the like were studied.[22] All served, as later under Peter the Great, the needs of the state, while the fine arts and handicrafts, those of the gold- and silversmith or of the potter and weaver, were but seldom considered, and among the scientists only the practicing doctor was encouraged to come. Herberstein mentions several foreign bombardiers and artillery men in Moscow—one from Spires in Germany, one from the Inn Valley, one from Italy. Mercenaries served in the armies of Vassilii III and, under Ivan IV, formed entire regiments of Scots, Germans or Scandinavians. Toward the end of the century they totalled, according to Fletcher, perhaps 8,500 men out of armies amounting to well over 100,000 and reaching perhaps 300,000.[23]

All foreigners were subject to many regulations; even merchants could not travel freely, could not trade except in those branches which were stipulated in their privileges, and had to stay in quarters specially set aside for them. In Moscow they, and the sprinkling of masons, architects, painters, interpreters and doctors who had come to Russia, were assigned to the later famous German suburb, which at the time of the death of Ivan IV was composed of perhaps little more than 150 houses.[24] Among the temporary western visitors we find travelers, of whom Adelung counts a total of 79 for the years before 1600, most of whom have left some kind of description.[25] There were, of course, many others of whom, for lack of a travel account, we know little or nothing. Furthermore, there were at times considerable numbers of war prisoners in Muscovy. Some of these ultimately stayed on and served the tsar in the army or the administration. A few entered the official class, among which—not counting Poles— a few hundred could be found at the end of the century.[26] Some Germans had by that time even been granted lands and had acquired serfs, entering thereby the pomiestie class.[27] In the time of Boris Godunov we can witness a rapid increase of foreigners.[28] Yet even then, the attraction of Russia was limited by the fact that all foreigners encountered difficulties when they later wished to leave Moscow.

The influx of foreigners might have been accelerated had the rulers set an example through marriage alliances. Significantly, Ivan the Great, Vassilii III, Ivan the Terrible and Boris Godunov all considered Western marriages—Ivan the Great and Boris for their sons and daughters, Vassili III and Ivan the Terrible for themselves. Vassili actually did wed, in a second marriage, Helena Glinskaia, daughter of a Lithuanian grandee who had been educated in Germany and Italy and had fled to Russia; Ivan the Terrible played with the idea of taking Elizabeth of England or one of her relatives as his sixth or seventh wife and Boris reached an engagement of his daughter to a Danish prince, who unluckily died in Moscow before the wedding. But it was in reality expense, customs and religion which up to the time of Peter the Great put insurmountable obstacles in the path of such an alignment of East and West.

Small as the influence of Europeans in Russia was thus bound to remain, the influence was smaller still in the other direction. To be sure, Russian envoys saw many parts of the West. It would be useful to know what interest in the East they evoked, what lasting impression they made and what they reported at home about Valladolid, Madrid and Toledo (where they visited the Emperor Charles V), about the Mediterranean Sea—where one mission fell into the hands of pirates—about the Netherlands, Scotland and England, and also about France—which they once crossed on their way home from Spain. But we have little information. Those who fled Russia, like some Judaizers, or Prince Kurbsky, or even the students whom Godunov dispatched to Germany, France and England and who never returned, certainly failed to exercise an influence on East-West intercourse.

The conclusions thus to be drawn from a study of East-West relations in the sixteenth century can perhaps be tentatively proposed as follows:

(1) As already stated, a new, factual approach seems desirable and even essential for a balanced appraisal since careless investigations often see contacts as causes for effects, while in reality we have no more than parallels, which can be explained on other bases and could be derived from economic or general human factors.

(2) The accent on Russian relations with Western nations does not lie with those with empire and papacy, interesting as these are, for they served Russian pride rather than the needs of East and West. It is the relations with northern, mainly Protestant Europe, with its commercial prospects, needs and realities, that are decisive. This point leads to a third, more important conclusion.

(3) It is not so much Russia that seeks Europe; it is Europe that must take Russia into account. The weight of the tsarist empire makes itself felt, based not on Moscow's foreign policies but on the inner strength of the country. As Platonov in his _Boris Godunov_ says: "One calumnied Moscow, one mocked at her, but no longer could one ignore her."[29] The fact that it was Russia's inner strength which impressed on Europe the impossibility of neglecting her is amply evinced also by the fact that, when an inner decay occurred after 1580, we witness a simultaneous renewed alienation from Europe.

(4) Important though the discovery of the northern route was, it was not the sea route from the White Sea that constituted the link between Russia and Europe. It was the Baltic sea lanes and the increasingly important ports of Narva, Riga and Reval which formed the major link.

(5) Religious disputations between Orthodox and Protes-

tants, as well as Catholics, were held chiefly for the sake of appearance. If they taught anything at all, they divulged to the West existing differences and led the Western world to desist from attempts at amalgamation, which offered no prospects, rather than to continue in the illusion that a common outlook and a common goal existed which could lead the Eastern and Western churches together.

(6) The role Europeans played in sixteenth-century Russia has to be reviewed. Some of them, like Herberstein, have written excellent accounts; others, like Fioraventi, have erected famous buildings; still others have been well-known doctors or artisans. Their names can be found repeatedly in many textbooks, thus suggesting that there were vast numbers of foreigners, of whom the most famous are mentioned. In reality there were hardly more than those few "famous" ones. Repetition does not increase their importance; actually their indirect influence was even less than their public impression. Since they lived by themselves they had little opportunity to inspire others whose traditions were different.

(7) Because of some external evidences, the effect of the Renaissance on Russia is still overestimated. Techniques, but not the spirit of the Renaissance, were adopted; its meaning remained alien to the East.

Some enlightenment concerning the essence of Russia's past and present history can be gained from these conclusions. A distinction can be made between those areas in which Russia remained Russian and those where she was open to foreign influences. Perhaps a parallel between sixteenth-century Russian and Western developments can be made. Perhaps the relationship of East and West is characterized by Russia using European techniques and methods while continuing to keep separate and emphasize her own spirit and culture.

Chapter III

THE ROLE OF NARVA IN THE SIXTEENTH CENTURY: A CONTRIBUTION TO THE STUDY OF RUSSO-EUROPEAN RELATIONS*

The sixteenth century, which abounds in important historical problems, offers the scholar of today a steadily growing area for research.[1] Publications in the area of sixteenth-century East European history are rapidly increasing in number; they can serve to improve our very incomplete knowledge of the relationship which existed between East and West, between Russia and Europe. Much has been written and philosophized about this subject, yet sufficient factual historical data have not yet been collected on which to base valid conclusions. It is a task for future historians to present these relations in their totality. Individual areas, however, can well be discussed on the basis of existing preliminary studies. To these areas belong the economic aspects for which we now possess a number of statistical studies that include the sixteenth century.

The historian who undertakes the task of dealing with the economic questions of that era will soon turn his attention to the comparatively unimportant port of Narva in Eastern Livonia —a port which offered few facilities to ships of more than 120 tons. In 1558, the Russians conquered Narva and, during the subsequent twenty years trade there, came to constitute the chief link connecting East and West. The conquest of the Bal-

---

*Reprinted with permission from Historische Zeitschrift, Vol. 172, (1951).

tic port of Narva by the Russians (and therewith the opening of an appropriate direct sea route from Russia to the West) occurred at almost the same moment that the discovery of the sea route from England past the North Cape to the White Sea also opened the possibility of direct traffic in the North.[2]

Narva's fall, and the appearance of Russia on the Baltic shores therewith, very soon had far-reaching consequences for the whole Western world. The Russian success affected the policy of Spain and the Netherlands, of England, Scotland and Denmark, of the German emperor and Saxonian electors, of the pope, the Scandinavian kings, of France, Poland, and Turkey—in short, nearly every part of Europe was quickly involved. And a study of the events related to Narva's conquest furnishes the historian with an occasion for considerations which, transcending local issues, can be of value in pondering general human questions as well as, more specifically, the course of international relations. Such a study also invites parallels between past and present—parallels, to be sure, which should not tempt us to premature analogies. For, notwithstanding the stimulating and engaging work of a Spengler, Toynbee or Berdiaev, we cannot in our judgment of present and future depend on our study of past events, nor even on an analysis of their rhythm. Neither individual facts nor broader currents of the past can offer a basis for a reliable judgment. But careful examination and evaluation of the past does give us a certain understanding for important and lasting characteristics marking human society. Once these traits are grasped, we may then attempt to draw further conclusions as to the effect under given circumstances of actions of an individual or of a nation.[3]

Even for the short period from 1558 to 1581 (during which, as a result of the conquest by the Russians, Narva came to constitute the center of East-West relations) the history of the town offers many opportunities for such considerations. It demonstrates the significance and insignificance of all human planning, man's wisdom and shortsightedness, the relativity of economic and ideological motives. It illustrates many great international problems, such as that of the "freedom of the seas," or that of the use, and the drawbacks, of naval supremacy. It bears on special political questions, as for instance on the issue of the "dominium maris Baltici," or the problem of the "Iron Curtain." All these topics play an important and lasting role in the relations between East and West.

The origin of the rise of Narva in the sixteenth century goes back to the year 1493. In that year news of the discovery of America spread throughout Europe. In the following year the Hanseatic office in Novgorod, up to then the most important trading center for all East-West commerce, was destroyed by Tsar Ivan the Great. Describing the destruction of Novgorod, the Russian historian Vipper has maintained that Ivan's action against the Hanseatic merchants there can serve as a proof for Ivan's determination to abolish the intermediary position they held and to establish a direct link between Russia and the West.[4] This statement is, however, untenable—even if we take into consideration that Ivan had already started to construct the fortress of Ivangorod, which was situated on the right bank of the Narova stream, opposite Narva. For it was strategical rather than commercial considerations which led to the subjection of Novgorod and to the closing of the Hanseatic office there combined with Russia's interest in establishing closer ties with Denmark. A letter written much later by Ivan the Terrible and addressed to Prince Kurbsky, cited by Vipper, in which the tsar affirmed that with his policy toward the West he was only following the example of his grandfather, should not blind us to the fact that Ivan the Great envisaged other aims than his grandson.

The effect which the destruction of the Hanseatic factory in Novgorod had upon the West differed from place to place. In general, the former situation had been rather satisfactory. It had given the Western powers extensive control over Moscow's foreign trade with the technically progressive countries in Europe. Once Novgorod was irrevocably lost, the greater part of the Hanse was willing to make Narva its successor, hoping thereby to be able to continue exercising old controls—though with the help of new means. In this connection, the admission of Narva into the Hanseatic League was repeatedly considered.[5] But a favorable decision was at no time taken because the Livonian ports of Riga and Reval opposed such a move. They aimed at becoming the heirs of Novgorod themselves and at securing the economic and political advantages which this town had possessed. In 1540, they established a monopoly for their merchants by which all overseas merchants were barred from carrying on direct trade with the Russians (trade "von Gast zu Gast").[6] Instead, all business had to be negotiated with the merchants of Riga and Reval, who in turn dealt with the Russians.[7] The greed which was evinced by the establishment of such a monopoly exasperated the other Hanseatic towns, and especially the town of Lübeck which for centuries had maintained direct trade with the Russians in Novgorod. The quarrel which ensued concerned issues so basic that it eventually wrecked the position which the Hanse had held so long in the field of Russian trade.

Ivan the Terrible followed this quarrel between the Livonian towns and the rest of the Hanse, including its headquarters in Lübeck, with greatest attention. He recognized that the policies of Lübeck opened the possibility to him for furthering his own projects and for restoring the interrupted direct traffic with the West. He therefore offered the merchants of Narva in 1557 the right to establish a factory and an office on the other side of the Narova river in Ivangorod. He assured them of all the privileges there which they had once possessed in Novgorod.[8] In doing this he pursued the aim of undermining the monopolistic position of Riga and Reval and reopening for Lübeck's skippers the direct traffic to the East. Narva, however, proved to be too shortsighted and insisted on insignificant but unrealizable conditions.[9] As a result, Ivan's peaceful efforts to find a harbor and outlet on the sea met with failure. Thereupon he took up arms. In January, 1558, he invaded Livonia; in April he started the siege of Narva, and in May he conquered both town and fortress. Since he subsequently failed to conquer the coveted ports of Riga and Reval also, he had no choice but to make Narva his main outlet to the Baltic Sea. This plan he carried out, and until its conquest by the Swedes in 1581 Narva remained Russia's most important "window to the West."

It would be incorrect to gather from these events that the tsar possessed great "foresight" and to conclude that he had a "far-reaching understanding for the historical significance" of his conquests. To be sure, proof is available that Ivan the Terrible understood better than Ivan the Great the essential problem which Russia faced. It was he who consistently pursued the task of bringing German craftsmen, engineers and doctors into his country; who energetically sought to strengthen the foreign trade of Russia; who had welcomed the English who had discovered the northern sea route to his realms; and who had allowed the Swedes to travel by way of Russia to India and China if, on the other hand, they were willing to permit to the Russian merchants passage to Lübeck, Antwerp and other Western cities.[10] Nevertheless, the words of Nicholas Dobroliubov, in his famous article about Peter the Great, Ivan's counterpart in Russian history, can be applied to a judgment of Ivan's actions. Dobroliubov wrote that the tsar's reforms and innovations "were inevitable owing to the very nature of Peter's activities;" and if "we credit . . . subsequent influence to the genius of the ruler," we implicitly presuppose that he "clearly foresaw all the consequences." Such a statement would, according to Dobroliubov, indicate that we "confuse the results with the deed." "Transcendental inspiration, sudden intuition . . . and clairvoyancy belong to the realm of the conjurer's art," but not to that of historical personalities.[11] It is in this sense that—just as with the work of Peter the Great—one has to reduce Ivan the Terrible's foresight and actions concerning Narva to the measure of what is possible in history, and to evaluate them within this framework.

An examination of the sources makes it clear that it was not only Ivan's military might, nor the accident of a fire or the carelessness of Reval and of all of Livonia, which forced Narva to surrender to the Russians. It was the free will of the inhabitants which contributed most to the fall of the town. Especially the lower classes of the population favored subjection to the Russians, for they expected milder treatment from them than from the lords they had. Yet they were not the only ones so inclined; even some members of the Order of the Livonian Knights favored an alliance with Ivan. And the Livonian Master of the Order, Wilhelm von Fürstenberg, correctly reported after the fall of the town that the most eminent people in Narva had conspired for more than a year to get under the protection of the archenemy.[12] In order to encourage the tendencies propitious to his aims, Ivan was wise enough to propose sufficiently generous conditions. In consequence, many additional citizens, as it is reported, lent an ear to his proposals.

Once the fortress was taken, the tsar acted in accordance with his promises and with a moderation such as his grandfather had never displayed. Instead of destroying, he built up. Apart from a series of minor incidents and occasional punitive expeditions, Narva was treated honestly; and soon the town saw an unprecedented economic upswing. It was not long before 50 Russian soldiers sufficed to defend it against attacks from the West—that very place which just recently had been considered a main bulwark of the West against the barbaric East.[13]

In 1558 Narva began to rise to a key position in European policies. Since Ivan was unable to bring his war in Livonia to a satisfactory end and failed to conquer Riga and Reval, the town of Narva kept its political role until its fall to the Swedes in 1581; its economic position was held for over a century.

As soon as the Russians had occupied Narva, the skippers from Lübeck began to by-pass Riga and Reval and to sail directly to Narva. Soon, those from Hamburg, Antwerp, London, as well as Swedes, Danes, Scots and Dutchmen did likewise; even some Frenchmen appeared in the port. Eventually, no matter how exposed she was to attacks from the Russian side, Reval herself began to trade with her enemy in Narva.[14]

The occupation of Narva brought a sudden new distribution of power, and Narva's rise exerted its influence upon the courts of the whole continent. The effect was threefold. In the realm of strategy, it became necessary for the West to recall part of the troops which were needed for defense against the Turks so that they might be used to protect Catholic Christianity on the north-eastern borders of the empire. This meant the end of all hopes for a common crusade by East and West against the Unbelievers. In the realm of diplomacy, it became unavoidable to give consideration to a Russia now possessed of free access to the Western powers, even though she was not yet admitted to the conference tables of the Western kingdoms. The existing balance was shattered. And in the realm of economics, a revolution of the whole existing order was brought about. New economic organisms came into existence and began to flourish, and bilateral treaties with the East, stipulating reciprocity, helped young powers like England and Sweden, as well as Russia herself, gain new prominence. All these events were the more important as no one could foresee the results. All of Europe—the Catholic as well as the Protestant countries —felt insecure; and questions connected with the exchange of goods with Russia, no matter whether they concerned war materials or everyday commodities, gained unexpected importance. The German emperor, who saw his first task as the protection and preservation of the existing order, accordingly sent directions and requests for help to Spain, Sweden, Livonia, Lübeck, Poland and Denmark. He asked for cessation of the dangerous trade in Narva; and in the course of time, his efforts, prohibitions and directions, as well as similar ones by other rulers, were duplicated on many sides. The effect was, however, indifferent.[15] No one was willing to abandon the Narva trade unless all other nations and merchants did likewise. For everyone feared that the abstinence of one would only serve the covetousness of others. Bitter competition resulted, and further deterioration in relations between the individual European trading countries occurred.

Perhaps it would have been better for the West had the nations taken the point of view which Charles V had once defended in relation to the Turks. As A. Winckler reports, Charles refused to prohibit trade with Turkey because, he thought, such a ban would serve only to weaken the trading towns and make it impossible for them to contribute their share to the general good.[16] But the political situation in 1558 and the quickly rising influence of new trading nations—such as England with her demanding, mercantilistically oriented joint stock companies—made corresponding action with regard to Russia impossible. Eventually a compromise had to be worked out: normal commerce was allowed, but the export of war material was prohibited. This compromise, however, turned out to be equally unsatisfactory, for no agreement could be reached as to what constituted "war material." In the sixteenth century, war was as all-embracing as in later ages, especially in the economic field. It therefore remained a question of whether or not grain, for instance, was to be excluded from, or included in, the list of prohibited goods to Narva; after all, it could serve the maintenance of the troops and horses of the enemy. And what about saltpeter, which was used for the production of amunition? Or gold, which was needed to pay mercenaries? Or salt, the want of which would have brought to a standstill large areas of the Russian economy?[17] Apart from wine and cloth, everything was bound to appear useful for the Russians in their war preparations; and even wine and cloth could help to strengthen the enemy by permitting him to increase his exports, and therewith his influence.

Further, the political situation as it had developed under the new circumstances held unsolvable contradictions. Since the end of the fifteenth century, pope and emperor had realized —and had considered in all their negotiations with Russia— that the Russian empire could act as a counterweight against Turkish might. Was it then advisable for the emperor to weaken a possible ally in the fight against the arch-enemy of Christendom? Other contradictory interests appeared elsewhere: trade with Russia constituted the backbone of Dutch wealth; should Philip II of Spain attempt to prohibit the trade to his richest provinces when because of their religion they were already in rebellion against him? Russia was also a most important trade partner of Lübeck; was it possible to allow the weakening of Lübeck if this would lead only to a gain in power for Reval and Riga—the two Livonian cities which turned out to be most unwilling to contribute to the defense of the Occident? English and Scottish merchants had only recently succeeded in gaining concessions from Moscow with regard to the much desired trade with Persia and India by way of Russia; could Queen Elizabeth dare insult the tsar and therewith endanger the new connections? Indeed, there remained, at best, Sweden and Poland; because as neighbors of the tsar they had the most reason to fear any increase in his might, they had cause to impede the trade in Narva. But even in Sweden and Poland insurmountable contradictions existed. The one, Poland, insisted on vigorous action against Russia, while the other, Sweden, which fought Poland over the Livonian inheritance, considered it more advantageous to carry on a policy of pacification and friendship with Russia and to try to gain permanent advantages from such a policy.

Thus, it was the occupation of Narva by the Russians and their entry into the economic and diplomatic affairs of the West which caused sharply contradictory tendencies within the European community of nations. Growing conflicts rendered increasingly difficult all common action against the presumed enemy. If the Western powers had intended to lower an "Iron Curtain" in order to cut off the Russian "barbarian" from the Occident, if they sought to limit Russia's productive potential and to hinder the increase of her military might by an embargo on ammunition, food and information, and by preventing craftsmen, engineers, and teachers from departing for Russia, then the execution of such intentions became impossible with the opening of direct connections via Narva.

The divergent tendencies among the European powers led, in 1563, to the outbreak of a war which soon engulfed nearly all of North and North Eastern Europe. The antagonists were Denmark, Sweden, Norway, Lübeck and Poland. This conflict is known as the Northern Seven Years' War. Very wisely, Russia not only kept aloof from any involvement, but opened her harbor to belligerent and neutral nations alike. This served to increase the rivalries among the states of Northern Europe and to sharpen their already existing hostilities over Narva. Soon the Danes, as well as the Hanse and Lübeck, depending as they did upon Eastern trade, began to experience severe financial reverses. Their difficulties were multiplied by the fact that their enemy, Sweden, with control of the naval bases in the triangle Stockholm-Åbo-Reval, dominated the whole eastern part of the Baltic. And while the belligerents suffered, the neutral nations, above all Russia herself, but also England and the Netherlands, were quick to understand how to exploit the situation. Soon, trade with Narva became so significant for England that in 1564 it could be called "the best traffic for the realm."[18]

The development of the Baltic trade via Narva and its

repercussions in Europe afford an example of human shortsightedness and the inability of man to anticipate the consequences of his political actions. Actually Narva's role was not more than a secondary phenomenon, following upon the contemporary voyage of discovery by the Englishmen Chancellor and Willoughby. Looking for a new route to China, they had been investigating the possibility of a sea route past the North Cape. The outcome of their endeavors was, however, that Chancellor did not get to China at all; instead he landed in Russia. Even this accident did not lead to the consequences which he thereupon envisaged. In fact, the significance of the newly found route for the establishment of relations between East and West is still overestimated. The true importance of the discovery of the Northern route lay in the unexpected result that Russia, and consequently also the Baltic sea routes, gained in importance. The attention of English and other foreign merchants was attracted by the extraordinary possibilities for profit which seemed to offer themselves there. The sea route to Archangel remained unsatisfactory; it was insecure and dangerous. But the fact that it opened prospects for direct contact between Europe and Russia and that such a contact appeared greatly desirable sufficed to stimulate activity also in other regions. Without premeditation, old routes increased in importance and attractiveness. Simultaneously, political conflicts of unexpected magnitude arose, and Narva gained a place which seemed to be justified neither by logic nor by the course of history.

During the years when the Northern Seven Years War weakened the five participants, Narva reached the climax of its significance, flourishing as never before. In preceding centuries, the Hanseats had exercised a virtual trade monopoly. This may have tended to lead to a deterioration of the quality of the goods which were traded in Baltic harbors and to a rise in prices. Now, despite all dangers threatening them by pirates, buccaneers and warring nations, merchants from everywhere came to Narva. They came from Hamburg, Breslau, Augsburg, Nuremberg and Leipzig; from Scotland, England, Denmark and Sweden; from Amsterdam, Antwerp, Dieppe, La Rochelle and Cadiz. All were welcome. The turnover of goods offered in Narva increased and prices sometimes fell below the level at which the goods were traded in other regions. Gold, for instance, was offered in Russia at a rate up to one third less than in the German empire; the same was true for damask, linen from England and other products.[19]

Of what magnitude was the trade in Narva? The statistics which we can derive from Nina E. Bang's Tabeller for the commerce to and from Narva offer perhaps a fair basis for a meaningful estimate.[20] Even though we cannot claim to present with the help of these records a precise picture, we may gain from them at least a point of departure for some reliable conclusions. They provide us with data regarding those ships which on their way to and from Russia paid dues in the Danish Sound. Thus, according to Bang's Tabeller 76 ships coming from Narva sailed through the Danish Sound in 1567—in the midst of the Northern War. By comparison, in the year prior to the occupation of Narva by the Russians there had been none, and after Russia lost Narva there was again none. Seventy-six ships—this meant 40 per cent of all the ships which coming from Riga passed the Sound, as opposed to zero per cent ten years earlier. At that, the year 1567 did not even bring record figures. Records had already been reached, as far as the sixteenth century is concerned, in 1566. Of course, the figures indicate no more than part of the whole traffic, for three categories which formed part of it do not appear in the Tabeller: first, those ships which, although sailing officially through the Sound, for political reasons gave incorrect information as to their place of destination or as to their port of departure; second, those which were smuggled past the Danish customs office, either by way of the Sound itself or by way of the Belt; and third, apart from the ships of the Danes themselves, those which did not touch Danish waters because they sailed from or to the Baltic harbors of Germany, Sweden or Finland. We read, for instance, that during the year 1567, 33 ships from Lübeck alone arrived in Narva.[21] Such figures make us doubt the statement by Forsten that by the middle of August almost 100 ships had been in Narva—an estimate which appears to be rather too low.[22] Moreover, for political reasons, many Western goods were sent first to Viborg, or even to Stockholm, or Åbo, where they were reloaded and shipped on to Narva. We may not be mistaken when estimating the total commerce in Narva at several hundred ships and the turnover at no less than that in Riga, which possessed the largest harbor of the entire Eastern Baltic.[23]

Owing to its conquest by the Russians, Narva thus developed within ten years into one of the wealthiest ports of the Baltic and, in addition, to one of the most important political focal points. Beginning with 1558, German emperors, imperial diets and Hanse diets were forced to consider regularly the issues which resulted from the Russian conquest. It was because of Narva and because of the Russians there that the German emperor had to turn to Spain, England, Sweden and Poland to implore their support; that the dukes of Pomerania and Mecklenburg, the king of Denmark and his brother-in-law, the duke of Saxony, had to engage in feverish activity in order to adapt their needs and their policies—especially those with regard to the house of Habsburg—to the newly created situation; and that the Queen of England found herself obliged to make concessions to Denmark in the matter of the Sound dues, which had an effect far beyond this question, though it alone seemed to be at issue at the time.[24] Then, too, Russia's expansion on the shores of the Baltic exercised a decisive influence upon Sweden's domestic and foreign policies. It was for Narva's sake that the Vasa empire had become involved in a war with its neighbors, which was to last seven years; but beyond this disaster, it was also in consequence of the Narva question that the Vasas had to deal with grave dissensions at home and with a dangerous split within the royal house.[25] Events in Narva help to explain the political actions of Poland and her kings Sigismund Augustus and, later, Henry of Valois and his deputy, Montluc. Like the German emperor, they all sought to put an end to the Russian danger and therefore tried to stop the trade in Narva.[26] Even Spain and King Philip II became involved. Philip's governor in the Netherlands, the Duke of Alva, is said to have expressed the feelings and mood of his time with regard to the Russian question, which developed out of the conquest of Narva, in the peculiar words: "l'Europe sera libre ou cosaque."[27]

After a few years, however, and in accord with the only valid historical law, namely that every historical situation is subject to continuous transformation, a change occurred in the views held regarding the Russian danger and the actual potential of Russia's ability to expand. The reason for this change should not be seen, though, in the dialectical effect which Russia's possession of Narva had upon Europe. It may be found rather in the internal conditions of Russia, in the weakening of the inherent strength of the country caused by Ivan's despotism. In the Baltic provinces, this despotism was especially felt after new attacks had been launched on Livonia. They brought a siege of Reval by Ivan's shadow king Magnus of Holstein and led to the final destruction of old Novgorod and the introduction of the Oprichnina in Narva.[28]

In the same year, 1570, in which these events occurred, the Northern Seven Years War came to an end. Peace was concluded at Stettin. Concerning Narva, the treaty provided that no one should interfere with the trade there. All traffic should remain free and undisturbed—except that the German emperor should have the right to prescribe exceptions if at any time the boundaries of the empire seemed threatened.[29] These regulations remained in force throughout the period of ten years during which Narva was still in Russian hands.

Soon trade in nearly all fields began to flourish anew. Scots and English, French and Dutch, merchants from Lübeck, Denmark and—notwithstanding all protests by the Polish kings—even those from Poland took part in it. From time to time, the emperor tried to prohibit the export of war material, "wehr, pantzer, harnisch, puchssenn, spiessenn, pulver, artolerey, saltz, salpeter, kupfer noch andere metall oder munition, ferners auch kein korn, selber noch reichs muntz."[30] But the prohibitions issued by him, which raised again the numerous questions that had been recognized as insoluble before, were not taken seriously, and he did not have the power to enforce his regulations.[31]

The reports of an attentive and sympathetic observer, namely the French ambassador in Denmark, Charles de Dançay, show the significance which, in the meantime, the trade in Narva had assumed in East-West relations and which it was to retain. Dançay realized that the commerce in Narva constituted an all-European problem which touched all countries—from Scotland to Hungary, and from Spain to Sweden.[32] But though evaluating correctly consequences and angers, he could no better than others point a way out of the dilemma in which the Western powers found themselves. For on the one side, the Western nations wanted to exploit fully the economic advantages of the trade with Russia, while, on the other, they were unwilling to face the political consequences. This dilemma was also pointed out by another Frenchman, the historian de Thou. When speaking of the Narva problem, he tells of the merchants of Lübeck who, like the English and Dutch and many others, "blind with greed," overlooked the grave effect which the role of Russia was bound to have for all the European nations in view of the immediate and future threat it posed to them.[33] And a contemporary Latin source compares the problem with another one which a century earlier had to be answered by the Ligurians and Greeks. At that time, out of greed, these two peoples had not wanted to renounce trading with the Turks and had thereby given the enemy the means to conquer them and, at the same time, all of the Balkans.[34] Likewise, whatever principles and ideologies were at stake, the Narva question was ultimately decided, as the events were to show, by economic advantage rather than by political foresight. No regulation regarding trade with the presumed enemy and in favor of the general welfare was observed if it did not allow for the desire for profit by the individual merchant or even for the wishes of mercantilistically inclined governments and the interests of state-subsidized joint stock companies.

Trade in Narva, consequently, went on unchanged during the seventies. During this decade a number of new problems emerged which ever since have with regularity afflicted the Western states. Thus, in connection with Narva, the question of the "freedom of the seas" emerged and was raised by Dançay in his correspondence—a question which had begun to play a role when the English had started their voyages past the North Cape, and which was enhanced when the Russians conquered Narva. In spite of all the well-sounding proclamations on the part of the English,[35] who subsequently were themselves to become the chief sinners against this principle of the freedom of the seas, no solution was found; on the contrary, trade with Russia led the English as well as the Danes to attempts at monopolizing the sea routes, both in the North and on the Baltic. No protest of Ivan the Terrible or, later, of Boris Godunov was to be of any avail. Another question which arose in connection with the Narva navigation concerned the "neutrality" of goods which were shipped under a neutral flag. Not only the English but also the Hanse[36] and the Dutch insisted that a neutral flag protects all goods, including war material, against seizure by belligerents. This principle, too, could neither than nor later find general acceptance.

Perhaps a consideration of these events is apt to induce us to speculate as to the course which the relations between Russia and Europe might have taken had Russia been able to consolidate its hold on the Baltic outlet. Although such speculations are unscientific and unacceptable insofar as they relate to that which might or should have happened, yet they serve a purpose if they afford us a deeper insight into what actually did happen. If Narva had remained in Russian hands, the possession of an open harbor would have made possible, apart from economic relations, a cultural, scientific and political rapprochment between Russia and Europe. Closer contact between Western and Eastern societies could not have been delayed for a century and a half, until the time when Peter the Great not only reoccupied Narva but then also conquered Riga and Reval. Furthermore, the disintegrating policy of a "European balance of power," instead of European cooperation, would have had to follow a different path if Russia had been included earlier in the European community. The problem of serfdom in Russia would likewise have had to be solved earlier than it actually was; and perhaps participation in the development of the West, such as Ivan the Terrible had envisaged, might have brought a measure of equalization between the stages of development in East and West. But actual events took a different turn: Russia lost Narva. Beginning with the year 1577, Ivan's power in Livonia waned. Soon a Swedish army stood at the gates of the town. To be sure, the Swedes had first to learn the lesson which the Russians, under Peter the Great, were to learn later when in 1695 they tried to take the fortress of Azov—namely, that land forces without sea forces were not enough to conquer a well-defended port town. As a result, the Swedes had at first no success.[37] Only in 1581, when they reappeared before Narva, were their land forces supported by a strong fleet. In the meantime, in

1580, Ivan had found himself compelled to withdraw troops from Narva in order to use them against Poland, which was attacking his Western borders.[38] The Swedes seized upon this advantage and now succeeded in conquering fortress and harbor.

Like its earlier conquest, Narva's surrender had far-reaching consequences. This observation does not refer primarily to the bitter quarrel which, as a result of Narva's fall, ensued between Poland and Sweden, for the Poles envied King John his conquest and could not conceal that they would have preferred to see Narva remain in Russia's possession than fall into Swedish hands.[39] Nor does it refer to the revival of competition between Narva and Reval, or to the relations between the Northern powers and England. The most important consequence which followed consisted in the effect which Narva's surrender produced on the position of Russia herself. Once more she was cut off for the greater part of the year from Europe; once more she became dependent upon the good or ill will of her neighbors. As before 1558, foreign craftsmen, soldiers, scientists and even diplomats could, as a rule, reach the empire of the tsar only with the permission of Poland or Sweden. The medieval economic structure pervading her trade and industry was thereby bolstered, and medieval practices were prolonged. Again, Russia was forced to orient herself economically and culturally toward the East; she was to seek compensation in Siberia for the losses sustained in the West. Tendencies toward the "Aiatization" of Russia were strengthened.

Statistics give us a picture of the development: In the year following the surrender of Narva, we do not find a single ship which upon passing the Danish Sound gave Narva as its port of departure. Reval revived; without Russia, Narva tended to be forgotten.[40] During the following fifteen years, we do not find in Bang's Tabeller a single year when more than five ships sailed from Narva through the Sound. Generally, there were no more than two or one. Riga, from which 135 ships had sailed in 1566 when 98 had come from Narva on their way through the Sound, or 205 in 1567 as against Narva's 76, showed a traffic invariably of the same magnitude: some 125 to 280 ships per year. Narva, on the other hand, showed figures of no more than one half of one per cent of those of Riga, while it had been 40 per cent to 70 per cent at the time of Russian rule. The commerce with Baltic harbors and Viborg is not even included in these figures.[41]

The fate of Narva and the role which the town was suddenly called upon to play in the sixteenth century—even if it lasted only a short time—serve to illustrate significant historical questions which have cast their shadow upon later and present problems. The sixteenth century gave a foretaste of the effect which Russia was destined to exert on the Occident once she gained access to the West.

Chapter IV

A MILESTONE IN EUROPEAN HISTORY: THE DANISH-RUSSIAN TREATY OF 1562*

For several centuries Denmark shared with the Hanseatic league predominance in the Baltic area, but the first three decades of the sixteenth century witnessed radical changes. The Hanse was affected adversely when new routes were discovered to important overseas markets, when European states underwent fundamental reorganizations in structure, and when for some reason the herring changed their course. Denmark found herself weakened by the political revolution following the Reformation, the expansion of Spanish, Dutch and English seapower, and the dissolution of the Kalmar Union due to the Swedish independence movement. As a result, the old balance of power in the Baltic area was destroyed. Had Sweden, Poland, Prussia, the Holy Roman Empire or any combination of these taken over the place which Denmark had held for so long, no significant new development would have resulted. The fact that Denmark's decline coincided with and partly caused the rise of Russian power in northern Europe marks the importance of the period.

Russia, for centuries split up into a number of autonomous states, several of them subjected to Mongolian rulers, had started on a path of consolidation under Ivan III, the Great. However, that otherwise discerning Muscovite ruler showed little comprehension of Russia's destiny in the Baltic area when

---

*Reprinted with permission from The Slavonic and East European Review, Vol. XXII, (1944).

he allowed the destruction of Novgorod with its important trade. The city's ruin contributed to an extension of the power and importance of the Livonian harbors of Riga and Reval, which resulted in the increased dependency of the tsar's realms on the Livonian state.[1]

With more clarity of vision than Ivan III, his grandson Ivan the Terrible set himself the task of remedying the situation. In 1548, he sent a German agent, Hans Schlitte, a resident of Moscow, to Germany to hire a number of artisans, doctors and engineers who were to come to Russia and instruct the people in western methods and ways.[2] But because the Hanse and Livonia feared Russian competition and economic growth, none of these people reached Moscow. Though allowed by Emperor Charles V to depart, some were intercepted in Lübeck when embarking for Russia, some—discouraged—returned, and others who actually got as far as Livonia, were taken prisoners there. One of them, who had been detained for years by the Livonians, eventually sought compensation for his sufferings through a German diet, but, of course, no action was taken.[3]

The failure of Schlitte's mission demonstrated to Ivan the necessity of a change in his political aims and measures. In order to eliminate the control which the rulers of Livonia had applied in the affair and which they could exercise at any time over Russian economic and political relations with central and western Europe, he decided to lay claim to the Baltic provinces as his own ancient heritage[4] and, if necessary, take forceful possession of the country with its important gateways.

The winning of the Baltic provinces was thus no aim in itself. Indeed, aside from its rich harbors, the country possessed little that could contribute to the growth of Ivan's empire. It constituted a medium only for free intercourse with the powers around and beyond the Baltic Sea, and it was on this ultimate goal rather than the mere acquisition of land that Ivan's attention was centered. The discovery of the route around the

North Cape, it is true, had aroused hopes for other possibilities of direct contact with foreign nations, but because of navigation hazards, the new route remained unreliable. The first great Russian mission which Ivan sent to England via the North Cape was shipwrecked. Richard Chancellor, who had piloted the fleet, was drowned, and the Russian envoy escaped death as if by a miracle.[5]

It was natural under these circumstances for Ivan to seize the first real opportunity which offered itself to him for co-operation with a Western power, and he saw his chance in Denmark, perceiving that possibilities for a satisfactory arrangement were more promising in connection with this country than with other Baltic states, the Empire, the Hanse, the Livonian Order, Poland and Sweden. The Empire had shown its weakness and unreliability in the Schlitte affair, while on the same occasion the Hanse and the Livonian Order had demonstrated their active opposition to any Russian progress. Poland was traditionally hostile to Russia and engaged in schemes of her own in the Baltic provinces. Sweden disputed Russia in Karelia on the Finnish border; wars had been fought repeatedly, and as yet Gustavus Vasa had not been recognized by Ivan as a king of equal standing with other European sovereigns.[6]

On the other hand, few points of dissension existed between Russia and Denmark. Some permanent trouble persisted on the northern border between Norway and Russia, where Russian settlers were accused of infiltrating into Norwegian territory and pushing out the original inhabitants.[7] The Livonian question was also full of material for conflict, because Denmark, out of fear of Swedish ambitions and profiting from the decline of the Livonian Order, tried to gain substantial holdings for herself and to re-establish her dominion given up in the fourteenth century. Furthermore, the Danes shared the prevailing distrust of Russia which, despite the Christian faith of the inhabitants, was considered a danger to western Christendom not unlike the

Turkish Mussulman; and Ivan himself, notwithstanding his often proved magnanimity and sense of justice, was generally described as a cruel tyrant, who had but little in common with the human race.[8]

But Christian III of Denmark realized that the necessity of gaining and preserving Russia's good will was more important than any other consideration. He depended on Ivan's friendly attitude toward Danish policy in the Baltic provinces and with him he shared opposition to Sweden. Prospects for better opportunities in connection with Russia's trade were opened by the weakened state of the Hanse. Moreover, Denmark's crucial hold on the Russian overseas trade with all its profits in dues would be endangered.

In view of such considerations, King Christian decided to seek an understanding with the Tsar. Profiting by the request for his mediation by the Livonian Order, which implored his help after the Russians had invaded the country and conquered the important trading centers of Narva and Dorpat, he dispatched an embassy to Moscow. The envoys, who left Denmark in October, 1558, were instructed to demand from the Tsar cessation of hostilities against the Order. But they were given additional tasks. In particular they were to ask for peace for the northern part of Livonia, namely Estonia, because Christian claimed it as Danish property. The latter point was of special importance, since the conquest of Narva had opened considerable opportunities for direct Russian trade and the problems which arose with the facilities and establishments of Narva's harbor in Russian hands threatened to become a central problem in Baltic policies. In exchange, the Danish envoys were to promise commercial advantages for the Russians and to guarantee all ancient privileges and liberties to Russian merchants, if they continued their business activities in Estonia and its important harbor of Reval.[9]

Under the leadership of Claus Uhrne and Wladislaw

Wobisser, the ambassadors proceeded to Moscow and in May, 1559, returned to Livonia.[10] Their task had not been accomplished because, except for a six months' truce, they had failed to secure peace for Livonia. Their claim on Estonia was categorically rejected by the Russians. Trade treaties had not been concluded because of Ivan's own claim on Reval, and the negotiations had finally been interrupted by the news of the death of Denmark's king.[11]

The Tsar was considerably disappointed. His chief ambition regarding freedom of trade for his subjects had not been fulfilled, and new negotiations were necessary if he were to gain any essential advantage.[12] An opportunity for the resumption of negotiations presented itself soon. In 1560, Magnus, the brother of Denmark's new king, Frederick II, had taken possession of the island of Ösel, which formed part of Livonia, and of two additional bishoprics in the Baltic provinces. In order to reconcile Ivan to the Danish occupation and to secure a guarantee for Magnus' realms, Dietrich Behr, commander of Ösel, was sent to Moscow in August, 1561, on a new mission.[13] Knowing well that Ivan attached great importance to questions of freedom of trade, King Frederick instructed Behr to point out in particular the service rendered by Denmark to Russia in refusing to comply with the order of the Emperor, as well as with the requests of the Hanse towns and the Livonian ports, to refrain from trading directly with the Russians in the conquered harbor of Narva. Indeed, the trade with Narva, which was as important to Russia as it was envied by all other Baltic powers, had in no way been hindered by Denmark,[14] and consequently King Frederick expected Ivan's co-operation in the pacification of Magnus' realms.

The Tsar did not fully comply with the Danish envoy's desires. In the absence of definite trade agreements, he accorded an armistice only until Whitsuntide, 1562. By then, Frederick was expected to dispatch a new embassy which should be authorized to discuss the larger problems. At the request of the Danish king, who was unable to equip the new embassy within the stipulated time, the armistice was prolonged for a few months and it was not until July 6, 1562, that the Danish ambassadors arrived in Moscow.

Composed of Eyler Hardenberg, Jacob Brackenhaus, Jens Ulfstand and Zacharias Vheling, the embassy had received its instructions in March. It was to stress once more the friendly feelings shown by Denmark in the Narva trade question and to ask peace for Magnus' possessions in exchange. Once Magnus' share in Livonia was recognized by Ivan, Denmark, although not recognizing any legal titles of the Tsar on the country, was willing to promise not to interfere with Russian policies in the other parts of Livonia, or to support Ivan's enemies. Both parties were to guarantee freedom of trade and intercourse, and if the Tsar personally ratified the treaty by kissing the cross, King Frederick himself would likewise take an oath.[15]

On this basis, after negotiations of slightly more than a month, the famous treaty was actually concluded. It shows a particular endeavor to avoid any point which could be construed as favoring one at the expense of the other. Indeed, with the exception of Article XIX, every single passage was ostensibly drawn in such a way as to accentuate the mutual interests. Significantly, Article XIX was the one which stipulated that free passage through Danish territory and waterways should be granted to all doctors and artisans who might be invited to Russia. The Schlitte incident had left a strong impression on the Tsar who realized its deep implication and did not hesitate to mar a treaty otherwise built on complete reciprocity.[16]

The larger part of the treaty dealt with the question of the Livonian frontiers. In the first seven paragraphs, amity between Russia and Denmark was sealed, and any co-operation of either side with the enemies of the other, especially with Poland and Sweden, was barred. No mercenaries from either of the contracting parties should be allowed to serve against the other. However, no formal alliance entailing help in war was concluded.

Articles VIII to XII delineated the frontiers of the Danish and Russian spheres in Livonia. While Denmark was allowed in the main to keep the possessions of Magnus,[17] Russia reserved for herself by far the largest and most valuable share of the country, including the harbors of Riga, Reval, Narva, and the fortresses and trading centers of Dorpat, Mitau, Vellin, Dünaburg and Dünamünde. Since Magnus was included in the peace, so was the governor of Novgorod. Only the decision regarding a territory called Kolk was postponed until later.

As a whole, the first part of the treaty concerned questions in which King Frederick of Denmark was more deeply interested than Ivan. Articles XIII to XVI as well as XXIV dealt with general questions of jurisdiction, amnesty, waterway regulations and fishery rights, and the treatment of fugitives. All these points carried equal weight for both sides. The remaining six paragraphs take up the questions of trade. With these, the Tsar was mainly concerned. Personal safety for all merchants and their unhampered movement in and through the countries of the contracting parties was guaranteed, including the passage through the Sound. Non-Germans and Letts were excluded from all privileges. When forced to land on a treaty partner's shores, subjects of both rulers were to be accorded fair treatment. Most important of all, either side was privileged to establish two warehouses ("factories") on the other's lands (Article XXII). Denmark was to open one in Novgorod and another in Ivangorod, Russia could establish hers in Wisby on Gotland and in Copenhagen. The latter stipulation was of special value, for previously Russia had never been entitled to more than one store house, that in Wisby. An additional paragraph provided for the Tsar's taking a personal oath by kissing the cross.

The treaty was outstanding inasmuch as it was the first

ever to be peacefully negotiated by Russia with one of the great powers of western Europe which was based on complete equality. Neither in tone nor in essence was the slightest difference made between the two parties, nor had victory or defeat forced either side to an agreement which otherwise might have shown a different tenor. The barbaric empire of the East, with its non-Roman-Catholic and non-Protestant inhabitants, was treated on terms of equality by one of the proudest nations of western Christendom. It did not come to seek contact by according special privileges, as in its treaties with the Empire, the Pope and especially with England, but without sacrifice to either side, it granted the same kind of advantages which it demanded.

So advantageous did Ivan justly consider these negotiations with Denmark that he took the greatest pains in having them immediately ratified by King Frederick II himself. A great embassy was dispatched on September 15, 1562, under Prince Ryapolovski Romodanovski, with Ivan M. Viskovaty, Peter G. Sovin, six other noblemen and 150 other members and servants.[18] They left in the company of Denmark's envoy, Eyler Hardenberg. Their instructions were complicated. They were to get the ratification of the treaty without any change in style or contents, and without permitting Frederic to keep the original, but only a copy to be written out in Denmark. Regarding the only point left in abeyance, the possession of Kolk, they were asked, if possible, not to discuss this question at all, and under no circumstances to renounce the territory, but to insist upon retaining it for Russia. They were to point out the historic rights of Ivan, and to refuse to look at the old treaties which Denmark might wish to show them in support of her own claims. These treaties between Denmark and the Livonians were to be disregarded because they had been made with people under Russian sovereignty who had no right at all to make treaties. If Frederic were to threaten to close the Sound, they were to counter by threatening to prohibit entry of all Danish merchants into

Russia. They were to impress Denmark with the might of the Tsar, and to be very meticulous as to the ceremonial. They were to insist that the factories for the merchants on Gothland and in Denmark be of the same size as the Danish factories in Russia. If asked what the Tsar was planning regarding Poland, they were to pretend ignorance of the subject, and in any case they must block any Danish attempt to mediate the Polish question. Finally, they were to investigate the commercial possibilities in Denmark.[19]

The ambassadors arrived in Copenhagen on October 14, but at first they refused to disembark, because their reception was not honorable enough. They then had two audiences with the king, but only after the second were negotiations started with Frederick's councillors. The Danes, while agreeing to most points of importance, tried to get concessions as to the possession of Kolk. Obviously, a question of principle rather than of material importance was involved, and just for this reason they were met with adamant resistance from the Russian envoys and had finally to give in. Early in December, 1562, the negotiations were successfully concluded, the oath was taken by Frederick himself, and presents were exchanged. The ambassadors left for Lund, where they stayed during the winter. Only in August, 1563, after almost one year, did they return to Moscow.[20]

The importance of the treaty, which was concluded without a time limitation, lay less in its practical aspects than in its implications. Indeed, its practical results were less than satisfactory. Within a year after its ratification King Frederick of Denmark entered into an alliance with King Sigismund August of Poland, and though this alliance was directed against Sweden, Russia's other enemy, it bore the germ of future dissension with Ivan. As a result of the Danish-Polish alliance, the Swedes attacked the Danish possessions in Livonia and conquered the province of Wieck. This meant an additional setback for the

Tsar, who considered the Wieck as his own, which he had "granted" to Denmark, which in turn had suffered it to fall into Swedish hands. Aside from the resultant increase in the power of hostile Sweden, Denmark was less able than ever to promote the Tsar's desires for expansion of trade and intercourse as envisaged by the great treaty.

Under the circumstances, the reception in Russia of Zacharias Vheling, a former member of Hardenberg's embassy and now charged with the execution of the commercial stipulations of the treaty, was hardly friendly. He stayed in Russia two years, and three months of this period, from February to May, 1564, were spent in Moscow.[21] Ivan, after having suffered a severe defeat by the Poles at Ula, had in the meantime concluded an armistice with Poland and was also attempting a rapprochement with Sweden. Denmark therefore no longer enjoyed the privileged position of two years before, and her representative, Vheling, was in a difficult position. His proposals met with little approval, and his explanations of Denmark's actions were disregarded. The Tsar in a letter to the Danish king spoke in the most deprecatory terms of his entire mission.[22]

Furthermore, the special friendship which supposedly had been established by the negotiations of Eyler Hardenberg existed no longer. Its decline was due, according to Vheling, to the lies which the great Russian embassy to Copenhagen had spread regarding Denmark. The improvement of the relationship became therefore a necessary objective and Vheling had to devote his attention to it. Upon leaving Moscow he declared that he had succeeded at least to a certain degree in this task, though the subsequent events do not bear out the correctness of his assertion.

Certainly his success did not suffice to promote his main purpose, the establishment of the factory which, according to Article XXII, Denmark was permitted to build at Ivangorod. In his endeavors he not only met with the opposition of the Swedish and English merchants, who as competitors for Russian trade tried to hinder him in every possible way, but he also failed to secure the co-operation of the Russian officials. The site which had previously been arranged for the factory was refused him, and obstacles of all kinds were put in his way.[23] Eventually he was accused of overstepping his proper rights and by order from Moscow he had to leave the country. His departure meant that the execution of the points of chief interest to the Tsar was indefinitely postponed.

The wrecking of the principal hopes which Russia had cherished in connection with the treaty with Denmark was closely followed by a similar collapse of Denmark's ambitions. More than half of the agreement of 1562 had been devoted to a delineation of the Livonian frontiers and Magnus' Danish realms. Ivan's subtle policies, however, succeeded in drawing Magnus to his own side, and the prince, created by the Tsar's grace as a "king of Livonia," recognized the Russian ruler as his overlord, under whom he held the whole of his dominions, thus implying the cessation of Danish suzerainty. In doing so he rendered useless the corresponding stipulations of the treaty. Thus, with the disruption of amity, the dissolution of the concord regarding the political boundaries, and the non-observance of the commercial arrangement, the work of 1562 lost almost all its practical meaning.

Yet the theoretical importance should not be underestimated. Having once agreed to full equality in arrangements with Russia, Denmark had not only committed herself, but also set a precedent for others. Sweden, Poland and the Empire eventually followed her lead. Had it not been for the military disasters during the later years of Ivan's reign and for the internal troubles after his death, Russia from then on might have been able to negotiate with all powers on the same basis. As it developed, more than another century passed before her position as a member of the European community of nations was firmly established.

As to Denmark, she continued in the spirit of the treaty of 1562, though with different objectives. In 1575 she dispatched an able envoy, Elias Eysenberg, to Moscow to re-establish the former friendship.[24] All the old questions regarding the trouble on the Norwegian border, the political situation in Livonia and the trade to Narva were once more discussed, and the alleged breaches of the treaty of 1562 were taken up by both sides. Though the negotiations, which lasted a month and a half, led to no result, they paved the way for a new treaty destined to replace that of 1562. It was concluded in 1578 by a great Danish embassy under Jacob Ulfeld.[25] The agreement, concluded by Russia's chancellor Sokolov and Ulfeld (who proved to be an incompetent negotiator) was not ratified by Denmark's king.[26] Nevertheless, it formed a basis for the future relationship of the two countries. It sealed Denmark's withdrawal from Livonia, leaving her nothing but the island of Ösel and some other small possessions formerly belonging to Magnus. All other parts of the Baltic provinces were abandoned in favor of Russia, which, however, presently lost them to Sweden and Poland.

Thus ended in failure Russia's first and temporarily successful attempt to be regarded and treated as a member of the European family of nations. True, the initial success was limited not only in time but also in effect. Yet, the treaty constituted an essential link connecting the past, when Russia was thought of as a strange, barbaric and un-Christian country and a menace to the Western world, with the future, when she was to form an integral part of European organization and civilization.

Chapter V

THE BEGINNINGS OF FRANCO-RUSSIAN ECONOMIC RELATIONS, 1550-1560*

Little is known about the beginnings of Franco-Russian relations. Much work has been devoted to a discussion of the subject, but most of it is based on the study of official diplomatic reports, which alone do not allow for satisfactory results.[1] Historians, too often dominated by the political interests which prevailed in their discipline at the end of the nineteenth century, have neglected broader investigations. In particular, the economic aspects of Franco-Russian relations have been lost sight of; the stimulation of their study is so recent that conclusions satisfactory to us today cannot yet be expected.

Most of the historians who investigate the subject of Franco-Russian relations mention the marriage between King Henry I of France and Anna, daughter of the Kievan Grandduke Yaroslav, in 1051. The event had no greater portent in history than marriages of other members of Yaroslav's family into various princely houses in Germany, Norway, Poland and other countries. Not a single trace of the establishment of a subsequent diplomatic link between France and Russia can be found; after the wedding the situation remained unchanged for the next five hundred years. It was only in 1586 that a new mission was sent. It was led by François de Carle, whose embassy has been verified and described by A. Rambaud.[2] But as F. de

---

* Reprinted with permission from _Revue historique_, CCII (1949).

Martens points out, it too has remained without practical consequences.[3] Not until 1615 did Russia officially reciprocate with a mission to France.[4] Even then an effective diplomatic intercourse was not initiated; regular relations had to wait until the reign of Peter the Great. In 1657, before Peter's day, relations were so weak that Louis XIV addressed a letter to Tsar Michael Feodorovich, not realizing that Michael had been dead for twelve years.[5]

The story does not differ much for the area of cultural relations.[6] France had little to offer to Russia and little to gain from contact with the far-away "barbarians." While doctors, scientists and artisans left Germany, England and Italy for Russia, and while these countries exchanged envoys and travelers, France remained indifferent to Russia. Friedrich von Adelung lists for the period from 1558 to 1610 109 travel accounts dealing with Russia, but he mentions among them no more than three very modest reports written by French visitors. From 1610 to 1650 one finds not a single Frenchman sufficiently equipped and interested in Russia to tell of his experiences there. Pierre de la Ville may be considered an exception, but as the chief of a regiment he served under a Swedish general, Jacob Pontus de la Gardie, who led his Swedish troops in 1611 to the gates of Moscow. A generation later, in 1647, we hear of another exception, a French sailor, de la Martinière, who, however, visited only the Arctic rivers of Russia.[7] Wilhelm Michael von Richter, who wrote a history of medicine in Russia, does not refer to one single French doctor, unless we include a physician of Italian origin, Paul (Citadin), who lived in France and made a trip to Russia. His journey has remained an insignificant episode.[8]

Perhaps one can attribute the absence of diplomatic, and possibly also of cultural, relations to the fact that up to the time of the reign of Ivan III the Great or, to a certain degree, up to that of Ivan IV the Terrible, a sound legal basis for diplomatic relations between Russia and the Western powers did not exist. Only after the liberation from Tatar rule and after the crushing of the independence of the various Russian principalities, their incorporation into Muscovy and the elimination of the power of the Bojars and that of the archbishop of Novgorod were the legal conditions created which permitted international diplomatic relations.[9] Likewise in France, internal conditions during the Hundred Years War, and even later up to the murder of Henry III, made it difficult for the French to enter into binding treaties with external powers. Under the circumstances, what regular diplomatic relations between the West and the schismatic Slavs of the East existed were confined essentially to those with the leaders of the Catholic Church and the Holy Roman emperors. As the spiritual and temporal heads of Christianity, they entertained, as might be expected, certain official relations with Russia.[10] Aside from them, only Russia's neighbors such as Sweden, Livonia, Poland and Turkey maintained regular, though not necessarily friendly connections.

If on the level of diplomacy the situation permitted for no more than limited and superficial relations, the situation was different on the economic level. German commerce with Russia was not only extensive in size but also of very considerable importance.[11] Ever since the twelfth or thirteenth century, Hanseatic merchants had established themselves in the frontier provinces of Russia and in adjoining parts. Through their factories or houses and trading centers in Novgorod, Riga, Polotsk and Vitebsk, as well as through their establishments in border towns such as Dorpat, they entered into lively commercial contact with Russia, and this turned out to be profitable for both sides. The Hanse imported large quantities of fur, wine, honey, and also of victuals, fish and tar; it exported chiefly cloth and salt from Germany as well as from other countries. As a matter of fact, the connection with Novgorod was everywhere considered the key to the predominant position which the Hanse held in all northern trade.[12]

Italians, Dutch, English, Scandinavians and Greeks were, of course, as aware as the German Hanseats of the great opportunities which the vast Russian realms offered to the trader. In the middle of the fourteenth century, Italians (from Lombardy) were carrying on business in Russia. The Venetians and Genoese carried on a vigorous trade via the Black Sea ports. At the end of the same century, the Dutch were acquiring such importance in the trade with the East that, at the instigation of the Hanse, all business with Russians was prohibited to them. Continuing Hanseatic complaints against their activities testify, however, to the fact that the Dutch maintained their connections and that their merchants were successful.[13] English traders appear at approximately the same period; they engaged in the cloth trade. Scandinavians profited by their proximity to Russian lands; their colonizing activities had given them a footing in eastern Baltic territories. Thus, the Danes, like the Germans, had established themselves in Livonia during the twelfth century and the Swedes in Finland. The latter, especially, seized the opportunity for commercial exchanges. Finally, the Greeks maintained a trade with Russia which dated back to the close contact which Byzantium had established with her northern neighbor at the very period when, for the first time in history, one could speak at all of a "Russia."[14]

But what about France? No doubt, a number of French goods did reach Russia. Among them were wines from Gascony, Poitou and other provinces that were shipped to the East in foreign bottoms.[15] But we cannot find additional exports, although France possessed a great wealth of other useful products. A document of the middle of the fifteenth century, the "Débat des Hérauts d'Armes de France et d'Angleterre," speaks of the fine harbors which France possessed and the excellent commodities which she could offer—gold, silver, saltpeter, coal, fish, paper, draperies and cloth—in addition to wine and salt.[16] However, little if anything was done by France to exploit her advantages for trade with Russia. Indeed, it has been argued that the prosperous condition of the French economy and the balance achieved in her internal commerce impeded distant ventures.[17] For, in contrast to England, which was forced by her geographic location and lack of natural resources to conduct an aggressive commercial policy, France could enjoy a large measure of autarchy. She did not depend upon imports, except for some luxury goods, and of these, Russia did not have an abundance. Actually, a parallel situation some three hundred years later contributed to the failure of Napoleon's Continental System. Despite his military might, Napoleon could not carry out the economic policy with which he had tried to win the tsars. He could not live up to the promise he had made—namely, to buy the goods on the Russian market which England used to buy and pay for them with French products substituting those of England.

Conditions prevailing at the beginning of modern times do not indicate, though, that France made no attempt to share with other nations the advantages they derived from their Russia business. Obviously, there existed in France, as elsewhere, a spirit of enterprise. But at a time when mercantilistic concepts came to the fore, support from above was as needed as a spirit of enterprise among those below. This support is what we find in many of the Western countries. But as far as France was concerned, authorities did not at this crucial moment during the sixteenth century take the appropriate action with regard to Russia. Only very inefficiently did they approach the question. Thus, Henry II in 1555 accorded an interview to Hans Schlitte, a German resident in Russia, who a few years earlier had been dispatched by Ivan the Terrible to Germany in order to hire doctors and artisans. Owing to the opposition of the

Hanseatic merchants, Schlitte's efforts had, however, come to nothing. He later proceeded to France, where he was well received but achieved no more than in Germany. In seeing Schlitte, Henry's real motive did not lie in his desire for the commerce Schlitte promised to promote and from which the French economy could have drawn considerable advantage; it was a political gain which the king hoped to make. Indeed, instead of seizing the chances which Schlitte's visit opened in connection with Russia, Henry was interested only in exploiting the interview insofar as it could be used in his struggle against the Habsburgs—a struggle which ultimately proved to be in vain.[18] At that, Schlitte's visit might have had the most important consequences. For in 1553, just two years earlier, English sailors had discovered a route past the most northerly point of Europe. Their discovery made possible commercial connections with Russia which were subject neither to the controls the king of Denmark exercised nor to the dues which he levied in the Danish Sound. Nor were they dependent upon the good will of the Hanseatic merchants who dominated all trade which in transit had to cross the Baltic regions and Livonia.

A second chance offered itself a few years later, in 1558. Having conquered Kazan and Astrakhan, Ivan the Terrible at that time began an assault on the ports of Livonia and the domains of the Livonian Knights. In the course of Ivan's campaign, Narva with its useful harbor fell into his hands. Russia thus gained an access to the open sea, and overseas merchants gained direct access to Russia.

The perspectives which this conquest opened were not ignored by the French merchants. They knew of the profits which other nations had derived from their first ventures to Russia, and even though a sizable merchant fleet was not at France's disposal, she had increasingly paid attention to the Russian market. Indeed, trade in the East had begun to gain national significance. In 1557, no less than 247 ships, out of a total of 1,150 which on their eastward voyage sailed through the Sound to reach Baltic ports, had come from France. Of course, the majority of them belonged to the Hanse and other foreign masters, but it was French merchandise that they carried.[19]

The years after the fall of Narva, however, did not bring a steady improvement. Troubled by civil war and by lack of understanding of commercial issues, the French kings and their councillors gave no support to the ventures of their merchants. Instead, they continued to devote their chief attention to politics and diplomacy. Preoccupied, they neglected a vigorous economic policy, and at the very moment when it would have been appropriate to send a mission to Moscow in order to exploit the situation for the sake of establishing close ties, they directed their attention to other projects, seeking to gain influence in Sweden, Poland and Turkey—all countries hostile to Russia.[20]

Soon it was demonstrated how risky such a policy was. In 1563, war broke out between Sweden, Denmark, Lübeck and Poland—a war which was to last for seven years. The conflict served to put an end to just those French projects, feeble as they might have been, which envisaged gaining by intervention ascendancy in northern European affairs. Moreover, the war had an adverse influence upon the economic position which the French merchants had tried to secure on their own in the Baltic. It interrupted the traffic which the Hanse carried on and thereby damaged French interests, since the major part of French goods was still shipped in Hanseatic bottoms. Indeed, the French merchants were forced to look for other carriers for their overseas ventures. This at least, brought one advantage: France was stimulated gradually to replace Hanseatic ships by ships of other nations (especially Holland) which competed with the Hanse; and she was also encouraged in her endeavors to employ ships of her own on the Baltic voyage. In 1562, French ships, on their way to Russia, begin to appear in the Sound.

Their number was small in the beginning, but gradually it grew. Figures from the registers of the Danish Sound Dues illustrate the development:[21]

Year	Total ships sailing eastward	Among these, ships coming from France	Among these, ships sailing under the flag of		
			France	Hanse	Holland
1558	1,059	218	--	211	1
1560	1,322	287	--	197	84
1562	1,824	193	10	124	56
1564	1,669	237	2	92	143
1566	1,945	288	27	82	171
1568	1,805	380	58	94	221

Unfortunately, it is difficult to ascertain precisely how many ships that entered the Baltic proceeded all the way to Russia. For the records of the Sound are not reliable with regard to the information which the captains of the ships paying dues gave as their port of departure, nor was any record kept about the ports of destination. To discover the ports to which eastbound ships were sailing, all we can do is try to draw conclusions by examining the list of ports from which they returned on their voyage westward. Whether a systematic examination of the archives in Dieppe, La Rochelle and Bordeaux can bring supplementary verification might be worth investigating. Certainly these archives would bring a considerable amount of new information. This much can be regarded as certain: that Dieppe held first place among the ports of departure, and that Calais, La Rochelle and Bordeaux played a lesser role. There is no doubt either that the port of destination for the majority of the ships was Danzig. Yet indirect evidence (as well as an examination of the ports from which the ships left on their return) indicates that a substantial number of the ships did go on beyond Danzig, heading for the great Livonian ports of Riga and Reval. After the conquest of Narva, they also sailed to this unique "Window to the West" of Russia.[22]

A large part of the cargoes carried from France to Russia at this time consisted, as the 1562 figures indicate, of salt and, to a lesser degree, of cloth. After 1566, one can also trace shipments of pepper, rice and other colonial products. Wine, too, begins to figure in the Sound Dues records. Dried fruit, figs, raisins and sugar played a minor role. As with all colonial products, trade in them was subjected to rather sharp ups and downs. Only occasionally do we find leather, glass and paper mentioned.[23]

One of the great difficulties which the French merchants encountered in their efforts to promote the Russia trade consisted in the fact that sales of their chief export article, namely salt, were subject to the vagaries of politics. They depended upon the political situation in Northern Europe and upon the good or ill will of the various northern governments. If war was being waged, or even when it was only threatened, then salt, to the extent to which it constituted a necessity for the belligerents, was used as a weapon, and each country tried to block its delivery to its opponents. When shipments arrived in the Baltic, they were, if possible, intercepted and re-routed by one of the belligerents to his own harbors. Obviously, French trade was primarily affected by this situation, and at that in a twofold way. On the one hand, war stimulated commerce, the demand for French salt rose and opportunities for neutral France increased. On the other, war impeded freedom of movement, shipping was endangered, boats which normally carried French goods could not reach their points of destination, and unaccustomed problems were encountered in the harbors to which trade was forcibly directed. The Russia trade was particularly sensitive to war involvements in the Baltic since the connecting lines between Russia and the West were at the mercy of the Baltic nations. Militarily and economically, access to the Russian market played a role in every Baltic upheaval, and even if Russia was not directly involved in such an upheaval, she was drawn into the embroilment because of her salt cargoes. For, although the Russians produced salt of their own in the mines of Staraia Russa or of Perm, and although they had a refinery at Astrakhan,[24] they did remain in part dependent upon foreign imports.

The long period of the Northern Seven Years War illustrates the dilemma. The struggle led to a confused situation. At first, France succeeded in consistently increasing salt shipments. Those which passed through the Sound amounted to:

1562	19.293	laest out of a total of	40.552
1564	25.623		32.895
1566	24.722		35.952
1568	27.243		46.271

Most of these shipments were dispatched in Dutch bottoms and went directly to Narva and from there to Russia. In 1568, however, when King Erik XIV of Sweden, a friend of France, was deposed and his brother John III ascended the Swedish throne, political sanctions were introduced and the situation for France was reversed. No more than 48 ships coming from French ports passed through the Sound in 1569, as opposed to 380 in 1568, and instead of 27,243 laest of salt, no more than 3,498 paid their dues there.

If French exports thus had to battle, in peace and in war, with factors which were outside the control of France, imports encountered almost equal difficulties. These difficulties were augmented by the indifference of the French authorities. The English were resolved, and prepared, to use their Russian contacts for the purpose of strengthening their naval power. Although the English merchants had originally undertaken their voyage past the North Cape in the hope of finding a commercially practicable route to "Cathay," and although after reaching Russia instead, they never lost sight of their initial plan of establishing a link with the Orient (or at least with Persia and India), they were not blind to the chances which Russia herself offered. They began to import timber, tar, wax, linen and hemp—all products useful for the construction and equipment of naval and merchant vessels. In their endeavors they received the full support of their mercantilistically inclined government. The French, on the other hand, wasted their energies in external and internal struggles. Under the insecure and selfish rule of the Valois princes and of Catherine de Medici, their merchants could not count on sustained support from the side of the monarch. Left to themselves, they imported linen and linseed, hemp, tar, leather, skins, rye, wax and sometimes, though seldom, timber.[25] None of these imports evoked in France any of the enthusiasm with which they were received in England, and none was accepted as an indispensable, or even an important asset for the economy of the country. For this reason, the quantities were not large; and this, in turn, accounts for the lack of attention Franco-Russian trade received both in Russia, which was not sufficiently impressed to offer special favors to French merchants, and in France, which proved equally unwilling to change its attitude.

Not until 1570, when the conclusion of the peace of Stettin ended the Seven Years War, was the dilemma in which the French had found themselves finally resolved. Only then could the former belligerents finally devote their energies once more to the normal demands of commerce. One of the principal figures recognizing the need and opportunity for a new start for France was the French ambassador at the Danish court, Charles de Dançay. Once the hostilities were over, he lost no time in entering into negotiations with the Danish king, taking up with energy the cause of the French merchants and seeking to extend their commerce and to increase France's prestige in the Baltic region.[26] An indefatigable negotiator, Dançay tirelessly evolved new plans. Among the foreign agents and representatives of France, it was he who embraced most vigorously the mercantilistic concepts of his age. After having participated, though without much glory, in the conclusion of the peace, he made it his task to attempt to gain a substantial share in the commerce with the East for the French merchants.[27] Unfortunately for him, his efforts were soon counteracted by a political move by the French court which once more sacrificed essential long-term economic interests to narrow, shortsighted political goals—a mistake which was all the greater as the political plans ended in failure. In 1572, France put forward the candidacy of Prince Henry, third son of Catherine de Medici, to the throne of Poland. The throne had been vacant since the death of the last Jagellonian king, Sigismund Augustus. The economic consequences of this step were likely to be serious, since a French alliance with Russia's chief enemy, Poland, was bound to ruin the chances for close economic links with the tsar's realms. Nor did the Poles fail to demand promptly that French shipping to Narva be suspended and that the French king see to it that his subjects, instead of seeking commercial links with Russia, establish them with Poland. Moreover, they expressed the expectation that they would be offered the products of France at no higher prices than Russia paid for them.[28] Such a situation could have led to war with Russia. Only the death of Charles IX and the ignominious flight of his brother Henry from Poland, where he had traveled to secure the crown, prevented the French from becoming involved in war. But one fortunate result came from the Polish intermezzo: the French withdrawal from Poland saved from collapse Dançay's commercial projects for French economic expansion.

The French envoy therefore turned to a new project. On April 12, 1575, taking advantage of a stop-over which the king's councillor and secretary of state and finance, M. Pinart, made in Copenhagen on his way to Sweden, Dançay submitted to him an interesting, though hardly practical scheme.[29] He proposed that France attempt the conquest of Livonia, whose ports largely controlled the traffic to Russia and constituted the key for any extensive trade with this country. Once seized, Livonia was to be turned into a hereditary French duchy. Dançay estimated that with her wealth in grain, linen, wax, leather, tar, and also oak and other timber useful for naval construction, Livonia herself could greatly contribute to the prosperity of France. In addition, she could provide the door for access to the rich Russian hinterland. Moreover, so he thought, Livonia could offer space to French emigrants and colonists. Inasmuch as Reval with its economically advantageous location, though now Swedish, was to become part of the new duchy, Dançay entertained no doubt that the merchants of Normandy and Brittany, of Paris, Orléans, La Rochelle and other places would gladly contribute, by lavish financial help, to the success of the enterprise.

The sources and strength of the French government and of the French people were obviously unequal to such a chimeric undertaking; and the strategic Livonian ports fell into, or remained in, the hands of Sweden and Poland. But Dançay, always on the alert, promptly worked out new schemes. In 1581, he proposed that negotiations be opened between the king of France and the tsar, with the purpose of securing trading privileges for French merchants in St. Nicholas on the White Sea. In corresponding with his king Dançay asserted that the voyage there was perfectly safe, that it took no more than four or five weeks, and that the business in wax, skins and linen on this route past the North Cape formed one of the most lucrative commercial connections anywhere.[30] A month later he repeated his arguments, pointing to the success of the English.[31] He also informed the king that the merchants of Dieppe had already requested information about the practicability of such a voyage. He warned, however, against the regrettable lack of harmony and cooperation among French merchants — a trait which he considered rather typical of the

French, even though others, including the Dutch, also suffered from it.[32] Finally, in order to further his plan by practical measures, and without waiting for definite instructions from home, he entered into negotiations with Denmark. In this he was prompted by the fact that the Danish king had in the meantime begun to assert rights to the northern route, and had begun to levy, at Vardöhus, dues parallel to those he levied in the Sound.[33]

At the end of the year, Dançay could report that the Danes were willing to allow French ships on the route past the North Cape in return for payment of a lump sum of 6,000 Thalers per year. Since, however, the extent of the traffic there was most uncertain, he continued the negotiations, insisting that the sum be reduced to two portugaises per ship. Another year later, he offered to send to France a man who had resided in Russia for twenty years and who could give a description of the customs and of business life in Russia. He hoped that the court and the merchants could, on the basis of the information gained from him, form a picture as to their chances in the Russian market. At the same time he emphasized that efforts must be made to secure for France the same commercial privileges which the English enjoyed. She was to secure a port on the Dvina and free passage for her merchants.[34]

At their best, the plans of Dançay represented a school of economic thought typical for the age. But no matter how sensible they were, he could not overcome the practical obstacles which presented themselves to the French. Before his death, which occurred in 1589, he had, however, the satisfaction of witnessing a few efforts which were in line with his proposals—at least in regard to shipping to White Sea ports. When Tsar Feodor had succeeded Ivan the Terrible on the throne, he had, in 1585, advised Queen Elizabeth of England that he would waive customs dues on merchandise coming from England, but that he would extend the same privilege to other nations. "Our kingdom is greate," he had written, "and merchaunts owte of many realmes have recours with their merchandize into our kingdomes."[35] Trusting in this promise, Jean Sauvage, a merchant from Dieppe, had undertaken the northern voyage in 1586. He had reached Archangel, but we do not know what results he had achieved, except that he had been well received and that he could exchange his goods for skins, linen, wax, tallow and hemp.[36] Other French merchants who undertook the trip during the same year, however, were less successful. They had used false passports and had tried to avoid the dues of the Danish king; so they were arrested by the Danish customs inspector in Vardöhus.

In the same year, 1586, Dançay had also witnessed the first French diplomatic mission to Tsar Feodor. Under the leadership of François de Carle, it had as its main purpose negotiations concerning the exchange of goods between the two countries. Not only had de Carle been charged to seek an improvement in existing relations, but also to seek guarantees for future freedom of movement and security of the French merchants. As a result of his efforts, the port of Kholmogory, not far from Archangel, had been opened to the French, and in 1587 commercial privileges were accorded to a company belonging to a certain Jacques Parent. This company was granted a 50 per cent reduction on all general customs dues levied on imports by the Russians.[37]

It is interesting to note, though, that all these concessions did little to change the pattern of Franco-Russian commercial relations; nor, for that matter, did all of Dançay's planning or even all of the enterprises of Henry of Valois in Poland. Unlike German or English commerce with Russia, French commerce with the tsars did not rest upon fundamental needs which imperatively demanded an exchange of goods. Franco-Russian trade depended far more upon temporary diplomatic schemes and upon changing political constellations than upon a general economic trend. No matter how well intentioned or logical official negotiators may have been, they could not change the path determined by the political situation within France. Therefore, even during the decades after 1570, which had brought general pacification, it was difficult for France to gain an important place in the Russian market. Interminable local struggles between Poland, Sweden and Russia for the possession of Livonia followed the great Northern War, and Baltic traffic was largely subject to the mercy of the Swedes, who held the strategic positions in the triangle Stockholm, Åbo, Reval. The figures for French trade therefore remain insignificant. As late as 1575, no more than 21 ships coming from France entered the Baltic; nine of them flew the French flag. Salt shipments fell by 95 per cent to only 422 laest, even though other products were not equally affected. The total of exports on French ships was in the neighborhood of only 10,000 Thalers. Imports were touched less, their value amounting to 22,912 Thalers.[38]

No improvement occurred until after 1575. Then, however, progress was made. Between 1578 and 1581 more than 200 ships coming from France passed regularly the Sound. In 1580 there were 294, of which 18 were French. The export of French salt climbed once more to a total of 10,986 laest. While the majority of the ships sailed to Danzig and Königsberg, considerable numbers did continue on their way—on to Riga, Reval and Narva. But just when recovery seemed to show a steady advance, a new blow was dealt French commerce with Russia: the Russian armies, which had kept Livonia occupied, were expelled by the Poles and Swedes, and under pressure of the two victorious nations, Denmark requested the French to give up their trade with the enemy via the Sound. In particular, the French were asked to stop sending war material for the tsar to Narva. And when shortly thereafter this port fell into the hands of the Swedes, French trade there was automatically stopped.

For six years not a single French ship reached the town. It was in connection with this impasse that Dançay had tried, as recounted, to open to the French the direct route to Archangel.

In 1584 the situation changed once more. In that year, Tsar Feodor succeeded Ivan the Terrible on the throne. During his reign the pacification of northern Europe made progress and French commerce began to revive. In 1587, 348 ships from France entered the Baltic; in 1588, 240; in 1594, 257; in 1595, 263. Of these 263, 91 ships sailed under the French flag. Exports of both salt and wine reached important figures, and those of dried fruit, rice and other colonial products amounted, in 1595, to 46.807 livres (out of a total of 102,997 livres for all nations taken together). Record figures were reached also for imports, especially in materials for naval construction, and in rye and other grain. The value for French imports and exports of ships flying the French ensign is estimated, for 1595, at 100, 050 and 29,475 Thalers respectively—sums far higher than the annual average values of a total of 20,000 to 30,000 Thalers.

Resolute French policies should have made possible further progress, and this is what we could have expected from a king like Henry IV, who in the meantime had come to the French throne. But despite the interest in trade which the king himself as well as Sully and others of his councillors showed, the important role which Russia could play both as a market for exports and as a supplier of imports was still not recognized. Again, one should not overestimate the influence of internal political disturbances under the last Valois and at the beginning of the reign of Henry IV, and see in them the chief cause for the lack of development in France's commercial activities.[39] As the example of the neighboring Dutch proves, civil and external strife alone certainly cannot explain the absence of economic progress; despite divisions in the country, despite war and the flooding of large parts of the land, and despite the desperate struggle for their independence and their lives, the commercial enterprises of the Dutch showed a remarkable vitality. Other factors must therefore be taken into consideration. In the first place, lack of cooperation continued to prevail among France's merchants, and cooperation would have been needed to establish large companies—perhaps joint stock companies—able to carry the load and the risks of that new type of commercial enterprise which was best suited for successful trade with Russia.[40] Local particular interests triumphed over those of the commonweal. As Professor Cole has demonstrated, a spirit which served the national well-being and which was so evident in England, was absent in France. No matter to what extent mercantilistic principles were studied and advocated in France, they were not put into practice. Moreover, liquid capital was lacking. Indeed, the whole economy was not organized in a way which would lend itself to meet the undertakings of English and Dutch competitors.[41] Yet, there were at the beginning of the seventeenth century enough products which France possessed and which, as in the sixteenth century, could have been sold in the Russian market—salt and wine and colonial products. Likewise, France, no less than Spain or England, could invariably have made use of the raw materials which Russia offered, timber and cordage in particular. But for stepping up such imports, she still would have had to decide upon concentrating her efforts on the construction of a large navy and merchant marine. Yet, during Sully's administration, all these possibilities were neglected. And Calais and other ports, which possessed geographical advantages certainly not inferior to those of many a Dutch port, were not developed as they could have been.

If one looks for further reasons for France's failure to put mercantilistic theories into practice, attention may be called to another factor applying to France around 1600. This was the defeat of Calvinism, which elsewhere, according to some historians, created a climate favorable to early capitalistic ventures. Could this defeat have been responsible for stagnation in France, while in Holland, England and other countries the triumph of the spirit of Calvinism furthered economic activity? The question may be raised, although no answer shall be attempted here. Besides such speculations, there are also more concrete problems to solve. French diplomacy in northern Europe too often neglected the need for friendly relationships with Denmark, Sweden and the North German towns. Furthermore, attention of the French merchants was directed largely toward ventures in North America and India, although even there they lacked the needed help from the political authorities, who often hindered rather than supported French expansion. A last reason for the failure of France has been stated by an author and economist of the age, colleague and rival of Sully, namely Barthélemy de Laffemas: his compatriots were at fault for "trop de paresse et de négligence."[42]

All these factors combined to neutralize cooperation between the political and economic forces in France—even if Henry IV on his part had been willing and capable of offering such cooperation. But the king knew little of Russia. A. Rambaud points out that Henry IV corresponded with the tsar. He did; but what has been preserved of the correspondence shows that only the most insignificant questions were discussed.[43] Henry also talked with the French mercenary, Captain Margeret, who had served the pretender to the Russian throne, the False Dimitri, and who possessed a solid knowledge of conditions in Russia.[44] Yet, the *Grand Dessein* of Sully and Henry IV hardly took Russia into consideration. Her religion, different as it was from that of Catholic Europe, excluded her in the opinion of the authors from being able to form a part of the *concert européen*.

Under such conditions, Franco-Russian exchanges

developed, as before, less in accord with the needs of France as a whole than with the often only too short-lived interests of an individual merchant who sought a chance for acquiring wealth quickly. The figures for French commerce in the Baltic during the reign of Henry IV show the following picture:

Year	Total ships sailing eastward	Among these, ships coming from France	Among these, ships sailing under the flag of France	Hanse	Holland
1595	3,161	263	91	14	143
1598	2,899	81	43	7	24
1600	2,134	348	16	20	293
1603	2,095	252	24	50	160
1608	3,334	427	116	25	278
1610	2,028	169	18	7	144

In 1609, the export of salt amounted to 21,989 *laest*, while during the same year that of wine reached a new record—3,086 *piber*. The share which exports to Russia had in this trade remained, however, very weak; they profited but little from the increase which the total of France's Baltic trade showed. For just at the moment when France was recovering from her troubles of the preceding period, Russia found herself plunged into the horrors of the *smuta*, her own "Time of Troubles." Commercial activities were interrupted. Almost no Western ships and cargoes at all could reach Russia. The majority of the ships coming from French ports did not get farther than Danzig, Königsberg and other ports in the western Baltic, and as so often in the past, all efforts had to begin anew when the *smuta* finally ended in 1613. By that time, Henry IV was dead.

The following period opens with the first great embassy which Russia despatched to France. It was led by Gabrilovich Kondyrev. Once more, the purpose was not so much the discussion of economic relations as the exchange of official compliments. Such an exchange seemed necessary inasmuch as both Russia and France had new sovereigns—both very young and neither secure on his throne. Michael Romanov who had ascended the throne of the tsars, owed his crown to an election by a Zemsky Sobor,[45] while in France, with Louis XIII succeeding his father Henry IV, the country had come under the regency of the Queen-Mother, an Italian by birth and a stranger to the customs of the French nation.

Kondyrev left Archangel in May, 1615, sailing with his entourage on a Dutch man-of-war. After visiting the Hague in October, he proceeded to Bordeaux, where he met the king, who was staying there with his mother because of the civil war.[46] A great deal of the ambassador's time was absorbed, as was typical for Russian diplomats, with petty questions of protocol, and no useful convention could be concluded. All the embassy did prove was a desire for an increase of contacts, including commercial connections; its despatch was, somehow, an indication of the fact that the possibility for such connections existed.[47]

It is difficult to ascertain, however, whether or not the merchants derived a practical benefit from the good will which the Russians had demonstrated. Figures show that French trade in the Baltic in the years following the Russian visit in France was relatively lively. In 1615, 254 ships coming from France passed the Sound, of which 20 flew the French flag. In 1620, there were 233 ships, 33 of them carrying the French flag. And in 1625, 201 sailed through the Sound with seven of them under the French flag. About 8 per cent of the total—French and Dutch, with most of the shipments from France being carried by the latter—sailed beyond Danzig and Königsberg all the way to Livonia, by whose ports Russia proper was served. During the period a record for the first hundred years was established: in 1623, 493 ships coming from France entered the Baltic on the eastward journey, transporting also record cargoes of salt (37, 643 laest) and wine (5,979 piber) Twelve of them were French ships.[48]

Yet the figures show that we can neither speak of a well-established, steady trade connection nor can we recognize a continuous upward trend. Richelieu, who shortly after the return of the Kondyrev mission came to play the leading political role in France, was no better disposed toward the Russian merchants than his predecessors. "Partisan de la politique de puissance," he concentrated his attention on the political struggle both within the country and with foreign enemies. Despite the influence which Barthélemy de Laffemas and Antoine de Montchrétien exercised upon him, his economic policy, though it has been praised by recent scholars,[49] was neither energetic nor comprehensive. It failed to allow France to exercise that role which her importance as an exporter, her attraction as a market for foreign goods, her wealth and her internal balanced economic situation should have permitted.

It is from this point of view, and in relation to Richelieu's professed aim of increasing France's naval power, that one has to evaluate the total of Richelieu's policy in regard to trade with Russia. Inasmuch as it was Russia which with her resources in timber, tar, pitch and hemp could more than any other country contribute to the building of a strong French navy and to the execution of a vigorous mercantilistic policy, and inasmuch as both England and Holland imported from there many of the materials which enabled them to establish their predominance, Richelieu should have considered more seriously the advantages which Russia offered. But he sacrificed naval power to other tasks, and France exhausted her timber reserves at home and let the Dutch build her fleet rather than draw on Russian resources and expand her own shipbuilding facilities.

Moreover, the French under Richelieu followed an inconsistent policy with regard to the creation of joint stock companies, in spite of their proven value for her rivals. There were times when such companies received official guarantees and when the supervision of a state which was becoming more and more absolute was extended to them. But there were other times when too little was done and too much freedom permitted to them. This was a mistake, even if, as has been suggested, such vacillation was the result of adverse experiences which the government had with monopolies granted, during the first decade of Richelieu's ministry, to merchants interested in the colonization of Canada.[50]

Altogether, the merchants were not afforded enough of that protection by law and by diplomacy which the businessmen of other countries enjoyed and which was especially necessary for countries engaged in the risky Eastern trade. In vain did the merchants complain; in vain did they insist that without protection the difficulties of trade with Russia were practically insurmountable; and in vain did they argue, though not quite truthfully, that about 60 years earlier (around 1568) "all the traffic with Moscow was in French hands; but wars and frequent revolutions . . . had forced them to give up that trade altogether."[51] The advances which the Kondyrev embassy had made were forgotten, and the complaints of the merchants fell on deaf ears. Nor did the French government pay sufficient attention to the fact that, with the smuta ended and Moscow freed of the Polish invaders, Russia began to exercise an increasing influence upon international politics and was on the way to becoming the leading power among the Slavic nations in Europe.[52]

In this manner, fourteen years following the Kondyrev mission were lost. Again and again, especially in the course of the last five or six years of this interval, the merchants demanded, as Richelieu's Mémoires prove, that a Muscovy Company be established. Only in 1629 was the embassy reciprocated. Even then, the main task given to the French envoys was not to seek a trade accord with the tsar but to enter into negotiations with him about access to the Near East. Indeed, it was rather an improvisation that the envoys were instructed to stop in Moscow on their way to the East and to discuss trade with Tsar Michael, "le Roy n'ayant nulle intelligence avec ce prince là."[53] The talks were to be keyed to the wish of the French king to get permission for the French merchants to trade with Persia and other Oriental suppliers by way of Russian territories. Actually this trade had never proved to be of much profit for those who had shared in it. Nevertheless, it continued to constitute a major aim of all Western importers.[54] It seemed interesting also to Richelieu, who thereby sought ways of avoiding the high commissions which the French had to pay to intermediaries in the Levant trade and who simultaneously wanted to re-establish French influence at the court of the Turkish sultan.

Unfortunately for French business interests, other factors of a very different nature were confounding the issue. In their desire to gain the support of the cardinal, the merchants had alluded to the possibility of converting the Orthodox Slavs to Roman Catholicism.[55] Poorly informed about Eastern Europe, Richelieu promptly thought of the effect this might have on Franco-Polish relations. Not the advantages which a rapprochement with Russia could bring, but the possibility of the French displacing Habsburg influence in Poland immediately became the matter of importance for him and made him determined not to promote the schemes of the merchants.[56]

The ambassador whom Richelieu chose for the trip to Moscow was Deshayes de Courmenin. He was charged to convey to the Russians the regrets of the French king for having seemed, in the past, somewhat indifferent to Russian interests and to excuse this indifference by the numerous wars in which France had been involved. Deshayes left and on his way stopped in Denmark. There he concluded a favorable treaty, which provided for the reduction of the dues levied on French merchandise destined for Narva. They were lowered to the minimum rate of one per cent, and this reduction was to apply equally to goods coming from Narva and destined for France.

In Moscow, the French were well received. But the results of their negotiations were meager. On the twelfth of November, 1630, a treaty was concluded by which the tsar granted to the French merchants in Russia the right to have Catholic priests in residence and the right to exericse their religion, if not publicly, at least in their homes.[57] He also exempted them from his jurisdiction in quarrels among themselves, though not in litigation with their hosts. But the tsar proved intransigent in most of the practical issues. Neither did he authorize the establishment of a French consulate in Moscow as requested, nor did he exempt the merchandise which the French merchants sold or bought from the tax of two per cent which was generally levied. Moreover, he insisted that the transit trade with the Orient remain in the hands of Muscovite merchants; all that he conceded was that these merchants were to furnish the products of the East at reasonable prices.

Several missions of still less importance followed that of Deshayes de Courmenin in the course of the subsequent twenty years. In 1631, for instance, a certain Captain Bertrand Bonnefoy was despatched to Moscow in order to make a purchase of rye for Louis XIII. He did not succeed because the tsar had promised the Dutch all he had at his disposal; but as a substitute Tsar Michael offered other grain, and Louis XIII gratefully accepted. Shipments were sent and repeated for several years. Other negotiations took place in 1632 and 1635, without, however bringing useful results for the French-Russia traders. As before, vigorous government action, such as was demanded by the mercantilistic principles voiced in Dançay's lifetime and thereafter, was not forthcoming.[58] Thus, the French merchants of the seventeenth century, like their predecessors in the sixteenth, were forced to rely on their own resources. Their conservative and individualistic tendencies remained, however, the same serious obstacle to the growth of their Russia trade that their particularistic and provincial attitude had been before.

Worse still, lack of toleration and the resulting revival of the struggle against the Calvinists, which had previously handicapped this economically important group within the nation, accounted for new difficulties. It must also be considered that with the re-establishment of order within France under the guidance of Richelieu, the internal market offered opportunities for profit which previously had seemed less attractive. All these factors combined to reduce the energy necessary for adopting and carrying out those measures which could have led to an expansion of the Franco-Russian trade. Actually, rather than stimulating efforts in regard to Russia, circumstances discouraged initiative. A first *Compagnie du cap Nord* was created in 1633 and incorporated in 1636, but its membership was economically weak, and adequate support for it was lacking. Moreover, the partners soon directed their attention as much to South America as to the northern markets. No wonder then that the best results and profits were achieved not on the trade routes to Russia but in the tropics, where the fort of Cayenne was erected by the Company.[59] A second *Compagnie du cap Nord* was organized in 1638. This, in turn, was replaced by a third one in 1643. Yet it was only in 1644 that a fourth *Compagnie du Nord*, founded "au profit du Sieur Claude Rousseau et autres," promised greater stability than its predecessors.[60] But it, too, took little action. While the expansion of trade with Russia was supposed to be one of its objectives, it put the chief accent on fishing ventures in Arctic waters, especially in whaling. As a result of this, and also of other extraneous undertakings, commerce with Russia lagged. Only rarely was the trip past the North Cape undertaken; and as far as the Baltic was concerned, the trade there, which the Company carried on with somewhat greater vigor than the White Sea trade, envisaged Scandinavian, German and Polish markets rather than Russian.

No wonder therefore that we notice a certain change in Franco-Russian relations. Beginning in the second decade of the seventeenth century, a steady decline of the number of French ships participating in the Eastern trade took place. Figures from the Sound Dues Tables bear out what has been suggested, namely lack of attention to the Russian business and lack of understanding for Russia's role as a supplier to the various nations of the means for creating a strong sea power. They indicate:

Year	Total ships sailing eastward	Among these, ships coming from France	Among these, ships sailing under the flag of France	Hanse	Holland
1628	1,088	44	--	5	38
1631	1,684	159	63	13	79
1635	2,182	134	6	4	121
1639	1,501	164	1	3	155
1647	1,716	261	10	26	217
1649	2,314	161	11	11	136
1651	1,663	218	--	3	213

After 1650, the numbers of foreign ships coming from French ports remain more or less stagnant in relation to the total tonnage, but ships sailing under the French flag disappear completely. What a difference as compared to the record year 1587 when 218 ships flying the French ensign passed the Sound! And this at a time when the French, like the Germans, could have profited from the difficulties experienced by the Dutch who just then were engaged in their desperate struggle against England.

The majority of all the ships passing the Sound still sailed for Danzig and Königsberg; the Dutch also sought to retain their hold on the trade with Riga. Salt still was one of the commodities exported into Baltic regions. In 1638, for instance, 20,940 laest paid their dues in the Sound, and in 1649 the amount was 17,041 laest. Wine exports for the same two years accounted for 2,488 and 1,344 piber respectively. Cloth, on the other hand, was represented only in less significant quantities—except for the period between 1618 and 1634. Pepper, rice and other colonial products reached important figures in the decade after 1640. Occasionally we find foreign nations using French carriers for their own products; thus, Rhine wine from Germany and fish and skins from other parts were transported in French bottoms. But such shipments were so small in numbers that they did not have a marked influence upon the curve of French commerce.

The handicaps under which the French suffered were emphasized by the absence of a French colony in Moscow. There, in the so-called "German suburb" of Moscow was to be found the center of Russian relations with foreigners. It has been described as a " sorte d'académie pour les hautes classes de la société russe."[61] The German language served as lingua franca, and the suburb harbored Germans and English, Scotch and Dutch. But few French people were to be found there.[62] The Catholic religion constituted an additional obstacle for the French, who would have found themselves, to a certain degree, isolated in the midst of an otherwise Protestant milieu. A last blow was dealt France by Tsar Alexis, who had come to the throne in 1645: under grave penalties, he prohibited the employment of Frenchmen in any position whatsoever.[63]

What conclusions then can the investigator reach when he tries to evaluate the extent of Franco-Russian economic relations during the first hundred years of their existence? They may be summarized as follows: the French lost many opportunities which presented themselves in the course of more than a century. Among the various factors which may be suggested as having contributed to this failure are these: lack of governmental support; absence of such impelling reasons for building up the Russian trade as the English on their little island felt; failure to realize the importance of sea power as one of the bases for modern economic development; undue attention to questions of prestige and political power. The French approached the problems which trade with Russia offered without the necessary determination. They did not sufficiently take into account the amount of corruption permeating Russian society[64] and neglected the even then well-known fact that the Russians of the seventeenth century did not possess that knowledge, know-how, capital and entrepreneurial spirit which would have been necessary for them to retain for themselves, instead of abandoning to foreigners, the major share of their external trade. Not even commerce on the route to Archangel was pursued with sufficient energy, although it was there that the basis had been laid for the close relationship between Russia and England. It was this route which Dançay had recommended as being at least as desirable as the Baltic route and that, as late as 1688, the Russians themselves encouraged the French to use more extensively.[65] The instructions of the great Colbert himself to his ambassadors illustrate the failure; he voiced the opinion that the differences between the two nations were too great to make possible the conclusion of useful commercial treaties.[66]

Yet, figures show that the contact between France and Russia was by no means as negligible as former studies have indicated. The individual French merchant had, after all, achieved something. It was he who prepared the way for those closer contacts which were to characterize the subsequent two centuries, both in the realm of economics and in the intellectual sphere.

NOTE

References to the foregoing article as well as to those dealing with Russia's foreign trade and the role of Narva are to be found in several writings. For instance: A. L. Khoroshkevich, "Vneshniaia torgovlia Rusi XIV-XVI vv. v osveshchenii burzhuaznoi istoriografii," _Voprosy istorii_, February, 1960, pp. 104-117; Pierre Jeannin, "L'économie française au milieu du XVIe siècle et le marché Russe," _Annales: Economies, Sociétés, Civilizations_, v. 9 No. 1 (January-March, 1954), pp. 23-43; Jeannin, "Les comptes du Sund," in: _Revue Historique_, v. 231, 1964, pp. 55-102 and 307-340; and, for a recent contribution to the issue, Dow, "A comparative note."

Chapter VI

ENTREPRENEURIAL ACTIVITY IN RUSSIAN-WESTERN TRADE RELATIONS DURING THE SIXTEENTH CENTURY*

Recent progress in the study of entrepreneurial history in the West has not been matched by an equal advance in eastern European, and especially in Russian, entrepreneurial history. Scholarly work has been confined essentially to the Baltic regions of Russia, and even there, chiefly to the periods of German and Swedish rule. Nor can definitive studies be looked for as long as public and private archives in Russia remain virtually inaccessible. Meanwhile, using existing publications, the Western historian dares propose no more than a few tentative considerations and conclusions.

The entrepreneur in Russia in the early modern period differed in some fundamental respects from his Western counterpart. The concentration of both political and economic power in the hands of the Russian ruler constituted the most prominent single factor in shaping his role and the course of Russian entrepreneurial history. In this respect, the nearest analogies to the Russian situation are to be found, not in the south and west, but in sixteenth-century Sweden, and perhaps also in Brandenburg, whose rulers undertook entrepreneurial activities similiar to those of the tsar.

The economic strength of the tsar was based on his per-

---

* Reprinted from Explorations in Entrepreneurial History, Research Center in Entrepreneurial History, Harvard University, Vol. VIII, (1956).

sonal wealth in bullion and in land; upon such special privileges and powers as his right of pre-emption and his control of trade monopolies; and upon his ability, as an autocratic ruler, to coordinate foreign policy and personal profit motives. Both Ivan the Terrible and Boris Godunov were among the wealthiest landowners in Europe. Their trade monopolies extended to exports and imports and included such commodities as grain, hemp, rhubarb, silk, , potash and caviar, and also skins, wax, honey, precious stones, metals and damask. The tsars reserved for themselves a right of first refusal of goods entering the realm and could buy at arbitrarily fixed prices, to resell at a profit. Ivan IV invested in the Muscovy Company and participated in its gains—especially those of the Persian trade.[1] His ultimate purpose seems to have been to use the pioneering work of the Company as a means for laying a foundation for a future all-Russian enterprise. As a financier, the same tsar is reported to have once offered the Fuggers a loan of 7 1/2 million Thaler at 5 per cent. Even though this offer may never have been made, reports of it were taken seriously enough to cause extensive discussions in South German business and political circles.[2]

Further, control of public policy enabled the tsar to promote his private economic interests. When in the 1580's Narva had fallen into Swedish hands, he rerouted trade via Pskov, to the detriment of the national economy. Historians have much disputed the political implications of the conquest and destruction of Novgorod; it warrants re-investigation with an eye to the extent to which the tsar's personal business interests were involved.[3] Likewise, the English alliance, the Persian trade and the border struggles on the Norwegian frontier were influenced by the commercial interests of Vassilii III, Ivan IV and Boris Godunov, respectively.

Conversely, political considerations influenced commercial policy. The tsar was not an entrepreneur in the ordinary sense. Personal power motives remained predominant for him, and led a ruler like Ivan IV to adopt policies which checked the evolution of groups which might eventually have constituted a nucleus for the development of a representative political system. For his own enterprises the tsar used foreign rather than native traders. Feeling that he could hire them under specific conditions and then more easily control them, he granted them a number of immunities.[4] Even for the role of agent, he preferred to rely on foreigners residing in Russia. Thus, in the middle of the fifteenth century, Ivan III used the services of several Italians, like Gian Baptista Della Volpe, and later Volpe's nephew Antonio Gislardi.[5] In the sixteenth century, we find a man like Paolo Centurione in Moscow. He was related to the Genoese banking house, was in the service of the papal court, and had connections also with German and Dutch banking houses, with the Fuggers, with Pompeius Occo and others.[6] In Russia, he was one of the tsar's most important agents. In the middle of the century, the German Schlitte lived at the Moscow court. He is well known for his activities as Ivan IV's agent commissioned to hire artisans for Russia, but less known for other enterprises which involved him directly and indirectly with plans of the princes of Stolberg and of Braunschweig, who in turn were interested in trade with Russia. Some of these agents were used to secure information on prices, business opportunities, possibilities of new trade routes, etc. —information which, as the largest entrepreneur in Russia, the tsar was anxious to possess.[7] Characteristically, some of the agents combined diplomatic with these economic functions. In view of the tsar's economic position, the borderline between commercial and political ventures in Russia was very narrow, indeed.

The Russian nobility felt as little compunction as the tsar in exploiting its position for business purposes. With no ideological barrier and fewer feudal customs to overcome than his

Western counterpart, the Russian aristocrat could indulge freely in commercial enterprises. Unfortunately, we lack careful studies of these activities similar to those we possess, for example, for the Livonian nobility. Yet we know that Russian noblemen controlled much of the salt, iron-ore and potash production; that they ran their estates as businesses and sold the produce on the market; and that they bought furs and fish, wax and leather and resold them to the Russian consumer as well as, with tsarist permission, to foreign traders. The Stroganovs in particular tried to build up an export market. For this purpose, they built ships and trained sailors, observed price fluctuations, hired agents abroad, and tried to supply those goods which were in international demand.[8]

Similiar activities can be traced among a number of monasteries. Some of them possessed vast lands and mines of ore and salt, which, as early as the fourteenth or even the thirteenth century, the monks exploited for sale on the Russian market. Other monasteries sold fish or oil. The monks of Pechenga traded in Vardöhus with Norwegians, Englishmen, Danes, Germans and Dutchmen. Indeed, their main income seems to have come from such trade.[9] The Church authorities looked complaisantly upon trading activities; and monasteries, favored by exemptions from taxes, customs and fees, did not content themselves with selling the products of their own lands, fisheries and subsoil. They even sent their buyers to faraway regions to purchase oriental products which they resold to Western merchants.[10]

The privileges and activities of the tsar, coupled with those of the nobility and the monasteries, had important social implications. Since Russia was a trading rather than a manufacturing nation,[11] the participation of granddukes and boyars, noble landowners and churchmen in trade, the very activity where profit could most easily be made, checked the growth of an independent merchant class.

The overseas trader was most adversely affected. While the upper-Germans, the Italians and the English had built up powerful agencies abroad (which stimulated home industry and enterprise through the trading and banking facilities they provided), the Russians entered the sixteenth century with no solid connections in Western countries. As opposed to their trade in the East, they had, as a rule, to rely in the West upon occasional missions abroad whenever they wanted to use their own, and not foreign, channels for the direct distribution of their products and for the purchase of imports. At these occasions much of the trading was done by the official diplomatic envoys. Thus the clergymen who left in 1438 for the Council of Ferrara-Florence, or the ambassadors who went to Rome in 1471 to negotiate the marriage of Ivan III and Sophia, or those who visited Venice in 1499, took along heavy loads of furs which they sold to secure funds for their own sustenance, for the account of the tsar and for their personal profit. In the sixteenth century, with an increase in diplomatic contacts with the West, business enterprise increased somewhat. Prince Zasiekin-Yaroslavsky and Simeon Borisov, who came to Spain in 1527, are described to us as vigorous traders.[12]

As a result, independent merchants participated only to a limited extent in the business transacted by diplomatic missions abroad. The embassy of Trusov and Lodygin in 1527 was accompanied by a merchant, Alexei Basei. When in the 1550's the envoy Napea went on his famous trip to England and was shipwrecked off the Scottish coast, two Russian merchants who sailed with him were drowned. Other instances could be given, but only seldom do we hear of independent voyages made by merchants only. A certain Vassili Posniakov combined business intentions with a pilgrimage to the Holy Land in 1558. Peter Pavlovich and Dmitri Kondratievich traveled to Holland in 1566 to engage in trade on their own account; and Tverdikov and Pogorelv visited England in 1567 to do business for the tsar and probably also for themselves. Still, the paucity of contacts of this kind suffices to show that Russian business initiative overseas was bound to remain weak as long as business organization remained unchanged.

The domestic trader, though less jealously watched, was not in a much more advantageous position. When visiting another town, he had to stay at certain hostelries and, for tax purposes, deposit his goods in designated warehouses. Often he was called upon to fulfill obligations for the fisc which were alien to his proper business. He was hampered by a licensing system for beer, wine and retail trade. Indeed, a significant specialized merchant class could scarcely develop. In the western outposts, in Novgorod and Pskov, there were merchants with a background and attitude not dissimiliar to those of western Europeans. Likewise, a small group of merchants emerged in old established centers like Kazan, where Eastern and Mohammedan influences played a role and set an example. In Moscow, under the eyes of the tsar, there lived a very limited group of entrepreneurs, who disposed of considerable capital. Of these "gosti" there may have been, in the sixteenth century, no more than 30.[13] The rest were seldom of other than local importance, and generally one and the same person may have been a "woodworker, farmer, shoemaker, trader."[14]

The policies pursued by foreign traders in Russia accentuated the disabilities of Russian merchants. For example, the Hanseats prohibited the formation of mixed companies at Novgorod as long as their own factory functioned there. (It may be tempting to speculate what the political fate of the town might have been had such business alliances existed.) In Pskov and in Livonia, likewise, mixed companies were not allowed. When the English opened direct trade with Russia, they avoided every kind of trade partnership with Russians. They even forbade their skippers to carry goods for Russian account. Yet as early as the fifteenth century foreign shippers had occasionally taken along Russian goods on a commission basis, and later this happened with greater regularity. Eventually, the English had to give in with regard to mixed companies and consent to agreements for sharing profits. By 1567 they were forced officially to allow the Muscovy Company to enter into a partnership with the tsar for at least one branch of its activity, the Persian trade.[15]

The activities of foreign traders in Russia have been studied with breadth and penetration by scholars working from Western sources, but much remains to be done from the Russian side. Only on selected topics do we find substantial research published by Russian historians. Thus, A. S. Muliukin has made a careful analysis of the legal position of the foreigner in Russia and has shown that the manifold restrictions which hampered his activities reduced his chances, though in different ways, to a level not much higher than those of the tsar's own subjects.[16] Foreigners had to live, in most cases, in special quarters, wear non-Russian dress, refrain from contacts with natives except for business purposes, hire no native servants except with the permission of the tsar, themselves accept no paid position without tsarist authorization, own no real estate, buy no goods from the producer directly but only through accredited Russian middlemen, carry on no retail trade, and enter and leave the country only with the knowledge and agreement of the tsar.[17] After the Reformation, questions of denomination could likewise become impediments. While the tsars had no love for the Protestants, they yet preferred them, for commercial and political reasons, to the Catholics.[18] Restrictive regulations against foreign merchants were, of course, not unknown among Western nations. Yet the effect of the restrictions upon foreign traders was far greater in Russia than anywhere else, and sharply reduced the numbers interested in the Russian market.

Nevertheless, those who came carried on a more varied trade than is generally supposed. The lists in Nina Bang's

Øresundtabeller[19] account for a large number of items which are worth studying separately. Furs, wax, honey, timber, pitch and tar dominated the exports; salt, silver, cloth, herring and colonial products predominated on the return trip. C. Mettig[20] mentions some lesser known commodities: nails, axes and other instruments, onions, horseradish. We also know that the Grandduchess Sophia purchased musical instruments for her terem[21] and that, in the early fifteenth century, such an unusual commodity as "Spanish bone" was purchased by the Russians for the manufacture of bows and arrows. After the Reformation Holland furnished broken church bells for the making of cannon.

In the list of Russian imports we should perhaps include services. These consisted mainly of those rendered by the carrying trade, but they also included the services of Western experts who came to Russia. Prohibited from accepting any position except those offered by the tsar, they helped to increase his entrepreneurial activity. Many were hired as instructors to aid with the establishment of new enterprises, the making of machinery, the production of bricks, cannon, leather goods, soap, hemp-oil, potash, etc. The investment of the tsar in this kind of service does not seem to have been very profitable, however; its value depended upon the capacity of the Russians to adopt foreign methods and develop them further. Chiefly in the field of the goldsmith's art do the lessons learned from foreigners seem to have benefitted native artisanship.[22]

Among the foreigners who engaged in the Russian trade the most successful were the Dutch. Of all the foreigners they built up the most durable connections. The father and brother of Alberto Campense, known for a letter to the Pope giving an early, comprehensive description of Russia, lived in Moscow at the end of the fifteenth century. Later, with the opening of the route around the North Cape, the number of Dutchmen greatly increased. Van de Walle, Adrian Kruyt, Gillis Hoofman and Justus de Vogelaar are some well-known names representing entrepreneurial activity of the Dutch in Russia. Other Netherlanders came from Brussels and Antwerp. A Claudius Monasta went to Moscow in 1561 to sell jewelry; Cornelius de Meyer and Simon van Salingen were two of the most successful foreign traders in Russia; Grammaye established a company in which at one time the king of Sweden, Erik XIV, and other Swedish royal princes were partners; Oliver Brunel served the Stroganovs. Others included Nicholas Verjuys and the very influential brothers, Melchior and Balthasar de Moucheron, who, coming from Antwerp, had settled in Middleburg.[23]

The Italians remained important throughout the sixteenth century even though proportionately they lost the prominence they had enjoyed a hundred years earlier. According to Adelung,[24] Marco Foscarini from Venice was in Moscow in 1537, and an uncle of Pope Urban VIII, the Florentine Raffaelo Barberini, visited Russia in 1564. A few years later another Florentine, Giovanni Tedaldi, arrived. Yet the fact that the Italians were Catholic, that the distance between their country and Russia was great, that German, English and Dutch competition was favored by direct sea connections via the Baltic and stimulated by the growth of modern entrepreneurial activity, and that the Poles opposed western connections with Russia and sought to block the overland routes—all this was responsible for the decline of Italian business in the East.

The German merchants were numerous and apparently successful. Much of their activity, especially that of the Hanseats and upper-Germans, has been extensively investigated and described. A few little known facts, however, throw significant additional light upon their affairs and the extent of their engagements. It is, for instance, interesting to note that Nicholas Poppel, generally considered the man who "opened up" direct diplomatic relations between the tsarist and the Holy Roman empires, may well have been prompted by business motives. He is pictured to us as a man of leisure and breadth of interest who liked to travel, and therefore came around 1490 on his peregrinations, as if by accident, to Moscow. But as a member of a medium-sized business firm in Breslau which was interested in Russian merchandise, he had perhaps a more practical aim in view than that with which he is usually credited.[25] He was promptly followed by other German merchants: a certain Martin Winter and Gotthard Stammler, recommended by Maximilian I; burghers from Frankfurt a. M. and Nürnberg; representatives of the Fuggers and others.

Interesting, though little known, are the manifold Russian activities of the Cramers of Leipzig and of the Tempelhof family of Berlin. Hans Cramer and Heinrich Cramer of Claussbruch maintained business relations with Russia. Their ventures, and the Tempelhofs', introduced a less solid, more speculative element than either Hanseatic or Fugger activities had possessed. They combined interests in copper and silver mines; traded in lead, fur, jewels and other commodities; and owned banking enterprises. They had dealings with the elector of Saxony, who was a partner in some of the enterprises of the Cramer of Claussbruch, and with the count of Schwarzburg, the duke of Braunschweig, the count of Mansfeld, and in the case of the Tempelhofs, with the elector of Brandenburg. Although they made most of their purchases of Russian goods at the fairs of Leipzig and Frankfurt, or in Berlin, they had agents in Moscow. In 1573, the Cramers were represented there by a certain Lorenz Buck and by Hans von Essen; the Tempelhofs in the following year sent Friedrich Aepinus and subsequently others. Yet though their undertakings may have contributed to stimulating large-scale business enterprise in central Germany, their activities, based as they were on a weak and occasionally a fraudulent foundation, served neither to establish durable connections with the East nor to set a model for other entrepreneurs.

Spaniards and Frenchmen were for the most part conspicuously absent in the Russian trade, notwithstanding the importation of considerable quantities of goods of Spanish and French provenance. A certain "Ivan Devaja Beloborod" from Spain resided in Moscow in the sixteenth century, and apparently there were also a few other Spaniards.[26] The French were hardly represented at all in the first part of the century; only during the last third do we see the arrival of men like Jean Sauvage and Jacques Parent.[27] Danes and Swedes were equally scarce in spite of the efforts of their respective rulers to set them up as middlemen of the trade.

It would be worth while to investigate more fully the activities of the English and German unlicensed traders. In the case of the English trade, our attention has been focussed on the Muscovy Company, and perhaps because of the masterly narrations by Hakluyt, we have gained, unconsciously, a somewhat distorted picture. For even the Muscovy Company (which gained a "monopoly" owing to its close relations with Queen Elizabeth, to whom the company extended loans and made other payments) did not secure as solid a place in East-West trade as the accounts of historians sometimes imply.[28] Unfortunately, the records of the company, which could have given us precise data, were lost by fire during the reign of Charles II. But we know enough about the extent of its difficulties, its numerous setbacks and intermittent enormous losses to realize why the company, which had started so auspiciously, could maintain itself for no more than half a century and make satisfactory profits only during a small part of this period. Much more interesting is the activity of the outsiders, the interlopers, whose risks were great, but who had the advantage of being subject to none of the official rules of the Company. At times, a member or representative of the Muscovy Company was simultaneously an interloper, entertaining on the side unofficial business relations to the detriment of his company. Political treaties notwithstanding, the tsar and his representatives were not adverse to suffering or even protecting such irregular channels; for these provided much desired competition and helped not only to keep down the otherwise monopolistic prices, but to secure for Russia, through free enterprise, types of goods—like armaments—which official regulations from time to time prohibited.

To study the Russian entrepreneur and his foreign counterpart from the point of view of the structure of the trade, as indicated here, may provide useful illustration of certain aspects of the economic process, and broaden our historical insight into the relative position of Russia and the West. However, a thorough investigation, especially in Russia, of possibly still existing customs receipts, account books and other trade documents would be necessary to gain a more comprehensive picture. This remains a task for the future economist and historian.

Chapter VII

FRANCO-RUSSIAN ECONOMIC RELATIONS IN THE EIGHTEENTH CENTURY*

The economic relations between France and Russia in the eighteenth century are of particular interest to the historian.[1] They reflect not only a dichotomy such as we rarely encounter between theory and practice, but they show also a wide divergence between the interests of the state and those of private enterprise. French advocates of closer cooperation between France and Russia acted as if whatever benefitted their private business interests automatically benefitted the state also; and it is therefore not surprising to see that French entrepreneurs, unlike English and Dutch businessmen, showed little inclination to take national policies into due account. They worked out numerous projects favoring the development of trade with Russia, and many of these were well conceived. They can now be found in the National Archives of Paris, but since they present chiefly the negative aspects of the issue, they serve the historian only to a limited degree. Only one article has been so far published on Franco-Russian commercial relations in the eighteenth century, namely that by S. Rodjestvensky and I. Lubimenko. It discusses events essentially on the basis of politico-diplomatic materials and thus enlightens us only within the limits narrowly circumscribed by official action.[2]

Rodjestvensky and Lubimenko themselves proposed addi-

---

* With permission from Revue d'Histoire économique et sociale, Vol. 39 (Paris, 1961).

tional research. It is in accordance with their suggestion that the present essay was conceived. By using available business papers, statistics, consular reports, and requests and criticisms brought by merchants to the attention of the government, it seeks to serve as a complement to their study. By providing a description of Franco-Russian trade—at least from the French point of view—it also seeks to lay a basis for further research. Documents of the type used for this study have been utilized by P. M. Bamford in his excellent work on French sea power.[3] His book also treats Russia. But inasmuch as he touches only those aspects which concern the trade serving the needs of France in her effort to create a navy, he deals only with one specific, though important, feature of a much wider problem.[4]

When studying the commercial connections between France and Russia in the eighteenth century, it is necessary to make a distinction between French and Russian aims. For the aim of Russia under Peter the Great and his successors was clearly economic; it consisted, once access to the Baltic sea routes had been assured, in providing the country with merchandise and technicians, on favorable terms, and in selling Russian products in exchange. It also had a fiscal aspect, namely, increasing the income of the tsar by the collection of import as well as export taxes. The aim of the French, on the other hand, was chiefly political. It consisted in making possible the building of a powerful navy so that France could challenge the sea power of her enemies—at first Holland and, later, particularly England. The appeal of economic gain, in line with the tenets of the age of mercantilism, was certainly an influential factor too, but the individual Frenchman was not sufficiently attracted from the point of view of his own personal profit by the possibilities which Russia offered.

I. Competition and Obstructions

The obstacles which presented themselves in all efforts

to initiate fruitful business relations between France and Russia seemed indeed overwhelming; and it is significant that despite the economic evolution which took place in the course of a whole century and despite organizational improvements during this time, all the efforts did little to change the conditions which the French had encountered at the beginning of the century He who reads the "mémoires" written by Frenchmen occupying themselves with Franco-Russian trade and thinking over its problems, will find that their points of view and, indeed, their whole perspective changed only slightly in the course of the century. At the beginning, as well as at the end, complaints about competitors are bitter. At the beginning of the century it was the competition of the Dutch and, to a lesser degree, that of the Hanseatic towns and particularly of Hamburg which rankled; during the second half of the century it was the competition of the British—a threat which was actually far greater than that of the Dutch.

Peter the Great has been given credit for initiating the establishment of commercial ties between France and Russia. His declaration of 1701 proposed negotiations and promised that he would treat France "better than any other nation."[5] Yet, in truth, he, even more than his predecessors, favored the Dutch,[6] whose competition is resentfully noted again and again in French memoirs. It is mentioned in statements dated 1713, 1718, 1726, 1730, 1745, 1766—in short, each time that a difficult moment in Franco-Russian economic relations arose, and often also during interim periods.[7] As late at the 1780's, a long diatribe asserted that not glory, prestige, religion or even lust for conquest are responsible for the wars in Europe, but that "commerce is the only reason for strife"; and the Dutch are branded as "natural enemies of all mercantile nations."[8] Their trade practices are often criticized. In 1718, for example, they were accused of diluting French wines and brandies and then selling them at a price lower than the French; or, in 1730, it was pointed out that they used, with permission, the Russian flag for their ships plying the Baltic Sea, and that thereby they gained undue advantages.[9]

Fear and hate of England, however, created a still more serious problem. Political motives and rancors were added to economic rivalries. First of all, the French, as did all other seafaring nations, bitterly resented the British monopolistic policies. In 1713, the British were indicted for their tobacco monopoly in Russia; in 1717, the French consul in St. Petersburg, Lavie, reported that English merchants had bought up all the tar the Russians would produce in the next three years; in 1724, the minister Campredon warned his government that the English and the Dutch had done the same with various other important products; and in 1731, Lavie's successor, Villardeau, wrote that the monopoly for exporting rhubarb and potassium had passed into English hands, to the detriment of Russia herself. Later, between 1760 and 1770, British monopolies existing on the sea routes to St. Petersburg, Reval and Riga, were gradually extended also to the trade with Russia by way of the Mediterranean Sea, the Straits, and the Black Sea; on August 23, 1779, the vice-consul Raimbert advised his government that the English were trying to secure for themselves exclusive privileges on the Black Sea route, and that for this purpose they had formed a mixed company, half English and half Russian.[10] In 1750, co-operation between France, Holland, Portugal and Spain was suggested to prevent the strangling of their trade by the British.[11] The proponent of this advice referred to the threat implied by the Anglo-Russian treaty of 1734 and denounced the conduct of the English as "unjust." Their statistics and their whole argumentation in their own favor were, it was charged, "pretentious," since they boasted to the Russians that they used more Russian products than the Russians used of English commodities. They left out the fact, however, that their imports were, for the most part, reshipped to other countries and that these countries constituted the real clientele of Russia. As was pointed out, the ill will of the British was also demonstrated by the fact that they had slyly spread the idea that France exported "trifles," for which she received in exchange gold and silver.[12] And the same memoir which had criticized the Dutch emphasized that all nations were alarmed by England, whose principal source of wealth was the Russian trade, and that the English were "the natural enemies of France." Even when in 1787 a treaty was finally concluded between Russia and France which at last contained the most-favored-nation clause, fear of competition was not definitely allayed. For the English still enjoyed various advantages—such as the right to display and sell their merchandise in shops at the various Russian fairs. They could also submit any dispute directly to the imperial Senate in St. Petersburg, whose jurisdiction was prompter and whose judges were considered less corrupt than the judges of provincial courts, to which the French continued to be obliged to submit their differences.[13]

The competition of other countries was less bitter, and it was also less felt—even though, from time to time, Spanish rivalry was denounced. Thus, in 1767, the consul-general, Rossignol, complained that a Spanish ship which brought a cargo of French wine had declared the wine as of Spanish origin and had therefore paid only a fourth of the import duties that were regularly levied on French wine.[14]

The bewailing of competition forms so constant an accompaniment to all French reports on Franco-Russian economic relations and has so much molded French official action that historical studies themselves tend to center around this issue. Nevertheless, competition alone cannot explain why Franco-Russian trade did not attain a higher level—particularly since the existing conditions made everything seem favorable to a growth of exchanges. For France could figure as a most important buyer of the goods which Russia wanted to sell, and on the other hand, as a valuable supplier of the tsar in those commodities, either from her own production or from that of her colonies, which he was anxious to buy. Actually a more realistic perspective, rather than the harping upon the question of competition, appears when one reads the opinions of French merchants engaged in this trade, which were repeated in consular reports.

First of all, a very definite lack of good will on the part of French merchants with regard to entering into economic relations with Russia is repeatedly pointed out. This situation does not seem to have changed in the course of the century, despite many official warnings. In 1726, Villardeau criticized his compatriots for not extending the credit to the Russians which was needed for successfully doing business in this country. In 1731, he complained that they sought too high profits and thus were "la dupe de leur avidité." In 1744, in his last message as consul, he insisted that French merchants had done nothing to encourage trade. In 1745, his successor, Saint-Sauveur, wrote that the French merchants were not interested in developing business connections with Russia; and in 1760, a French businessman, J. Michel, reported on the dissatisfaction of the Russians with France, particularly because French firms demanded excessive prices. However, Michel took sides with the French insofar as he pointed out the heavy supplementary expenses which burdened their transactions. He estimated them at 81 per cent, to which he considered it equitable to add a modest 10 per cent for profit. He also felt that it was necessary to allow an additional margin in order to make up for bad debts or for losses resulting from adverse currency exchanges, from investment and immobilization of capital, from unfavorable discount rates and ultimately from the dishonesty of the Russian trade partners.[15]

Several years later, the Chargé d'Affaires Rossignol again noted the reluctance of the French merchants with regard to doing business in Russia. But he added that he did not consider this unjustified, since the Russians derived greater benefits from the intercourse than the French. As a matter of fact, he considered it unnecessary to enter into new agreements with them, since all business from which France might derive profit could be done without such agreements. Twelve years later, in 1778, it was pointed out that an expansion of trade with Russia would necessitate an increase of credit transactions hardly warranted by the smallness of profit which could be expected from it.[16]

Undoubtedly, lack of experience accounted to an appreciable extent for the unwillingness of French business circles to adjust to the needs of the Russian market. Or perhaps one can also argue the other way around and state that lack of attention to the Russian market accounted for lack of experience. In any case, attempts to secure the necessary experience seem to have been much too feeble. Occasionally some French official sought to gain at least some information about trading conditions in Russia. But they seldom went beyond inquiring. Among them was the Marshal d'Estrées, who bombarded France's first consul in Russia, Lavie, with questions about Russia's trade with China and Persia, about her laws and about the men directing Russian affairs, as well as about the arrivals of ships, purchases of tobacco and the weights and measures used in Russia. He even asked for maps of the country and for samples of gold, silver and copper coins and he also showed an interest in Russian books and icons.[17] But little came of it, and French businessmen seem only rarely to have followed his example. There were far too few young people anxious to visit the country, to inform themselves about living conditions there, and to learn the Russian language. In vain did Campredon and Villardeau at the beginning of the century suggest such studies. Nor did the same suggestion, repeated toward the end of the century, meet with greater success, even though the need for knowing the Russian language, or at least the German and the Dutch, was again emphasized. Hanseats and Dutch had always sent their apprentices abroad; by doing likewise the French could have gained a knowledge of Russian methods—they could have informed themselves about the most suitable dates for sending their buyers there, about the right selection of Russian goods, and about the appropriate moment for the shipping of return cargoes, but few among them dedicated themselves to the study of the Russian market.[18]

Perhaps the establishment of a French center in Russia, or of a bureau, office, or warehouse there similar to those which Germans, Italians, Dutch and English owned and ran in different parts of the world, could have served to facilitate such studies and to open the way for a better understanding of Russia. Such an office or depot could at the same time have assured the French of a permanent base in the country. Theorists in France and consuls in Russia were in accord with regard to the need for a center and repeatedly advised its establishment.[19] But they were not listened to. Perhaps the time had passed when it was still possible to set up such commercial bases abroad. More important, however, was the fact that neither the merchants nor the government itself appreciated the value of the suggestion. The French were perhaps too individualistic to co-operate in practice; and perhaps the French merchant, mistrusting his government too much, feared excessive interference from its side.

It is true that the government could indeed have used this type of establishment for all kinds of interference. Yet governmental intervention might at the time not have been undesirable. However, lack of funds and lack of credit, especially at the beginning of the century, forced the government to be cautious, or indeed rendered it incapable of action. Moreover, blinded by the ideology of mercantilism, it was too easily satisfied with existing conditions, for the balance of trade (or at least the one indicated in statistics) was active. But, as Saint-Sauveur pointed out in 1745, this famous surplus in the commercial balance, which meant a deficit on the part of Russia, in reality perhaps constituted a liability. For the Russians could use French merchandise, but as they could not export more than they imported, they seemed determined to hold to their already tested relations with the English and Dutch, which, at least on superficial examination, showed a balance favorable to Russia.

Still, even under the circumstances, the French had other good chances for improving their trading position with the Russians. If they did not want to increase the amount of their purchases from Russia, they could, for instance, have increased the size of their merchant fleet in the Baltic Sea. This would have changed their status in the eyes of the Russians. It would have raised France's value as a business partner, it would have opened the door for an increase in profits, and it would at the same time have served the purpose of demolishing the British claim that England was a better client than supplier of Russia.[20]

Furthermore, even in the face of the theoretical position held by the French government—a position which conflicted with the bitter reality that the treasury was empty, that credit was lacking, and that an unstable currency prevented permitting an increase in imports and thereby aiding the merchant—the government could have worked out some means of assisting trade. As numerous memoirs pointed out, it could, and should have organized convoys or by other measures assured the safety of the French merchant ships on dangerous routes in times of war. It could, and should, have lowered, or altogether suppressed, import and export taxes on merchandise bound to or from Russia; or, as England did, it could at least have paid premiums to exporters instead of collecting dues from them. It could, with due allowance made for the pressing needs of internal and financial policies, have also exerted some pressure on the farmers general in order to facilitate the admission of Russian merchandise into France. Actually, it did occasionally take one or two steps in this direction: in 1718, for example, through the mediation of the Bureau of Commerce, it remitted the duties fixed by tax collectors on a cargo of salted meat and skins; and in 1733, it cancelled a tax of 20 per cent which was to be levied on imported rhubarb. A consistent policy was, however, not adopted.[21]

Finally, there was the problem of the export of bullion or currency. It was complicated by the fact that the prevailing ideology condemned the exportation of silver and coin. Nevertheless, French agents emphasized again and again the necessity of supplying cash both for the purpose of having on hand necessary means of exchange and for the purpose of being able to satisfy the demands of the Russian customs offices. The first purpose had to be served because silver coins (German or Dutch rigsdaler) and bronze coins (Russian kopeks) made up a large part of the cargoes, particularly on Dutch ships. To be sure, much of this was smuggled into Russia, but it yielded large profits, indispensable for making up for the expenses entailed in the costs for interest rates, which ranged as high as 12 per cent in cases where collateral was given, and which otherwise amounted to 24 to 40 per cent. The second and more important purpose, however, was to have coin available for paying to the Russians the customs duties which were demanded in rixdaler. This demand by the Russians was all the more burdensome for the French, as the international money market was dominated by Amsterdam and the ruble, on the basis of which customs duties were fixed, was overvalued by Russian officials and had to be converted into rixdaler at a fixed rate. In 1716, for example, the ruble, whose par value had been as high as 5 livres and 5 sols, had fallen to 3 livres and 15 sols. This meant, as Lavie pointed out, that more rubles would be needed in order to buy the demanded rigsdaler—equivalent to a 50 per cent increase in customs dues for the French. In 1717, he even spoke of a doubling of customs dues owing to the fact that at that time the rixdaler was exchanged outside of Russia for 95 kopecks instead of 50. A similar doubling of dues was denounced by Villardeau in 1726. In 1757, the French business firm of Godin suggested that the French should start to mint a currency equivalent to the rixdaler. This new currency could then be expected to serve without disagio for the payment of Russian customs duties. Godin also advocated that the French establish an exchange office for their own currency in Russia. That the problem was again brought up in 1778 indicates that even then a solution had not been found.[22]

To these difficulties, which had their origin in the internal conditions of France, must be added others over which the French had no control, since they originated in Russia. A first difficulty was caused by the level of the Russian customs rates which, for lack of a trade treaty, were very disadvantageous for France. It is not surprising to find that merchants, traders and consular agents continuously protested against the existing situation, even though in one case at least—in Villardeau's memoir of May, 1726, referred to above—a more impartial point of view is expressed. In fact, the author frankly admitted that the new customs tariff published in 1724 should not serve as a pretext or an excuse for the French, since it did not affect as severely French exports, such as brandy and indigo, as it affected those of other countries. Yet, it is true that, as a rule; Franco-Russian trade suffered from the high rates fixed by the Russian customs tariffs. They continued to rise, reaching their maximum in 1757. In comparison with those of 1753, they represented at that time an increase from 6 to 70 per cent. They particularly handicapped the sale of fabrics, jewelry and French wines.[23]

But difficulties, for which the Russians were responsible, were not caused by tariffs alone; the injustice, the favoritism in the Russian customs' administration hindered French trade no less. After the death of Peter the Great, the new minister,

Shafirov, promised to improve the administration of customs. But nothing was done about it. The Dutch, the English, the Hamburg merchants, with their long experience in Baltic trade and with their long-standing relations with Russia, knew how to get around arbitrary taxation; the French did not. They also lacked the experience necessary to cope with unexpected situations. One such occasion occurred in 1732 when officials of the Russian customs office conducted a raid against the foreign merchants whom they accused of fraud.[24]

Inequalities also resulted from the way in which taxes had to be paid: the English were allowed to settle their tax debts in Russian currency, but the French had to pay, as mentioned, in rixdaler. They proposed plans for a change to the Russians several times. In 1760, Joseph Raimbert presented a memorandum to Count Chernichev; but like Shafirov, the count did nothing. No settlement was reached until 1787, when finally a treaty of commerce was concluded with Russia. But then it was almost too late; for with the beginning of the revolution in 1789, France had to concentrate on political issues at the expense of economic questions.[25]

More important still than the problems connected with custom duties and manners of payment were those relating to Russian monopolies. They presented more serious difficulties at the time of Peter the Great than later, but they persisted more or less throughout the century, and they were the result mainly of the ruling that certain products could be imported only by some privileged companies and that other products, for political reasons, could be exported only by certain other privileged companies—generally Dutch or English. Certain products could be sold and others could be bought only by the tsar's treasury. Moreover, at times the tsar would buy up the entire Russian production of a given product for his personal use, and foreign buyers would find nothing left. This happened in 1717 with Russian leather. In addition, the tsar's treasury would often set arbitrary prices for Russian commodities and make these prices dependent upon the person of the customer. It would prescribe specific routes by which the goods had to be shipped, requiring, for instance, that all merchandise be transported by way of Archangel rather than by way of St. Petersburg or vice versa. This proved an impediment, especially to those countries which were less well equipped as far as shipping was concerned than the Dutch or the English, and it often entailed additional expense.[26]

When Peter II came to the throne in 1727, hopes for a change were raised. In August, Villardeau announced that anyone could come and sell salt and that, with the exception of rhubarb and copper, trade was to be allowed even in Siberia. This information, however, turned out to be premature, for in reality the monopolies were more or less maintained.[27]

The worst difficulty for the French, and the one which the historian has the greatest trouble in evaluating from an economic point of view, was the lack of honesty and the pettifogging of the Russian merchant as well as of the Russian official. In 1716, Lavie sent a report describing Russian usages. In his letter he furthermore explained the role which the Russian nobility, as opposed to the nobility of Western Europe, played in the economic life of the nation. In the same year another Frenchman, the consul in Danzig, Louis Mathy, sent information on the economic practices of the Russians. Nothing was to change in this respect in the course of the century, unless it was that dishonesty and corruption increased further. In 1758, the unreliability of the Russian debtor was pointed out; twenty years later, in his "Remarks on the Causes which Oppose the Progress of our Commerce in Russia," the author of this pamphlet (probably the consul-general of France, Lesseps) explained that all duties collected in Russia were divided in three parts: the largest was pocketed by commissionaries of the merchants, the second by the employees of the customs offices, and only the third, the smallest, reached the Russian treasury. Other complaints referred to the hazards in the relations with Russian customs officials, as mentioned in a memorandum dated August 27, 1776. It pointed out that all merchandise arriving in Russia was declared below its actual value and below its weight and size; as a result, in the one port of St. Petersburg alone the government suffered a loss of a million rubles on import taxes each year. Another million or more escaped the Russian treasury through smuggling, which undoubtedly could not have happened without collusion on the part of the officials.[28]

To be sure, neither were French merchants blameless. In 1769, a search was made in the establishment of one of the three most important French firms, that of Vice-Consul Raimbert. It was undertaken, as Raimbert insisted, at the instigation of the English and as a result of their jealousy and schemings. He was accused of not having paid the prescribed duties, of having hidden merchandise and of having sold goods at retail. It took more than three years to settle the affair. Meanwhile, a merchant from Sedan was accused of having made defective deliveries—an act which could only lead to discouraging the Russians from buying French merchandise.[29]

II. Treaty of Commerce and Consulates

In order to resolve at least some of the most important problems, the French government as early as the beginning of the eighteenth century thought of proposing the conclusion of a commercial treaty with Russia. It expected that, if a treaty existed, the French merchants would be better able to meet the competition of the English and the Dutch, that they would overcome their reluctance against the establishment of a French commercial center in Russia by which they could obtain the necessary base there, and that they could gain reductions in the customs tariffs. The government furthermore assumed that a treaty would secure for the French a seemly share in the merchandise which was sold through the monopolies of the tsar.

This is not the place for recounting the history of these negotiations; they are part of the diplomatic game which was played according to the rules of the time. But it is interesting to note that the tsar had proposed a treaty in 1701, and that it took 86 years, in fact almost a century, to attain it.[30] Negotiations were vigorously pushed from time to time, particularly in the years 1706, 1713, 1724 and 1725, 1744 and 1745, and then again especially in 1761. But political aims always took precedence over economic interests. The latter remained confined to a lesser place, with results for France's international position that would deserve more detailed study. The treaty was finally signed by Ségur and Ostermann on December 31, 1786 (January 11, 1787).[31]

With the exception of the first twelve years, when negotiations were conducted by Russian agents in Paris according to instructions issued by Peter the Great and Menhikov, the French consuls in St. Petersburg were the principal backers of a treaty. As a whole, France was rather fortunate in her choice of consuls. The first, Lavie, was perhaps the least competent; it was he who had led the negotiations with Lefort, nephew of the famous tutor of Peter the Great and chamberlain of Menhikov, who had come to France in 1713. But once Lavie had become French consul in St. Petersburg, he did not occupy himself much with economic issues—at least not in the reports which he sent to Versailles starting from 1716. As time went by, perhaps under pressure from Paris or Versailles, he concentrated in his messages more and more on political problems. Being paid no regular salary, he was soon loaded with debts, which the government eventually undertook to settle. In 1722, he asked the later ambassador, Campredon, to take care of consular affairs.[32] Campredon's letters give evidence of perspicacity and intellect as well as of a broad understanding of men and affairs; his recommendation of Villardeau as successor of Lavie proved to be judicious. And, in order to avoid repetition of past difficulties he prudently suggested that the consul receive a regular salary of 6,000 livres.

Villardeau (Villehardeau) served efficiently for nearly ten years, until 1733. His functions were then interrupted by political embroilments, and on January 19, 1734, and February 6, 1735, respectively, boxes and files containing the consular papers of the French were remitted to the papal legation. They did not reach France until the end of 1743.[33] The same year Cury de Saint-Sauveur was appointed consul. He was alloted a salary of 14,000 livres in French money and was asked to take up his post at St. Petersburg without delay. Villardeau drew up for him a long memorandum in which he revealed the reasons for the misunderstandings that had arisen between France and Russia in 1733 in connection with the quarrel over the succession to Poland's throne. He emphasized in particular the consequences of the Anglo-Russian commercial treaty of 1734 and the inaction of the French merchants.[34]

Saint-Sauveur's work began under inauspicious circumstances, in view of the La Chètardie affair of 1744.[35] Later, it was disturbed by his strained personal relations with D'Alion, who was Chetardie's successor.[36] Saint-Sauveur worked in vain for the conclusion of a treaty of commerce until he was appointed to a new post in Amsterdam in 1748. Notwithstanding the high regard which the Tsarina Elizabeth had for him, he succeeded no better when he resumed his post at St. Petersburg in 1756, where he remained until 1764. He was replaced first by Rossignol (1764), then (at least on paper) by Boyetet, then by Hason de Saint-Firmin, then by Lesseps (1774), by d'Avisday de Chateaufort (1788) and finally by Saint-Didier (1790). The last named, it is true, never reached St. Petersburg as he was stopped on the way by the Austrians. In the meantime, the Consulate had become a Consulate General, and the salary had been raised, at the request of Chateaufort, to 15,000 livres from the 10,000 livres which apparently had been payed to his predecessors.[37] However, during this whole period, from 1764 to 1792, the most important figure in the French consulate was, with the exception of the time of Lesseps, the Vice-Consul Joseph Raimbert.

The duties of the consul were so broad and the need for a more effective representation had become so evident that as early as 1720 Lavie had appointed a merchant by the name of Rademaker vice-consul in Riga. Other consular correspondents, vice-consuls or consuls, whether with official rank or not, could be found as more or less permanent representatives in Archangel, Moscow, Cronstadt, Reval, Pernau, etc. The most important among them, though not necessarily the most competent, was Pierre Martin, who in 1760 became vice-consul in Moscow; the best known was the son of Lesseps, who was vice-consul in Cronstadt before he started out on his voyages around the world and across Siberia.[38] Martin's successor in Moscow was de Boffe, who proposed that the vice-consulate there be raised to the rank of Consulate—a change so much more necessary as vice-consuls rarely received a fixed salary and were seriously hindered in their work by their financial preoccupations.[39]

The services rendered by these consuls were considerable and the information which they gave on the economic aspects of Franco-Russian relations were generally of high quality, as can be seen from their reports and notes, which are available in the archives. For the most part, their opinions coincided less with that of the diplomats than with that of the businessmen. Numerous reports reflect their views. A copy of the most remarkable and by far the most extensive and detailed report can be found in the archives of the Du Pont family in Wilmington, Delaware. It can be considered as a summing up of a century of projects.[40] Of course, the majority of the reports always made the same suggestions for putting an end to existing difficulties: they demanded the conclusion of a treaty of commerce and greater attention on the part of the French merchants to ways for acquiring better experience in the Russian market. They advocated the creation of a French economic center in St. Petersburg, the suppression of export taxes, and the providing of silver money and of foreign exchange for the purpose of equipping ships and having currency ready for customs payments. But most of these reports also add other constructive proposals.

Among the additional proposals, the issue of increased governmental help and support holds an essential place. Throughout the century, the tendency was toward freedom of commerce. Lavie's proposal, at the beginning of the century, to introduce in France navigation laws similar to those of England, represented rather an exception. In general, "free commerce" was advocated, while monopolies, privileged companies, and governmental interference were condemned. Even in England, state interference, particularly in the Moscow trade, had been under attack for a long time.[41] Nevertheless, some of the consuls, and some businessmen, believed that at this stage in the relations between France and Russia during the eighteenth century, governmental direction or help could be useful. This was certainly true—particularly on those occasions when local practices in France needed to be adjusted to ever changing international situations. Local practices often caused difficulties. For instance, tax farmers had practically ruined France's first efforts in 1758 to buy tobacco in Russia; or, in another instance, the town of Marseille had jeopardized the first French attempts to initiate trade with Russia via the Black Sea. At that time, Marseille, instead of charging the lower taxes which were customary for Russian goods shipped by way of the Baltic, had arbitrarily collected the same high taxes on cargoes of Russian merchandise arriving by way of the Mediterranean as on cargoes which came from ports of the Levant.

Governmental action could also be useful whenever it stimulated commerce without controlling it. In this connection, ever since 1750, Peter the Great was cited as an example of a statesman who had secured "almost unbelievable" advantages for Russian commerce. It was suggested that the French government maintain two salaried commercial agents who would be charged with supervising France's economic interests. In 1788, Chateaufort extolled as examplary the role of the Russian Empress Catherine II, who had taken the initiative in encouraging trade on the new route connecting southern Russia with the South of France.[42]

Other constructive proposals dealt less with innovations than with improvements in traditional practices. They concerned chiefly three aspects of commerce: types of merchandise suited for importation and exportation, means of transport, and trade routes.

As to merchandise, emphasis was put on the possibility of buying products in Russia which were normally imported from other regions.[43] Among these was in particular salted beef which could be obtained in Archangel. As some imports in 1753 and 1754 had shown, it cost less than that imported from Cork, Ireland; and even though subsequently it appeared that its quality needed improvement, it continued to attract the attention of the French. Other commodities which interested partisans of closer economic ties between France and Russia were Ukrainian tobacco,[44] rhubarb and caviar.[45] Likewise, it was recommended that the selection of French products to be offered in Russia be enlarged; the rapidly Westernized, elegant high society could be attracted, particularly in the times of Catherine II, by all kinds of French luxury items. In addition to fine wines and jewelry, which had always found a wide market in Russia, emphasis could be placed on exquisite fabrics of all kinds and on exceptionally luxurious cloth. It was even hoped that fabrics from Abbéville, the Andelys, and from Louviers, and the light materials from Languedoc would find good sale in Russia.[46]

Along with the thought given to commodities which could be bought or sold in Russia, attention was also focussed on those products which could, via Russia, be imported from or exported to countries located beyond Russia, among them, Persia, Mongolia and China. As early as the time of Peter the Great when Consul Lavie had come to St. Petersburg, he had been charged by the French government with the task of investigating the possibility of trade relations with the Middle and Far East. Campredon and later the new consul, Villardeau, were in turn interested in connections with Oriental markets. Their successors also never lost sight of the possibilities. In 1743, the chances of trade with Persia were again investigated; the English experiences, disappointing though they had been, were examined anew. In 1757 and during the 1760's, in connection with plans for initiating shipping by way of the Black Sea, attention was again attracted to these matters and to the opportunities which offered themselves for commerce with Persia; and during the 1780's, the development of trade with the Orient by way of Russia was once more considered. As before, it was deemed an important goal of French business.

At the same time, the possibilities of re-exporting Russian merchandise imported into France—a long-neglected branch of business—began to be investigated. Had not the English built their privileged position in Russia on the amount of goods purchased in that country—goods which England, rather than consuming, re-exported to other peoples outside the British Isles, France among them? Had not the Dutch shown themselves as important buyers of furs in Russia, although they hardly needed more furs than the French? Thanks to their knowledge of German markets, they re-exported their purchases to the Empire. A French re-export, via Nantes, of 1,200 barrels of salted beef to the American colonies or to Mozambique had actually met with great success in 1754.[47]

With regard to means of transport, improvements were likewise suggested in order to overcome the existing difficulties which hindered the development of Franco-Russian commerce. Among the difficulties was the weakness of French shipping equipment. This aspect of the problem was well understood, and recommendations were correspondingly made. Some were obviously advanced for patriotic reasons, with an eye on the state of the French navy and the "gloire" of France; others, however, were primarily conceived from the point of view of bettering commercial conditions. It was pointed out that French ships were outdated and that heavier ships—of perhaps 600 tons—were needed. Dutch ships of this size could serve as models. They carried larger quantities of goods and required a smaller crew, and this reduced expenses considerably. Even though the heavy ships were used by the Dutch only for their navigation on the Baltic, they seemed equally suited for the Black Sea route and were proposed for that purpose when trade along that seaway began to interest the French. It was even suggested that existing war frigates be transformed into commercial ships of this type.[48]

As to the third issue—that of trade routes—it, too, occupied the attention of the memoir writers. Its discussion was often combined with appeals for a livelier spirit of inventiveness, for greater alertness to existing opportunities. After the founding of St. Petersburg, Peter the Great had tried to channel as much trade as possible to that city, and the majority of the French skippers had complied with his wishes. Yet, these memoirs argued, interesting opportunities still remained for traders in ports such as Archangel, Riga, or even Reval and Pernau. Some of them indicated, for example, the advantages which the Dvina estuary could offer to merchants importing salted beef, or the harbor of Riga to those purchasing grain. More revealing, however, is the growing interest shown in the Black Sea route.

This route had been vaguely considered as a possibility at the time of Peter the Great's capture of Azov, but all projects collapsed when Azov was again lost by the Russians. They were revived in the second half of the century. To be sure, by utilizing the Black Sea route, the French hoped to gain primarily political advantages in their fight against England. Yet economic considerations played a role too. In particular, the French expected that with the help of Black Sea trade they could realize the important object of substituting Ukrainian tobacco for tobacco imported from Maryland and Virginia. The matter was discussed from 1758 to 1760, and a few deliveries of Ukrainian tobacco were made.[49] Altogether, the route seemed most promising, permitting also, as it did, a shortening of communication lines with Persia. Success depended on the cooperation of the Turks, who controlled the Straits, but who were unwilling to agree to removal of the obstacles to passage through the Straits which French ships encountered there.[50] Nevertheless, the project was, because of its inherent merits, systematically pursued. When Russia had succeeded in conquering a large sector of the Black Sea coast and had incorporated the Crimea, the matter of commerce via the Black Sea, at least by means of Russian ships, gained further importance. Besides tobacco, other commodities—particularly timber for masts and additional products for naval construction—aroused the interest of the French. A memoir of 1781 draws the balance sheet of the numerous advantages of this route: it could be kept open for navigation longer each year than the Baltic route; it was safer in time of war, at least as far as danger from England was concerned; it constituted a more direct approach to those regions which constituted the base for Russian power; and goods could be bought at lower prices in the South of Russia than in the North.[51]

Nor did the French consuls overlook in their reports advantages of lesser, or only temporary, importance.[52] Thus, at the beginning of the century, they pointed out the possibilities of promoting French economic interests by taking advantage of the misunderstandings between England and Holland and, in the second half of the century, of the quarrels between England and Russia. They took up the various legal problems, emphasized the privileges the English enjoyed in Russia, and endeavored never to let a moment go by without asking for analogous advantages for France. They likewise called the attention of their fellow-countrymen to the advantages which some of the Dutchmen enjoyed thanks to connections these Dutch traders had been able to establish in many cities in the Russian provinces where they had stationed relatives who could act as their middlemen in buying coveted Russian products.[53]

III. Enterpreneurs and Employees

Naturally France's success depended largely on the merchant himself, on his qualities as an entrepreneur, on his initiative and energy—which played the decisive role, whether he lived in France or acted as agent in Russia. Research on this aspect of the question would offer a large field of study to historians of French economic developments in the eighteenth century; and the provincial archives of Rouen, Nantes and Bordeaux could probably supply many useful data. Materials in this area are, as a matter of fact, rather rare in the National Archives, but even these can furnish much interesting information.

It was a banker from Rouen, Thomas Le Gendre, who, as early as 1701—the very year that the first official steps were taken by Peter the Great—seized the initiative and, addressing himself to the Bureau of Commerce, proposed the opening of direct trade with Russia. Responding to his request, the bureau deemed it opportune to conclude a treaty of commerce with Russia, and prepared a few paragraphs for such a treaty. These first efforts were, however, halted by war, which disturbed even that trade which had previously been conducted with a measure of success. Reports of the bureau of Commerce for the years 1705 and 1707 show that new action was needed, if for no other reason than to maintain the previously existing connections. It was with this aim in mind that the merchants of Bordeaux, for instance, asked for special permission to use Dutch and Hamburg ships to carry their wines and brandies to Muscovy. Not until 1713, when Lefort started on his mission, could the bankers of Rouen and their merchant friends resume their efforts. They took part in the conferences which Lefort conducted, and the firm of Planterose, in cooperation with MM. Pajot of Paris, prepared a plan which envisaged the despatch of four vessels, at the cost of 500,000 to 600,000 livres to Russia.[54]

A more modest enterprise was prepared simultaneously by the merchants of St. Malo—among them a certain Jean Gaubert. Having participated in the negotiations with the Russian envoy, they envisaged a transaction in goods totaling 200,000 livres. They planned to exchange them for approximately 4,000 pounds of silver in rigsdaler. They had some experience in this type of exchange since in the past they had carried on transactions with Russia through the port of Archangel. Unable, however, to obtain exemption from customs duties for their return cargoes to France, they had given up the traffic. They now decided to avail themselves of Dutch middlemen and in 1715 sent two ships to St. Petersburg. Unfortunately these ships were intercepted by the Swedes, and the owners of the cargo not only had to carry on difficult negotiations in order to recuperate their merchandise, but they also had to face unexpected additional expenses. For they had to provide freight for other ships which could sail to Archangel in order to bring back the return cargo. Unfortunate experiences of this kind destroyed hopes, with the eventual result that all plans were given up. Individual enterprise seemed of no avail, and gradually the idea that a larger, more experienced company was needed to take over the trade with Russia took hold. Consideration was given to charge the Compagnie des Indes and give it some special privileges. This idea was taken up also at various later times in the history of Franco-Russian economic relations. But it was always rejected while still in a stage of preliminary study. One of those who opposed it was Consul Lavie.[55]

Half the century thus went by before new attempts, of a more serious nature, were undertaken. But even then, only a few firms took part in them. Among them was one named Godin & Company of Rouen, who were the authors of the meticulous and carefully worked out, and very Anglophobe, memoir, dating from December 15, 1757, which has often been cited here. Godin & Company possessed a branch in St. Petersburg; they cooperated with Vidal & Company of Montpellier. A second Rouen firm, which was interested in trade with Russia, was the one of Nicolas Baudouin. It was associated with Beaujon and Goossens of Paris, and with the Hope banking house of Amsterdam, which had experience in the Russian trade. Baudouin personally went to St. Petersburg and set up an office there. Other French merchants, however, fearing the risk, refrained from organizing a network of correspondents in Russia. They contented themselves with selling their merchandise through customary channels, ready to complain violently whenever an incident occurred or a difficulty arose. When the new customs tariff was imposed in 1757, they bitterly decried it. But whether they were from Bordeaux, whose wines were so appreciated in Russia, or from Lyon, with its silk products, or from Sedan, with its fabrics, they undertook nothing which demanded the least imagination or included any risk—thus refusing to follow the example of Godin or Baudouin.[56]

Perhaps the general attitude would have changed if thriving French enterprises could have been set up in Russia. But those which did exist there at the beginning of the century never gained, by all appearances, much importance. In 1715, the firms of Salomon and de Vernezobre & Company in Moscow and Baudouin, Petit and Company in St. Petersburg, were among those which Lavie deemed worthy of his recommendation. If they had been better supported by the French merchants, these firms could, in his opinion, gradually have replaced the Dutch middlemen whom the French normally used. But this was not the case. Even a generation later, the situation had not changed: there still was no French firm of any importance to be found in Russia. In 1747, Ambassador d'Alion and Consul Saint-Sauveur agreed to ask the Bureau of Commerce to support the establishment of a new French firm in St. Petersburg "in order to deprive the English and Dutch thereby of this part of their commerce." They recommended for the purpose two Frenchmen, Michel, who was 26 years old, and Navarre, who was 33. They considered them perfectly capable of assuming the management of the firm.[57] Both of them had been authorized to adhere to the "Dutch and German convention" so that they could occupy a position adequate to launch themselves successfully into this venture. But the Bureau lacked confidence in the partners, judging them too young and inexperienced, and hesitated. As Saint-Sauveur had to confess to the Bureau a few years later, the hesitation was justified, for the enterprise failed. The consul put the blame of the failure on the "debauchery" and the "negligence" of Navarre and expressed the hope that a new company, to be founded by Michel, would prove itself more worthy of confidence and would have a better fate.[58]

The project for a new firm materialized. Ten years later, at the same time that Beaujon and Goossens were thinking of founding a branch in Russia, Michel was in charge of one of the three most important French firms then existing there, the other two being those belonging to Godin and Raimbert.[59] In 1761, the trade the three carried on reached the following totals:[60]

	Imports	Exports	Banking
Michel	3,500,000 livres	500,000	1,000,000
Raimbert	2,850,000	1,500,000	
Godin	1,050,000	625,000	2,200,000

Yet, even the combined efforts and enterprises of these three firms would still not have been sufficient to provide as firm and solid a basis as France needed to expand her influence in Russia. This is also proved by Rossignol's request of 1765, supported by Raimbert, for the founding of additional French firms. But it is understandable that businessmen were not much attracted, for they witnessed that even the already established firms failed to secure a large share of the business. As Lesseps indicated in 1778, Michel's profits never surpassed a very modest level—a fact not known, however, until after his death. As for Raimbert, he was not a rich man either. With his usual causticity, Consul Lesseps indicated that if he were in Paris, he would not be willing either to conduct his business through the French firms of St. Petersburg.[61]

Actually, the reputation enjoyed by the French as a whole seems to have been rather low, not only in the eyes of Lesseps, but also in general. In 1765, the Russian vice-chancellor complained about their bad conduct; a few years later, Lesseps declared that they did not inspire confidence; and many among them, including tutors, valets and footmen who had come to Russia, discredited their country by engaging, to the very limit of the law, in petty business deals such as selling French merchandise from house to house.[62]

It is not surprising to find that under such circumstances the idea of charging the Compagnie des Indes with the Russian trade came up again. But, even with the expectation of substantial business by way of the Black Sea route, nothing was done. Commerce by that route was finally left to the enterprising spirit of a small merchant by the name of Anthoine, who perhaps had good ideas but lacked both capital and experience.[63]

In view of the failure of the attempts of French businessmen to build up an adequate network of representatives who would assure the successful exchange of merchandise, the solution impressed itself on Russians as well as Frenchmen to try to produce at home what could not be imported from abroad. Various efforts, sometimes successful but more often unavailing, were made on both sides. Among those undertaken in France, the one by an Alsatian tanner, François Theibert, merits mention. Having spent some time in Russia and having perfected himself in the craft of tannery to the point of being able to "prepare cows' leather as in Russia," he asked the Bureau of Commerce in 1727 for a monopoly. He pretended to be in possession of the secret of the solvents ("drogues") necessary to reproduce and recreate Russian leather. The Bureau accorded him the privilege in 1731, hoping thereby that at least in this field France could be freed of her economic dependence on Russia. This dependence had seemed the more annoying as the tsar could block, as he had done in 1717, the entire production of an item each time that he needed a product for himself. It seems that a successful enterprise was thus born; to all appearances, it was set up in Saint-Germain, and its ultimate fate, which affected all French leather imports from Russia, would deserve separate studies. Several times in coming years the Bureau of Commerce had to deal with Theibert—the last time in 1745. The attempt of a certain Jacques Roquette, who got in touch with Consul Villardeau in 1728 and offered to transfer from Russia to France the manufacture of stockings according to a new process, met with less success. His proposals were rejected because he demanded inordinate support and extravagant privileges.[64]

More important than these limited endeavors of France to acquire Russian skills was the transfer of French industries to Russia. It occurred in the face of the objections of the French government and merchants who, like the Russians, were apprehensive lest competition hurt the sale of their creations. Nevertheless, even after Peter the Great had died and the impulses he had given the Russian economy were exhausted, French adventurers under the prompting of the Russian government continued with their endeavors to introduce French techniques and industries in Russia. This led to attempts at establishing factories, for example, sugar refineries, textile works and other branches of industry. Some of them prospered, others failed. Among the latter was that of Joseph Reuillis, who had emigrated in 1745 with the intention of starting a manufacture of velvets and silks in Russia and who was found later living in Moscow in the most complete destitution, his only hope being to obtain permission to return to France. In each case, the reaction of France jealous of its production was vigorous. In contrast to modern theorists, the mercantilists of eighteenth-century France did not recognize that a more industrialized Russia with a higher standard of living could have offered her commercial partners far wider profit potentials; they only saw the immediate losses which competition would cause for France.[65]

Another aspect of Franco-Russian economic relations concerned the French workers whose livelihood depended upon France's connections with Russia. They were workers who were either employed in France in enterprises which in turn depended upon the steady flow of raw materials from Russia, or they were workers who, seeking to improve their living standards, had decided to leave France in order to migrate to Russia, where they hoped to find employment in jobs calling for their technical abilities.[66]

As far as the ones who stayed at home working on Russian raw materials were concerned, the development of Franco-Russian commercial relations could not help but have an influence on their lives. Repeatedly—especially when interruptions in the trade connections with Russia occurred—their employers had to file appeals to the government, many of which are still to be found in existing records. Manufacturers of soap, for instance, who needed Russian potassium for their production, or those of morocco-leather goods who used the leathers of Russia, were haunted by the fear that their workers might have to be laid off for lack of supplies and would then leave for good. On given occasions, they therefore addressed requests to the government for special import permits or for the waiving of customs dues. The damage resulting from an interruption in the arrival of needed imports is again and again reported by them to the Bureau of Commerce.

As to the others, namely those who left their country in order to seek work in Russia, the problems which confronted them were still more serious. Like the government and the businessmen of Switzerland and other European states, those of France were chiefly concerned with the risk of losing markets if skilled workers left the country. Even normal commercial contacts could bring about this danger. When, for instance, the merchants of Rouen entered into contacts with Russians in 1713, they opened the door to agents of the tsar who, it was feared, could seize the opportunity and try to attract, by questionable means, French workers. This was, at least, a fear expressed by Lavie. When Lefort came to Rouen and Paris for negotiations, he, in his political short-sightedness, recommended therefore that the French act with the greatest caution. Three years later the French consul in Danzig issued another warning stating that Moscow was looking for 3,000 French workers in order to produce at home what up to then had been imported. Nevertheless, the appeals of Russia did not go unheeded. A number of French workers escaped the vigilance of the authorities and left secretly; others obtained permission to go. Thus, in addition to all kinds of household help, artists and scholars, even dyers and printers left for Russia.[6 7]

In the times of Catherine II, Russia redoubled her efforts

to procure foreign labor. Again French workers emigrated, their ranks swelled by the arrival of agricultural colonists. Their number was substantial even though it was not quite as high as Vice-Consul Martin indicated in a letter in which he speaks of 104,000 families who had come from all corners of Europe and had settled in 104 colonies, 52 on each of the banks of the Volga above and below Saratov. Of these immigrants, only four or five thousand, he claimed, survived, the others having died or having been abducted by the Tartars.[68] In reality, the figures were much lower. As far as Frenchmen were concerned, information likewise furnished by Martin gives us a basis for an estimate. In 1777, he listed about 300 families as residing in Moscow; some of them consisted of immigrants who had originally gone to the Volga region where, like all the others who had lived in the South of Russia, they seemed to have led an existence plagued by endless privation, misery and vexation.[69]

IV. Ships and Cargoes

If the many contradictory elements in Franco-Russian economic relations during the eighteenth century are duly taken into consideration, it is possible to obtain, with the help of existing statistics, a fairly clear picture of the importance of Franco-Russian trade and an approximate view of the amounts involved in the transactions. Up to 1744, to be sure, statistics are somewhat scanty; thereafter, they become more abundant. Naturally, they require a careful analysis. Such an analysis could benefit from a study of supplementary data which might be gained from research in French and Russian provincial archives.

For the period before 1744 the Sound Dues Registers give us, if taken jointly with occasional observations by French agents, much useful data.[70] We can deduce from them that between 1700 and 1712 no ship coming from a Russian Port, when passing the Sound, gave a French port as its place of destination. During the next ten years, three to eight ships sailed each year from Riga to France and, occasionally, one from St. Petersburg. Thereafter, this latter port assumed greater importance. In some years, five to six ships coming from there declared when sailing through the Sound that they were bound for a French port. In the same period, the number of ships coming from Riga increased up to fifteen ships, and some additional ones came from Narva. In comparison—and the comparison is very unfavorable for France—up to 90 ships left each year from St. Petersburg for England, while 100 sailed there from Riga and 30 to 50 from Narva. During the years 1738 to 1743, a definite increase in the number of ships coming from Russian ports and bound for France occurred. The total figure climbed to forty. The cargoes consisted mostly of linen, hemp, timber, cinders, tar and skins.

The impression one gains from these figures is confirmed by the reports of French observers: in 1720, when a vice consulate was established in Riga, Lavie complained about the small number of French ships which had up to that time reached that port; in 1726, Villardeau declared that no more than one French ship had arrived in St. Petersburg within the last two years; and in 1728, he reported two arrivals for the past four years, and five departures of French ships from St. Petersburg (the difference of three is explained by the fact that three ships had arrived in 1723). At the same time, Villardeau complained in another report that French commerce had diminished by three-fourths; and other reports confirm this impression.[71]

Beginning with 1744, trade with Russia is recorded separately in French statistics and is no longer combined with that carried on with other northern countries. The statistics show the following totals for the period up to 1756:[72]

Year	Imports from Russia	Exports to Russia
1744		141,978
1745	3,440 livres	310,566
1746	37,355	470,709
1747	3,600	132,200
1748	304,183	184,714
1749	461,150	437,833
1750	310,753	228,267
1751	859,616	236,772
1752	1,339,831	532,943
1753	856,253	780,873
1754	1,392,691	780,550
1755	1,574,554	1,754,513
1756	962,623	378,353

The accuracy of the amounts here indicated is difficult to judge. They are based on declarations made by merchants who had to report their exports and imports to the various bureaus of the tax-farmers. The quantities they reported were added up, and their "intrinsic value" was fixed by the directors of the Chambers of Commerce. Correct or not, one can only state by way of comparison that French trade with Spain, when compiled in the same fashion, was 30 to 40 times higher and that trade with each of the three countries Italy, the Empire, or England was 10 to 20 times higher.

The totals show an unfavorable picture also from the Russian point of view. Those which we possess for the trade of Russia with other countries indicate that in the ports of St. Petersburg, Riga and Archangel, commercial activity of Holland, England and the Hanseatic towns was several times as large as that of France.[73] In 1757, after what is known in the political sphere as the "reversal of alliances," tension between France and Russia made room for greater cooperation; but that same year the customs tariff, which was so violently condemned by the French, was put into effect. Statistics do not reveal the influence which these two factors exercised on the economic relations of the two countries. Perhaps they cancelled each other out, even if during several of the following ten years the commercial balance appears to have been larger and to have inclined to the advantage of France. The official figures are:[74]

Year	Imports from Russia	Exports to Russia
1757	1,143,670 livres	796,978 livres
1758	1,413,994	474,476
1759	574,336	740,120
1760	153,871	527,858
1761	197,650	815,888
1762	51,525	900,997
1763	1,256,942	541,788
1764	1,167,996	689,050
1765	1,389,299	1,354,612
1766	880,768	900,466

The figures in the records of the Sound dues are no longer very helpful; for the first two years, they show a serious decline in French sea traffic. But neither these figures nor the official French statistics are supported by the detailed data which are, for instance, provided by the firm of Godin & Company under December 15, 1757. Godin reports there that twenty French companies could find enough business if they could get into their own hands only that trade which was carried on between St. Petersburg and France through English middlemen. Godin and Company estimated the value of this commerce at more than 8 million livres. To these have to be added freight rates collected by England. For the year 1756, Godin carried out a detailed examination of French exports to St. Petersburg, reporting the following figures:[75]

Velvets, silks	655,000 livres
Brandies, etc.	255,000
Liqueurs, etc.	150,000
Jewelry	750,000
Gallons of gold and silver	950,000
Ribbons and notions	300,000
Coffee, indigo	2,500,000
Hats, stockings, embroideries	350,000
Dyed wood	150,000
Oils, fruits	150,000

Sugar, syrup	2,000,000
Wines of Bourgogne and Champagne	300,000
Wines of Bordeaux	1,000,000
Light materials, hardware	490,000
	10,000,000 livres, or 2,000,000 rubles

A census of ships, listed by countries, which reached St. Petersburg in 1776 likewise furnishes figures in contradiction with official indications:[76]

Countries	Exports from St. Petersburg	Imports to St. Petersburg
England	3,498,633 rubles	1,183,731
France	216,638	165,217
Hamburg	321,157	384,452
Holland	359,778	662,343
Lübeck	250,924	362,853
Russia	512,096	1,782,960
Other countries	616,130	714,965
Total	5,775,356	5,256,521

With the approach of the 1770's, a considerable change occurred. Perhaps because of better accounting methods, the twelve years show a very large increase in the official Franco-Russian trade figures. They begin to agree much more with what can be deduced from other sources of information. They clearly indicate the vast surplus of the balance of Franco-Russian trade in favor of France. The total reaches several millions and occasionally surpasses 10 million:[77]

Year	Imports from Russia	Exports to Russia
1767	605,177 livres	709,838
1768	2,246,078	1,130,345
1769	1,950,116	1,855,803
1770	1,626,145	6,388,767
1771	3,138,846	13,056,830
1772	3,048,293	10,409,374
1773	4,193,028	10,614,282
1774	4,710,259	5,384,853
1775	2,728,763	3,134,838
1776	4,464,345	2,204,967
1777	4,472,002	3,856,640
1778	2,401,338	1,884,243

However, the distribution of ships does not seem to have changed considerable; for the port of St. Petersburg the year 1773 can serve as an example, although figures vary a great deal from year to year. Of 682 foreign ships arriving in the port, 75 came from France; and of 674 foreign ships which departed, only 34 gave French ports as their ports of destination.

Trade by way of other Russian ports hardly alters the picture: their importance was too small in comparison with that of St. Petersburg. Even if the exports via Reval, Riga, Narva, Viborg, Archangel and Fredrikshamn were to be added to those which, by land or by sea, left Russia via Astrakhan, Kislan, Orenburg, or across the Ukrainian and Chinese borders, they still would not reach the total value of those of St. Petersburg alone:[79]

Ports	Imports into Russia	Exports
St. Petersburg	8,548,034 rubles	8,908,775 rubles
Riga	1,761,570	3,738,806
Reval	384,194	106,533
Narva	38,733	245,909
Viborg	166,965	100,357
Archangel	375,090	2,057,490
Fredrikshamn	35,770	24,996

A check among the various French customs offices of the distribution of imports and exports which went to or came from Russia may also be of interest. The totals for the year 1775 are:[80]

Ports	Imports	Exports
Bayonne	40,475 livres	
LaRochelle	84,376	1,734,225
Bordeaux	174,852	
Montpellier	46,943	4,400
Rennes	371,876	
Nantes	333,541	360,740
Rouen	1,676,700	815,786
Flandre		14,412
Paris		198,865
Saint-Quentin		6,440

Despite the increase of Franco-Russian trade in the years after 1770, the place which Russia held in the total picture of French foreign trade remained insignificant. As before, Spain, the Near East, the Northern European countries—Holland, England, the Netherlands—and lastly the Italian states remained France's chief suppliers. In 1773 Russia held thirteenth place, in 1774, twelfth, in 1775, sixteenth, in 1776, thirteenth, in 1777, eleventh and in 1778 the fifteenth place. During the following twelve years, up to the time when the effects of the Revolution began to be felt, trade with Russia represented no more than one to two per cent of France's total external trade. Statistics indicate:[81]

Year	Imports from Russia	Exports to Russia
1779	3,106,897 livres	2,365,978
1780	1,485,561	2,040,724
1785	6,412,339	5,485,675
1787	6,547,735	6,630,079
1789	6,139,000	6,963,000

The weakness of Franco-Russian commercial relations thus persisted up to this very last period. As a contemporary memoir shows, France sent scarcely twenty ships per year to Russia, while Holland sent more than 400. Many of these, to be sure, carried French products. A pessimistic report also came from the French consul in Helsingör, de Brosseronde. From his excellent observation point, he could survey the traffic through the Sound, and he, too, was impressed with the small number of French ships. Likewise, one cannot help notice the persistent weakness of French shipping on the Northern route to the mouth of the Dvina. In 1784, for example, only two ships, with cargo estimated in an official report at 113,549 livres, left Archangel, bound for French ports. The total freight sent to France from Russia in 1787 has been estimated at 162,000 livres for that on French ships, and at 1,105,600 for that on ships of other nations. As to the goods shipped by Russia to

France and destined for re-export to other countries, the balance was still more unfavorable.[82]

The usefulness of the statistics here given, chosen though they are from a considerable number of documents which have come down to our own days, is, however, limited. It is good, to be sure, to have figures at all, especially when it is possible to cross-check them against other sources of information such as written reports, impartial opinions, etc. Yet, we learn from them proportions rather than actual values. For the monetary values were often fixed arbitrarily, the currency was not stable, much smuggling occurred, and cheating was common. Statistical errors are therefore numerous, and false declarations were the basis for many statistics. In 1786, Raimbert wrote that, while 39 ships from St. Petersburg bound for France appeared in the official reports, in all probability there were 24 ships, or 60 per cent, more. These ships had given the Sound as their official destination, but afterwards they sailed on to France.[83]

It must also be pointed out that the picture of Franco-Russian economic relations was strongly affected by those transactions which show only in the balance of payments and not in the balance of commerce. They too must be taken into consideration. To them belong official subsidies as well as bribes. The latter were of great importance, even though the French used them too parsimoniously and, for this reason—as the consuls complained—less effectively than the British. There were also transfers of funds by emigrants, salaries and expenses for diplomatic and consular services, and a certain number of other expenses of a similar kind. Generally, the sums expended by the French were higher than the Russian outlay.

On the other hand, there was a certain amount of "tourism" which, on the contrary, favored the French. As Lavie had already indicated in 1713, many rich Russians were living in

Paris and were spending money recklessly. One of them, it was said, had lost no less than 50,000 livres in six months. Later reports, dating from 1731, likewise indicate the presence of Russian tourists in France. At that time, permission was given to several young noblemen (a Naryshkin, a Kantemir, an Argamatov, and a Chernichev) to go to France and to take funds along. A survey of Russian students registered in French universities, as has been made for those studying at the German universities of Rostock, Jena, Leipzig and Marburg,[84] could probably give further information not only on cultural relations but also on economic transactions.[85] Moreover, light is thrown on the problem of the balance of payments by certain court proceedings such as the one started in 1746 by Sieur Saint-Léger, who paid in France to the French creditors of his St. Petersburg agent, Navarre, debts totaling 740 rubles.

Far higher sums were involved somewhat later in the century, during the reign of Catherine II. The most important transaction carried out then consisted in the purchase by the Empress herself of a painting collection belonging to the Baron and Baroness de Thiers. The agent attending to this matter in 1771 was her regular correspondent, Denis Diderot, a member of the Academy of Sciences in Berlin. This collection, of unbelievable value, included five paintings by Raphael, one by Leonardo da Vinci, ten by Titian, two by Dürer, three by Holbein, fourteen by Rubens, twelve by Rembrandt and hundreds of other treasures. It was sold for 460,000 livres in French money, "espèces sonnantes d'or et d'argent."[86] Another purchase for the empress was negotiated by the Baron de Grimm in 1787. It did not have the importance of the other one, but it, too, reached the sum of 15,864 livres. It included two enamel miniatures of Charles the First and his wife, each worth 3,000 livres, one of Hugo Grotius painted in the style of van Dyck, for 720 livres, one of Venus "d'après nature," and others. Included in the sale were also maps, grammars, beds, totaling the sum of 176 livres.[87] Baron de Grimm was also charged with a number of other transactions which implied the export of currency from Russia to France, such as the payment of pensions to former French members of Catherine II's household or to administrative, scientific or artistic personnel abroad.

SUMMARY

A study of Franco-Russian economic relations, even if limited to an examination of selected documents which can be found in the National Archives of Paris, thus presents a variety of perspectives which are of interest in many fields of historical research. Some tentative conclusions can be arrived at which may serve to modify the impression which straight political and diplomatic documents studied in the past have given.

The first conclusion is that, in spite of a sometimes feverish activity, in spite of official efforts, of the ups and downs of diplomatic negotiations, Franco-Russian economic relations show a rather consistent picture. Secondly, a curve derived from the records of the Sound dues as well as a curve showing the sums involved in Franco-Russian commercial transactions would more or less establish that in the course of the years, with the exception of short periods around 1745, 1760 and 1780, the curve of Franco-Russian economic relations is ascending. Next, it becomes clear that, though the commerce between the two countries may not have been satisfactory in the eyes of the authorities, it nevertheless was not without importance. Attempts to increase trade did not primarily run afoul of the political situation and of the conditions which prevented the conclusion of official agreements, but above all they were checked by a double handicap: French businessmen sought less risky enterprises and judged their chances better in their customary commercial markets which did not include Russia; and, on the other hand, while Russian merchandise could have been of vital interest for France—particularly from the military point of view—Russia did not absolutely need any of the French commodities.[88]

This double handicap could have been overcome if France had had entrepreneurs more daring and more concerned with the public interest, such as Holland, Prussia, or England at the time possessed. But in the France of the eighteenth century, the combined interests of the merchants, the tax-farmers, the port authorities and the privileged nobility were so strong that no government, not even that of Turgot, could have overcome the obstacles without starting a revolutionary change which would have endangered its very existence.

APPENDIX A

The curve shows the number of ships which gave Russian ports as ports of departure and French ports as ports of destination on their westward voyage through the Sound.

(Source: N. E. Bang, Tabeller)

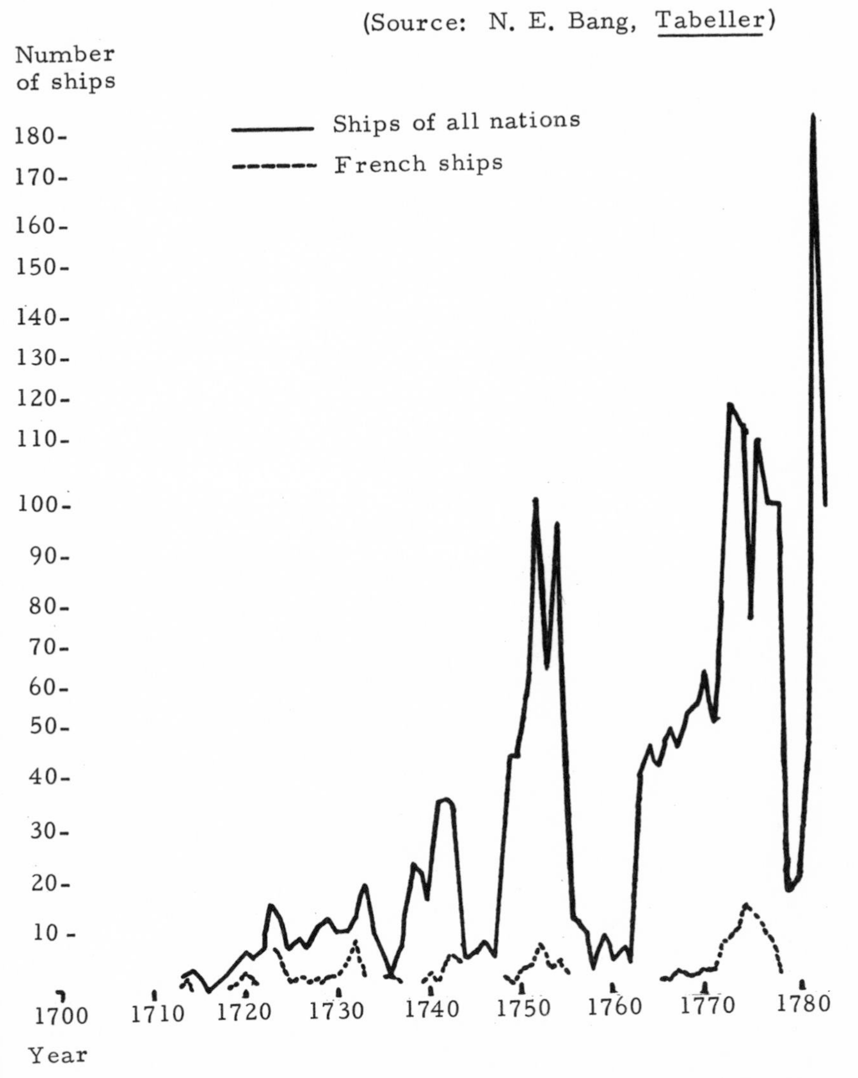

Note: Ships which give French ports as their home ports include, at least until 1724, also those few ships whose home port was actually in Portugal, Spain, or in Italian states.

APPENDIX B

Number of ships passing the Sound on their westward voyage.

(Source: N. E. Bang, Tabeller)

——— Ships giving Dutch ports as their home ports

------ Ships giving English and Scottish ports as their home ports

········ Ships giving French ports as their home ports

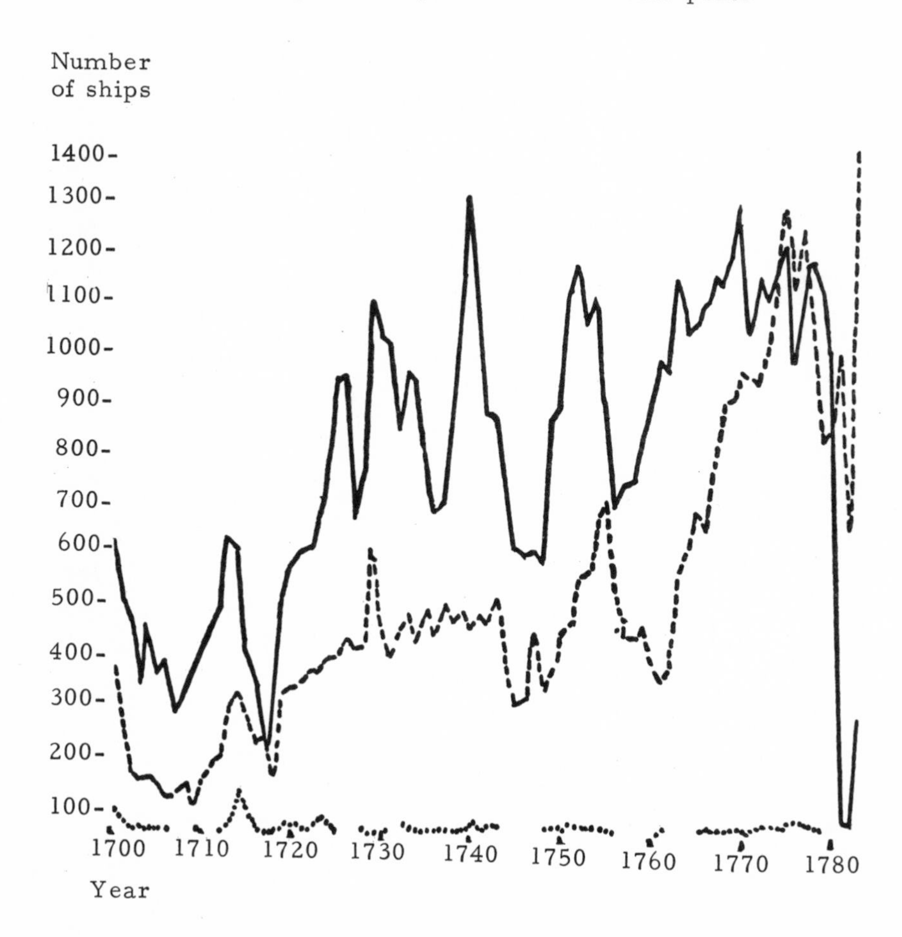

APPENDIX C

French imports from Russia and exports to Russia in 1775.

Imports	livres
Azure	3.042
Wheat, rye, etc. (bled)	116.463
" " "	53.037
Timber	1.016
Pitch, tar (brayes)	50.137
Chandelle*	4.304
Hemp	893.348
Wax	41.420
Glue	15.185
Horsehair	113.832
Copper	2.480
Iron	124.000
Black Sheet iron (fer noir)	1.080
cereals (grains)	28.543
Herring	9.562
Linseed (houpes de graine)	1.240
Ham	1.044
Wool	19.394
Books	1.626
Linen	17.200
Various merchandise	10.151
Masts	177.920
Furs, ermine	21.150
"	3.632
"	1.314
"	1.282
Boards	5.280
" , pine-	31.045
Feathers	8.383
Pig bristle (soye de porc)	40.384
Tallow (suif)	665.409
Sailcloth	82.177

Exports	livres
Stockings	1.308
Silk stockings	13.000
Cocoa	2.560
Coffee	895.339
Hats	1.920
Preserves (confitures)	3.092
Lace	6.475
Woolen fabrics (draps)	4.560
"	3.710
"	1.685
Brandies	72.960
Muslin	1.260
Silken Fabrics (etoffe)	7.670
Indian Fabrics	14.340
Other Fabrics	2.345
" "	30.765
Cheese	1.488
Fruits	9.129
Mirrors	91.800
Herbes**	1.530
Indigo	276.487
Books	1.992
Various merchandise	67.953
Notions	23.290
Paper, white	465
" for music	1.400
Wall paper	8.012
Other papers	1.187
Gypsum	1.771
Face powder	1.030
Sugar	77.848
"	24.825
" white (terré)	886.352***
Cotton or linen fabrics (toile)	6.440
same of Valenciennes	14.412
Glasses	5.860
Wine, Bordeaux	134.562
" "	354.300
" Bourgogne	9.300
" Champagne	38.066
" Nantois	6.500
Vinegar	6.982

* The meaning could be shipbuilding material ("chandelle") or tallow.

** " " " " (medicinal) herbs or spices.

*** Considering the importance of sugar exports from France as late as 1775, when sugar held first place among all French exports to Russia, one understands the dismay of the French when they learned, through news from Consul Lavie, despatched beginning November 10, 1718, that the tsar had the intention of having his own sugar refineries constructed.

Chapter VIII

UKRAINIAN TOBACCO FOR FRANCE*

In the course of the eighteenth century, the patterns of trade between Russia and the West changed fundamentally. Trade had always been lively, and it continued vigorously in the eighteenth century. But suppliers and markets changed; new procedures were introduced; the carrying trade came to depend upon shippers of other nations than those who had dominated in earlier periods; and, most important, traditional commodities were replaced by others befitting new needs. The balance of trade had generally favored Russia. But her place came to be threatened, and if she wanted to maintain her export surplus, she had to turn her attention to possibilities offered by unconventional products. Tobacco seemed in this connection particularly promising. [1]

As later events were to prove, Russian or, specifically, Ukrainian tobacco never did become a factor of significant practical value in the Russian export trade. But outside of the issue of commercial gain, the attempt of the Russians to secure a market for their tobacco had broad ramifications. It influenced international politics by involving Russia in the struggle for empire between France and England. It touched economic questions, for it affected, besides Russia, France and England, also Denmark and Holland—the former because of her control

---

*Reprinted with permission from Jahrbücher für Geschichte Osteuropas, Vol. 10, 1962. The article was published in honor of Professor Waldemar Westergaard on his eightieth birthday.

of the Sound, the latter because of her role as chief carrier on Baltic sea lanes. Russian tobacco exports raised issues of international law—particularly that of the freedom of the seas, for in the course of their tobacco shipments via the Danish Sound, the Russians and their French trade partners came to challenge the legality of the dues levied there. The tobacco issue throws light on internal Russian affairs, on the weaknesses of the Russian administrative apparatus and on the forces impeding the advance of a modern economy within the country. And in historical scholarship, it furnishes the student of eighteenth-century economic thought an example of the gap between economic theory and practice; moreover, it involves the investigator in complicated problems of research and forces him to a reevaluation of sources.[2]

The tobacco issue was raised almost immediately after the famous "renversement des alliances," which led to the ill-fated military alliance of France and Russia. To be sure, the possibilities of growing tobacco in southern Russia and exporting it had occupied Russian minds for quite some time,[3] and the consumption of tobacco in Russia herself was considerable. In 1697, an English company had received a monopoly for the importation of tobacco into the country. But despite making this grant, Peter, in line with mercantilistic views, had also promptly prepared steps to free his realms from dependence upon the British.[4] Not much was done, however, in this respect until the middle of the century when Count Peter Shuvalov received from Empress Elizabeth a monopoly for all Ukrainian tobacco exports via St. Petersburg.[5] For payment of 70,000 roubles, Shuvalov and his heirs were to enjoy the monopoly for a period of twenty years.[6]

Availing themselves of the opportunities offered by the grant, two leading French merchants in St. Petersburg, Raimbert (who acted also as vice-consul) and Michel (who occasionally was likewise charged with official missions)[7], started negotiations with Shuvalov. The matter quickly caught the imagination of other Frenchmen; for, did not tobacco constitute one of the great assets of England and could not the hated enemy be deeply hurt by discontinuing, or at least diminishing, imports from his colonies in Maryland and Virginia? In 1758, the French ambassador at the court of the tsarina, the Marquis de L'Hospital, intervened in the negotiations with Shuvalov.[8] Although he had at first considered using a foreign firm as agent or intermediary, he soon bent his efforts to eliminating the competition of an English house and to making it an all-French enterprise.[9] Samples of Ukrainian tobacco were sent to France.[10]

Difficulties arose, however, in France, and their study can throw light not only on internal conditions in that country under the ancien regime, but also on interdependence of political and economic forces in the policy-making of its leaders. The tax-farmers, M. Rollin and his company, "jealous to maintain their hold on the farm," proved reluctant. First, they insisted on receiving additional samples; then they argued that, since import dues on tobacco constituted a substantial part of the French king's income, imports even from the English enemy had to be encouraged, and that everything which might lead to a decrease in revenue, such as could result from unsatisfactory deliveries from Russia, must be avoided.

The argument, though selfish, was logical, and L'Hospital and the French merchants in Russia found themselves in a dilemma.[11] They had made a treaty with Shuvalov on March 23, whose ratification had to take place within four months. Fulfillment of the demands of the tax-farmers would, on the other hand, have meant a postponement of almost two years. This might have played into the hands of English competitors. A "Mémoire sommaire" was drafted in April which, after a resumé of the unsatisfactory conditions of past French-Russian commerce,[12] emphasized the unique chances that now presented themselves to France. Not only had France's chief opponent in Russia, the minister Bestuzhev-Riumin, been removed from office and replaced by Count Vorontsov,[13] who was favorable to the French tobacco plans, but the Russian tobacco growers had become interested in exports. The new chance, the memorandum therefore argued, should not be lost of forming "les premières liaisons d'un commerce directe entre les deux Puissances, et de jetter les premiers fondements solides du nôtre (comme il dépend de notre ministère de le faire) en favorisant de toutes ses forces le traité que les Srs. Rimbert et Michel viennent de signer avec M le Cte Pierre Schwalow pour l'exportation annuelle de 100 Mille quintaux de Tabac d'Ukraine propre . . . ."[14] Implied in the argument was the twofold desire to weaken the British enemy (to whom France was in "esclavage" and to whom, so to speak, she had to pay tribute) and to force Russia to consent to a favorable general trade agreement.

Simultaneously, steps were taken to change the attitude of the tax-farmers. Friends at home were charged with interceding personally with the government at Versailles. Moreover, it was suggested that the king should reduce French import and export dues on all transactions which Raimbert and Michel were to undertake and possibly to furnish them with a loan of up to 1,200,000 Livres, to be used for tobacco purchases as well as other speculations. Lastly, in order to press the issue, Michel was sent to Paris to negotiate with the tax-farmers.

In the meantime, a rather imprudent step was taken in St. Petersburg. At the instigation of L'Hospital (who seemed to be primarily obsessed with the thought that the French, as a contemporary memoire stated,[15] might easily remain "uniquement les tristes . . . spectateurs" of the Baltic commerce with Russia), the French merchants in Russia made a large advance payment to Shuvalov.[16]

In due course, the final decision of the tax-farmers arrived. To the investors it seemed most unfavorable since the total of the deliveries allowed into France was reduced from 300,000 to 60,000 poods (pud) and these had to be distributed over two years, with 30,000 poods for each.[17]

Anticipating a decision which would limit Russian deliveries at first to trial quantities only, Raimbert had, already before receipt of the answer of the tax-farmers, approached Shuvalov. Originally he had considered proposing to him a two-year postponement of the ratification of the agreement in order to allow for a trial period. In exchange, he was willing to promise regular orders thereafter of 500,000 to 1,000,000 poods a year. In order to finance such large quantities, the tax-farmers were then to advance 250,000 to 300,000 Livres. But he now found himself unable to make any promise for the future; and notwithstanding apprehensions regarding the effect on Franco-Russian relations (it was in the midst of the Seven Years War), the treaty of March was cancelled. No matter how great the disappointment of the French merchants in St. Petersburg, who argued that even if the Russian tobacco is bad, it would be used in France since people had become accustomed to tobacco consumption, nothing was left but to propose a mere 30,000 poods per year during 1759 and 1760. On this basis, a new agreement was concluded.[18]

Before deliveries began, the idea was ventilated of shipping the tobacco, in view of the British menace, to the port of Ochakov and then via Black Sea, Dardanelles and Mediterranean to Marseille rather than to St. Petersburg and through the Baltic to France's Atlantic ports. For the time being, however, this plan was dropped.[19]

The first shipment, consisting of 10,000 quintaux, began to arrive on the Neva at the beginning of the summer, 1759.[20] The quality was definitely inferior to the samples, and the unfortunate position of the French merchants in St. Petersburg became immediately apparent. Having advanced payments to Shuvalov, they now found themselves at his mercy. Notwithstanding the fact that they realized the shortcomings in the quality of the tobacco, they found themselves forced to accept it lest they lose all their investments. Not only did they have to take tobacco which was freshly harvested rather than seasoned for two years, but they noticed also that "tampons" of green or decayed leaves were mixed in with the tobacco. The weight was thereby increased, the product cheapened, and decomposition caused. At their own cost, they subsequently sent an agent to the Ukraine with instructions for the growers suggesting improvements for the next year. Steps were taken also with Count Shuvalov, but they brought no better results than that in later shipments the fraud of the tampons was, at least in part, eliminated.[21]

In the meantime, new troubles had occurred. Five Dutch or German ships had passed the Danish Sound on the sixteenth, seventeenth and twenty-eighth of August and on the fourteenth of September respectively, carrying a total of 38,445.72 poods, figured at 1,527,870 lbs. They were charged with dues amounting to 3,136.18 rigsdaler.[22] This amounted to about 9 per cent of the entire value of the cargoes, which meant that the whole enterprise became practically worthless from the point of view of the merchants, who saw their anticipated profits turn into a loss. To be sure, upon hearing of the Danish imposition, Raimbert and his associates at first thought that an error had been made, but they soon had to convince themselves that this was not the case. The ensuing correspondence with its French complaints and its Danish replies took several years and is of special interest inasmuch as it touched, besides the specific incident, the entire problem of the legality of the Sound due. Apparently, the French had figured on dues of 3/5 of one per cent, or at most on 2 per cent. They blamed the levy of 9 per cent on the "défectuosité du tarif" which made no distinction between "tabacs bruts & les tabacs manfacturés," [23] and they drafted a strong denunciation of the Danish action, in which they explained the legal position of France and Russia in the Sound as they interpreted it. [24]

They met, however, with still other difficulties than the rates at which the dues were levied. For the Danes insisted on employing weights different from those used by the French, figuring the pood at forty pounds—and at that, their pound differed from that of Paris. [25] Moreover, their exchange rate for Banco-rigsdaler, in which specie they demanded payment of the French dues, was higher than the French considered warranted. The whole matter was put before the French government which, on the twelfth day of May, 1760, lodged its official protest with the Danish government through its ambassador, the President Ogier. [26] The moment was awkward for France, since she was in the midst of alliance negotiations with Denmark, which the adverse course of events in the Seven Years War had necessitated. It was also unfortunate insofar as the director of the Øresund customs house, Wilhelm August von der Osten, upon whom the answer depended, may not have been quite impartial because of political involvements of a relative of his, who was ambassador in Russia. [27]

The correspondence about the issue of the Sound dues, both between France and Denmark and between the various French authorities, need not be followed here in detail. [28] What is interesting in the adamant way in which Denmark refused any correction, in spite of the French argument that building up the traffic in Ukrainian tobacco could lead to very large profits for the Danish treasury. On June 9, 1760, Baron Bernstorff[29] sent Denmark's official decision to President Ogier. He insisted that the duties levied on the tobacco were fixed in conformity with the treaties made with the United Provinces (Holland) in 1645, 1701, and ever since, and that they were valid for all "most favored" nations.[30]

While the whole question of the dues in the Sound was still in suspense, the shipments of the year 1760 began.[31] Again, the quality was unsatisfactory. An agent of Shuvalov, Teplov, had in February assured Raimbert and Michel of improvements; but obviously not much had been done. Nor had the advice of the French inspectors in Russia, who had been charged with the supervision of the deliveries, been heeded. On the contrary, French workers sent to inspect the products had been insulted and beaten by Shuvalov's officials. Further difficulties had arisen with regard to the packing and loading of the ships. Bales had been made of thirty poods each, and these proved to be too heavy for handling in France; bad odors had penetrated through the packing material and spoiled the quality; additional fraud had been committed by the Russians, who allowed rain and melted snow to seep in which, as well as spoiling the merchandise, increased its weight; and the Dutch skippers had packed the goods either too tightly or too lightly—depending upon whether they were paid by weight or by space. Nor did the Danes relent in their demands. They insisted that there was no reason for Russia to feel discriminated against. The tariff of 1701, they stated in a letter of October 28, 1760,[32] "regarde moins le Tabac cordé et preparé que celui qui est encore en feuilles," and leaf tobacco, they maintained, constituted also the larger part of English and Dutch shipments. In their refusal, the Danes were obviously motivated, at least in part, by fear of a reaction on the part of these two nations, since concessions made to France or Russia would force Denmark to reduce the tariff for all.[33] The trial period thus closed with France's hopes dashed for defeating her English rival in an area where the British had seemed especially vulnerable.

Too much was involved, however, to give up all efforts; nor would this have seemed justified on the basis of the concrete facts, which included Russia's capacity for producing tobacco and France's need for importing it. Consequently, plans were laid for an improved connection. As early as August, 1760, a draft for a new treaty with Shuvalov was prepared.[34] The new agreement provided for five distinct points: that the tobacco be fermented for two years; that the fraud of adding "tampons de feuilles vertes ou pourries" be discontinued;[35] that the other fraud of wetting the leaves be likewise discontinued and that Shuvalov use his full authority to enforce the prohibition; that the French workers should no longer be exposed to maltreatment; and that shipments be made in barrels, which would preserve the tobacco better than the bales previously used, and which would make impossible careless storage on the boats. In connection with this last point, the French declared themselves willing to attend to the packing themselves, provided a corresponding adjustment in the price were made.[36]

Simultaneously, the question of the Sound Dues was pursued further. In line with the tenor of his previous explanations, von der Osten had restated the Danish position again and again. While he agreed that the treatment of Russia was not the same as that accorded England and Holland, he explained that it was not worse than that given to Sweden, Prussia and other powers, and that there was no reason to allege that the Sound "was closed to Russia more than to others." This last point was of special importance. It was confirmed a few years later when Bernstorff, upon renewed inquiry, was once more assured that all nations were treated alike, except for three points in which the Russian position differed from that of the four privileged nations (which, at that time—1768—included England, France, Sweden and Holland).[37]

The Danes defended themselves equally energetically against the reproach of treating France unjustly. A memoire of April 18, 1761, even stated[38] that, warned by the complaints of President Ogier, the officials of the Sound Customs Office had, at least in one case, actually leaned over backward in favor of a French captain. It also rejected the arbitrary way in which the French apparently wanted to equal a rigsdaler with 4.10 livres of France and the Danish weight with weight "de marc." The tariff of 1701, it was, however, maintained, left complete freedom to Denmark in these matters, and therefore 127 1/2 Danish pounds had to be accepted as the equivalent of 100 French pounds. Were Denmark to agree to weight "de marc" for France, then other nations could come with parallel demands and endless disputes would result.

It was with considerable foreboding that, under such circumstances, the French merchants in St. Petersburg looked forward to the 1761 season. To their relief, they had found that, as the previously cited "mémoire sur les feuilles" of 1762 stated, some of the growers in the Ukraine had shown themselves interested in the improvements which the French tried to teach them. They had also succeeded in persuading the tax-farmers, in view of the possible advantages for France, to permit a third try and to allow the admittance of another 1,000,000 pezant. On the other hand, the needed radical reforms could hardly have been effected in so short a time, and Shuvalov himself showed little interest in the small volume proposed for the year. Nevertheless, delivery was made. The tobacco, the memoire says, arrived in St. Petersburg later than in other years, luckily escaping a fire which would have meant its total loss, but causing delay to the ships and thereby other losses, so that the tax-farmers now refused categorically to accept any further shipment of Ukrainian tobacco.[39]

Considering the latest failure, the same "mémoire sur les feuilles" could not help but concede that, after all, the tax-farmers in France, responsible as they were to the king for his income, had proved themselves justified from the beginning with their hesitancy, caution, and warnings, and that the first agreement with Shuvalov had been too hastily concluded. It also agreed that unless something could be done to improve the quality of the Ukrainian tobacco, which seemed difficult in view of climate and type of plant, it had to be considered unfit for consumption. Yet, the memorandum suggested that the whole issue was so important for France that perhaps a compromise could be worked out. After all, so far the tax-farmers had suffered no losses, for they had been able to mix the small quantities of the Ukrainian product, which had been imported, with the better Virginia and Maryland tobacco. Such mixtures might also in the future be salable—especially in the South of France and among soldiers and sailors. It was therefore considered desirable that small quantities should continue to be introduced every year and thereby help the merchants who had invested so much in the venture. New arrangements with Shuvalov could provide for better supervision, for incentives for the individual grower, for better overland transportation, and for adequate packing; and perhaps the transport could eventually be effected by the Black Sea route, avoiding the Danish Sound.

Even though nothing came of this proposal, the matter was not forgotten. It came to the fore again four years later when Shuvalov had died and Teplov approached the French anew in the matter.[40] By an ukase (ukaz) of February 11, 1763, the Russian government had already provided for the free distribution of seeds and had promised premiums to successful growers.[41] Moreover, Teplov had been charged in the same year by the new Empress, Catherine II, with improving the cultivation of tobacco in the Ukraine. Teplov's new proposals were supported by the French consul in St. Petersburg, Rossignol, and by a director of the Compagnie des Indes, Gilly, both of whom advocated another try. The possibilities of at least mixing Ukrainian tobacco with American tobacco were once more emphasized.[42]

Two years later, nothing having been done in the meantime, Teplov, now senator, wrote again about the tobacco exports from the Ukraine to France. He urged the French to forget the prejudices they may have retained from the time of Shuvalov, since the quality had been much improved. Indeed, the French were invited to send samples which should be matched in the Ukraine and even to dispatch representatives of the general tax farmers who could inspect and supervise the plantations in the Ukraine.[43]

It took, however, almost ten more years until serious attention was again paid to tobacco imports from Russia, and then the revival of interest was mainly due to new plans concerned with sponsoring traffic via Black Sea, Dardanelles and Mediterranean to the South of France. By that time the American War of Independence had broken out and the whole tobacco issue had changed. The anti-English argument no longer held, since the British were on the verge of losing altogether their position as tobacco producers; the revolutionary events had altered the conditions of the carrying trade; and the Black Sea route was no longer a mere dream. It had come within the reach of France and Russia owing to the success of the Russian arms against Turkey and the so-called "First Partition" of Poland. Ruthenia having fallen again to Russia, prospects for new trade facilities and new trade routes were opened to the tsarist empire. How important and lucrative connections via the Black Sea promised to become, at least in the minds of some Russians and some Frenchmen, is demonstrated by the willingness of Teplov to participate, through the purchase of twenty shares or one tenth of the total capital, in a proposed Company for Mediterranean Trade.[44] It is also demonstrated by the fact that the Russians counted on being able to sell the tobacco of southern Russia at the mouth of the Dnieper at about half the price charged in St. Petersburg.[45]

Unfortunately for both France and Russia, the new possibilities could not be promptly exploited. The establishment of the Black Sea route necessitated preparations which, as it turned out, took several years to complete; and the Baltic tradeway with all its disadvantages in being subjected to Danish dues remained the only path open for profitable Franco-Russian intercourse. The route was again used for tobacco in 1777, 1778 and 1779. The deliveries were quite substantial, amounting, according to a statement of the Danish customs director, to a total of 2,657,298 lbs.,[46] i.e., to not much less than in the crucial years of the first trials 1759 to 1761. As to 1779, the original Sound Dues records indicate that on July 22 a Dutch captain, sailing under the Russian flag, passed the Sound bound for Bordeaux with a load of 330,511 lbs. of tobacco, and that on the eleventh of October another ship, bound for Le Havre, followed with 295,520 lbs. It is probably this latter ship whose dispatch was confirmed by a letter which Raimbert sent on the twenty-fifth of September to Paris. Additional shipments left St. Petersburg for Amsterdam, and no doubt part of these were also sent on to French ports.[47] Altogether, tobacco shipments from the Baltic westward played an important role during this time. Statistics submitted in 1780 by the director of the Danish customs office show the following figures:

1773	27,538 1/2	lbs.
1774	--	
1775	11,610	lbs.
1776	466,787	lbs.
1777	6,229,225	lbs.
1778	5,618,828	lbs.
1779	5,512,639	lbs.

On the other hand, shipments from the West eastward into the Baltic region decreased, owing to the political situation, from a maximum of 3,949,052 lbs. in 1774 to a minimum of 1,394,063 lbs. in 1777; and if they somewhat increased thereafter, they stayed nevertheless far below the values of the cargoes traveling in the opposite direction, while they had been many times as large earlier.[48]

The same "Pro memoria" of the customs director which

gives these statistics also contains a new warning from him against concessions in the matter of the rates charged Russia or France. His position, however, became untenable. Notwithstanding the fact that developments in America made it less urgent than in earlier times for France to secure a reduction in the dues, the French ambassador had undertaken new and energetic steps to have them lowered.[49] Bernstorff again rejected all demands—arguing that Holland, which bought far more tobacco than France, had lodged no complaint and that, moreover, the Sound dues were actually so low that they in no way impeded Russia's tobacco exports.[50] But in the following year, which brought Bernstorff's removal from office, a first step towards a reversal of his stand was taken. Perhaps the change was hastened by the fact that the results of the year 1780 had been particularly disappointing. The total of the tobacco shipments westward through the Sound had decreased from 5,512,639 lbs. to only 1,246,727 lbs.[51]

Pressure did not come only from the side of France, or even from the fact that tobacco shipments had declined—there was a good prospect of their climbing again; it came also increasingly from the side of the Russians. On June 20, 1781, Catherine's minister plenipotentiary, von Sacken,[52] submitted to the Danish foreign minister Rosencrone[53] a clear exposé, in which he suggested that not only Russian but also Danish interests were better served if the excessive dues, which he figured at about 10 per cent of the value, were reduced. The Danish argument that Holland had seen no need for protesting he justifiedly rejected on the grounds that Holland acted only as a carrier of goods. Moreover, he pointed out that the existing Danish-Russian relationship, which was based on friendship and political co-operation, peremptorily demanded a revision of the rates.[54] Under such mounting pressure, the first step for redress was undertaken. On the twenty-second of September, Baron von Sacken was advised that even though

Denmark considered the dues she levied as both legal and fair, she might deem it possible to make an adjustment, and that this could be done within the framework of a general trade agreement. This idea of coupling the question of lower dues with that of a general trade treaty was not very kindly received by Russia, and the Danes had to defend themselves against the suspicion that they were using a concession in the matter of the dues as a lever to force Russia to come to terms on a general trade agreement.[55] But the fact remained that the ultimate settlement did come in connection with such a general treaty. Concluded in October, 1782, it provided that Russia be accepted among the most favored nations, that her ships be freed of all visitation by the customs officer in the Sound, and that the tobacco dues be radically reduced.[56]

To the extent to which Ukrainian tobacco played a role in the worldwide struggle for empire, power, markets and dues, the story ends here. All countries involved were the losers: France, because she found herself unable to replace the American product by that from the Ukraine and remained dependent upon imports from Virginia and Maryland; England, because she lost America and therewith her control of the centers of tobacco production; Russia, because she proved unable to establish plantations where an acceptable quality of tobacco, fit for export, could be grown; and Denmark, because she not only had to make concessions in regard to the rates collected on leaf tobacco in the Sound, but also because in the course of the vain battle to maintain them she found the entire legal basis of her system of dues questioned.

Perhaps a postlude should be added. Just at the time when Denmark concluded her trade treaty with Russia, a Frenchman, Anthoine (de St. Joseph), completed negotiations with Prince Potemkin about the establishment of the route—the Black Sea route—which was to by-pass Danish (and English) waters altogether; and in 1782, he could open a factory of his own in Cherson near the mouth of the Dnieper. He secured the same privileges which the French merchants in St. Petersburg enjoyed, and far larger privileges than those granted to other foreign merchants established on the Black Sea coast. With the motto: "Liberté, Egalité, Concurrence, voilà, comme on scait, les grands, les plus simples moyens, pour avoir un grand Commerce, une grande Navigation,"[57] he prevailed upon the French government to support his ventures with loans of money and ships. Negotiations with Turkey did not lead to a satisfactory arrangement, to be sure, yet within five years some nineteen ships sailed in the course of six months from Cherson to Marseille. Timber, masts and cordage as well as other naval stores useful in defeating English monopolistic endeavors formed the freight; but tobacco, which had so much excited the French imagination, which had held great expectations for Russia, and which had been a prime mover in the relationship of the two nations, was practically forgotten.

Chapter IX

EMIGRATION TO RUSSIA*

The problem of immigration into Russia has occupied the successive Russian governments since the time of Catherine the Great and has posed interesting questions to the student of Russian social history, questions which, with their manifold ramifications, scholars have investigated in isolated instances only. It is known that the Russian governments repeatedly tried to attract skilled and industrious workers and peasants, but their efforts were continually checked by apprehensions both within and outside Russia. On the one side, it was feared that politically and religiously undesirable elements might enter; on the other, the home countries of the prospective immigrants wished to avoid the transfer of valuable skills abroad.

A concrete illustration of the difficulties involved in the eastward migration movement and of the type of countermeasures employed is furnished by documents to be found in various Swiss archives. They reflect actions and attitudes encountered in many European countries, and they deal with problems which are typical of all emigration activities.

The account which the Swiss documents give us begins in 1762; for, notwithstanding earlier Russian interest in European immigration, it was only during the reign of Catherine II that methodical efforts toward large-scale immigration were successfully undertaken. From the very beginning of her reign

---

* Reprinted with permission from *The American Historical Review*, Vol. LV, No. 3, April, 1950.

Catherine directed her attention to population problems. Aware of the "the wide extent of Our realms" she issued a proclamation within four months of her coming to the throne inviting all but Jews to come and settle in her lands,[1] and by 1765 the first traces of the activities of her agents in Switzerland were apparent.

The agents were charged with three different tasks, two of them important but affecting few people, the third one far-reaching in every respect. The first concerned the introduction of educators into Russia. A Major General von Bülow,[2] about seventy years old and a scion of the prominent family in Mecklenburg, was commissioned to engage "some ten widows and ladies of a certain age" to go to Russia, accompanied by domestic servants, and to instruct young people of good families in French and other fields of learning.[3] The ladies had to possess good minds and good manners and were expected to be of Protestant faith; Orthodoxy was, indeed, not required of them, and Catholicism was considered undesirable since it was assumed to lead to superstition. They were given living quarters and board, clothing, 200 rubles a year, and the help of two servants;[4] and were assured of time for leisure and recreation. Carriages for going to church were put at their disposal. After the fulfillment of their obligations they had the right to return to their home country.

Bülow's undertaking assumed considerable importance, for the emigration even of the few persons in questions[5] was stopped by the Swiss authorities. We need not attach too much value to a Russian condition that the servants be of "agreeable face, pure virgins, and, in due time, of fruitful body, to understand French and to be well inclined toward the Orthodox faith" and that, as a complaint of August 23, 1765, shows, Swiss authorities felt that the country was not able to spare sufficient young women fulfilling these requirements. But the problem of depopulation seemed to be an urgent one and the principles involved in Bülow's action presently overshadowed the otherwise very limited extent of his work. When two ladies coming from Geneva passed through the territory of Bern, they were arrested and eventually, after some correspondence,[6] sent back to their home towns. Such procedure justly aroused the ire of Catherine's agent, particularly because a tradition of long standing in Switzerland had generally made Swiss citizens the freest of all, and apparently the bailiff of Geneva had assured Bülow that everyone was his own master and "could go wherever he pleased and do whatever he wanted."[7] But despite vigorous protests and insistence that Catherine, the empress, could expect better treatment from the Swiss, Bernese authorities remained firm in refusing an exit permit even to a few elderly widowed teachers.

How important the issue became is sufficiently evidenced by the fact that Catherine's prime minister, Count Panin, took a personal hand in the matter. He was aware of the fears of the western countries and their repeated efforts to prevent Russia from sharing in the achievements of the West. At about the same time that Bülow was busy on his mission, another plan to secure Swiss skills for Russia miscarried. It concerned the engagement of a Geneva watchmaker and his journeymen, who were not permitted to depart for Russia lest industrial abilities be spread to the tsarist empire.[8] On October 12, 1765, Panin therefore dispatched a personal letter to the Bernese authorities.[9]

The letter complained of Switzerland's unwarranted lack of co-operation. While not denying that every country had the right to restrict emigration, Panin stressed the gain which every country could derive from the activity of those who left their homes for a limited time to return richer in experience as well as material possessions. At no time, he insisted, had Switzerland, whose citizens could be found everywhere, disregarded resulting advantages. How much less reason had it then to arrest persons engaged abroad not as artisans or workers but as instructors and educators. The perfection of education, incompatible with national rivalry, constituted, as Panin emphasized, a common concern for all nations. All were to gain by it; and the employment of Swiss citizens for education abroad did only honor and justice to the happy state of Swiss institutions.

Panin's letter expressed convictions and sentiments which the enlightened West itself was beginning to preach. But not only did Panin sound his appeal in vain; he also had the disappointment of witnessing the collapse of a third and far broader scheme which the Russian government sought to promote simultaneously. It concerned the settlement of southern Russia by Swiss colonists.

In the course of the year 1765 there appeared in various cantons this public announcement:

Avis au public.

> Un Prince offrant a une personne pauvre et infortunée, qui ne possède qu'une misérable Chaumière, et ne trouve aucun secours, ni auprès de ses Supérieurs, ni auprès de ses Parents, du très-bon Terrein en Prés, Champs et Bois, avec une Maison d'Habitation, des Bestiaux et Ustenciles nécessaires pour son besoin, et cela héréditairement pour lui et les Siens; comme fair à présent SA MAJESTÉ L'IMPERATRICE DE RUSSIE, suivant l'Imprimé ci-joint: Il n'est pas douteux que tout pauvre homme, indigent et nécessiteux en état de travailler, n'accepte tel offre gracieux à bras ôuvert, et avec la reconnoissance la plus respectueuse.[10]

More detailed information was contained in a long "Report and explanation of the advantages and benefits for the peopling of Catharinen-Lehn, or principality created according to Swiss tradition." This report, distributed in both German and French, described the establishment of a settlement in the province of Astrakhan.[11] Between 50° and 52° latitude, in a climate similar to Lyon in France, with excellent communication lines to the Baltic Sea as well as to Persia, and in the midst of the black earth region, with winter hardly noticeable for more than three months and the grass by the middle of April half a man's height, a colony was to be founded near Saratov on the Volga. The soil was said to yield sixteen-fold returns; late planted peas were supposed in 1765 to have brought a hundredfold harvest. Horses could be bought at five to six rubles, cows at four. Wheat, rye, beans, oats, hemp, grapes, mulberry trees, wild cherries, and even to-bacco could be planted. Flowers of many kinds could be found on the meadows, fish abounded in the water, and fur-bearing animals were plentiful in the forests, affording the settler manifold opportunities. A "sweet life," indeed, could be had there, ideal for the rearing of children and a haven for Widows and orphans.

To induce colonists, whether peasants or artisans, to settle in such pleasant surroundings, Catherine offered liberal land grants and sweeping guarantees. Each colonist was entitled to a plot of ground ranging from 10 to 75 dessiatines.[1 2] Freedom of faith; freedom from taxation for thirty years; freedom to leave upon repayment of subsidies received; exemption from import duties on all goods brought along; permission to hold fairs without paying the customary dues; non-interest-bearing loans to defray traveling costs and first year expenses; gratuitous distribution of seed for the first winter and summer sowing and of working materials and utensils; two horses, money for chickens, and cows, sheep, and pigs according to the number of the members of a household—all this was promised to him who would come.

Recruiting centers for the new settlements were set up in Amsterdam, Utrecht, Hamburg, Lübeck, Cologne, and Frankfort. None was established in Switzerland, and the agents appointed by a Baron de Caneau de Beauregard de Brockhuysen, who directed their activities from Holland, soon found themselves in grave trouble with the Swiss authorities. The chief figure among them was a Captain François Mottet from Murten, hired as a lieutenant colonel with a salary of 7,900 rubles and the promise of 800 arpens of land; another agent was a Captain Schnorff.[13] Their activities were soon interrupted by the Swiss authorities, who reacted violently to plans that could lure away some of their best, their most enterprising citizens. All public advertising for emigration was prohibited and a great witch hunt began. Mottet himself was arrested in December, 1765, and his wife was confined to her house and forbidden to speak to anyone. Printers all over the country were warned not to work for the Mottets under penalty of arrest.

The colonization of the Volga district in Russia by Swiss citizens was thus badly hampered. No more than forty-three families, about 115 persons, all of whom immediately became Russian subjects,[14] managed to evade the restrictions. By 1772 this number swelled to somewhat over 1,000, but even then the total remained far short of Catherine's original expectations. Nine villages were founded and received Swiss names,[15] but the Swiss identity of the immigrants in these villages as well as in the whole district was soon lost, for like small Swiss groups of settlers in the American colonies, they were absorbed by the more numerous contingents of colonists from southern Germany. Almost all of them remained farmers and thus failed to establish any of the steel and iron works or tabacco factories contemplated by the Russian government.

What ruined Catherine's grandiose plans was not apathy on her part, but reluctance on the part of the western states to allow their citizens to avail themselves of Russia's attractive offers and contribute their skills and energies to the growing power of the tsars. Swiss authorities seldom failed to take a stand with regard to emigration questions. They had a long tradition and experience, and their attitude, with regard not only to Russia but also to America, is a subject well worthy of much further study. Despite difficult conditions at home the

Swiss generally tried—at least up to the middle of the nineteenth century—to discourage rather than to further emigration, and in the course of the nineteenth century they contributed much valuable investigation, evaluation, and discussion of population problems.[16]

Whatever the attitude of the Swiss authorities, the movement to settle Russia with Swiss colonists was interrupted during the second part of Catherine's reign. The peculiar contradictions inherent in an essentially agricultural society, with its land hunger on the one hand and its shortage of farmers on the other, came to the fore and discouraged persistent further efforts. Soon political considerations intensified the problem, for after the outbreak of the French Revolution in 1789 the tsarina withdrew her invitation in fear that Swiss immigrants would be carriers of the revolutionary virus. Emperor Paul followed her policy; and, even if he had sought to promote immigration, the ragged crowd of Russian soldiers which made its laborious way through Switzerland at the end of Suvorov's Italian campaign in 1799 would have constituted a poor advertisement for Russia. Not until 1803 when Alexander I, disciple of the Swiss Laharpe, was occupying the throne, do we find fresh efforts to attract Swiss colonists.

On July 25 of that year, a proclamation was published in the tsar's name by one G. v. Escher, a Swiss with the rank of a colonel in the Russian service; all Swiss were once more invited to come and settle in the tsar's realms. New colonies were to be established in the region of the Black Sea, the Sea of Azov, and in the mountainous regions of Tauria. The promises this time made to the settlers were based on the experiences during Catherine's reign. They included 60 dessiatines of land or as much as they needed for vineyards and other plantations; freedom of religion; 350 to 500 rubles cash advance per family[17] for the trip and a foothold in the new surroundings; exemption from import duties on all personal belongings; guarantee of their being settled together in one district; exemption from military service; right to found factories and engage in domestic and foreign trade; legal administration of their own, as long as it was in accordance with the criminal legislation of the land; free return to Switzerland, if so desired, including all property originally brought along; fifteen years' freedom from taxation; and exemption from quartering of soldiers. Swiss noblemen were to receive Russian noble rank, although their title to serfs was limited.[18]

Again the Swiss authorities interfered. The enterprise was labeled a private speculation, Escher was denounced as unreliable, and unfavorable reports from many disappointed emigrants were spread.[19] The needy, who were only too willing to accept the offer, received stern warnings. The canton of Zurich went so far as to prohibit emigration altogether, pointing out that without a certain amount of funds and without certificates of good conduct no one could expect to be admitted to and prosper in Russia.[20] The canton of Aarau did not imitate Zurich; it even aided prospective emigrants in getting the necessary permits and certificates. But it demanded that unless the emigrant relinquished all his property in the community (*in der Gemeinde besitzenden Mittel*) he was to renounce his *Bürgerrecht*, a provision which made return almost impossible.[21] Other cantons passed similar laws, and the crowning blow came when emigration's main proponent, Escher himself, was arrested.

It would be erroneous to believe that the Swiss authorities displayed in this matter a lack of a sense of responsibility. Conditions had changed considerably since Catherine's time. While the economic situation in Switzerland, as opposed to 1765, made restrictive measures inadvisable, the needs of Russia had also changed, and the reception of colonists was not so cordial as before. Furthermore, Escher's promises exceeded what Russia in reality was willing to offer, and the tsars had become more selective. An edict issued in 1804 decreed that Swiss criminals would under no circumstances be admitted,[22] and another clarified the regulations according to which colonists in Russia were to be received in the future.[23]

These regulations differed considerably from Catherine's invitation. Only good agriculturists and agricultural artisans but no artists or craftsmen were to be admitted, since the latter, in the opinion of the Russian government, could not expect to make a satisfactory living. Refund of travel costs was no longer promised; on the contrary, every prospective immigrant was required to have at least 300 imperial guilders of his own. A small subvention for sustenance after he had crossed the Russian frontier was the only help he could expect. Exemption from taxes was limited to ten years. Trade was permitted within Russia but no longer with foreign countries. As to ownership of land, possession with full property rights was still guaranteed, but whoever met disappointment and wished to return was required to sell his land before leaving. Under the circumstances, it was suggested that some colonists come first to inspect the land and to report to other prospective immigrants on what they had seen. As a whole, it can be said that in 1804 Russia permitted, but did not encourage, colonization.

As a result of the new regulations, a great number of impoverished emigrants who had already settled their affairs at home and had proceeded to Constance, Ulm, Vienna, and other assembly centers, returned rather than risk the venture. They became a burden to their cantons[24] and thus provided a justification of the attitude their governments had initially taken. Others reached Hungary only to die there during the harsh winter. A small group reached an estate near Feodosia on the Black Sea, from which they moved in 1805 to a colony called Zürichthal in the Crimea.[25] Although one of Escher's relatives, Friedrich Ludwig von Escher, wrote that colonists were well received and happy and that no good was served by the spreading of disparaging reports on Russia—"for where, in Europe, does one find milder views (Gesinnungen), more magnanimous and more justice loving?"[26] —facts reveal that even in Zürichthal conditions were adverse. The death rate remained exceedingly high, funds were lacking, many settlers proved unfit for the work, others were cheated by native Tatars and Turks. Only after 1822 did conditions steadily improve; the growing of wheat, vegetables, and grapes eventually brought a fair degree of prosperity.[27]

After the end of Escher's activities we do not hear of new Swiss colonization efforts in Russia until the Napoleonic wars were over. All of Europe had suffered terribly from the destruction and disorganization brought about by Napoleon's armies. The reconstruction of regions pillaged and devastated by the French took considerable time and was further delayed by unfavorable weather in the postwar years. A fearful period of hunger hit both Switzerland and southern Germany in 1816 and 1817. As a result, distress prevailed in many parts and necessarily led the poor to seek relief. In the prevailing romantic atmosphere many wild schemes to escape hardships found willing ears; one of the schemes was that of the Baroness von Krüdener, of Holy Alliance fame, who arrived in Switzerland in 1816 and proposed "to the faithful" emigration to the Caucasus where, as she asserted, God had charged the tsar of Russia to set up a kingdom for them.[28] She actually sent her son-in-law, Baron Berckheim, to St. Petersburg in order to further the plan, and eventually a small group of adherents found their way to Russia, where they settled in the neighborhood of Tiflis.[29]

Another movement, this one of greater importance, bore an official character and was directed toward Poland. "Considering . . . that the establishment of industrious foreigners could not but contribute to the progress of agriculture, manufacturing, artisanship, and all kinds of useful industries,"[30] Alexander I, in his capacity of king of Poland, published in 1816 an edict inviting Swiss citizens to settle in his realm. He promised to newcomers exemption for six years from all public burdens (impot public), from taxes, provided the land was carefully cultivated, and from import duties on goods brought along. If the colonist fulfilled all his obligations faithfully, he was guaranteed free return home after six years, although in this case his exemption from taxation was revoked and he had to pay taxes in proportion to his profits. All had to observe the existing passport regulations; Jews, however, were not admitted at all.[31]

Notwithstanding renewed warnings by Swiss authorities, many citizens were again taken in by the promises. They left and crossed the frontier into Baden, but there they found themselves once more confronted with often insurmountable difficulties.[32] For in 1817 Alexander published another proclamation, which was intended to clarify doubtful issues and thereby succeeded only in destroying many hopes. It bears witness to the changes in Russia, showing the political, economic, and social stabilization achieved in the previous fifty years and the resulting gradual tightening of immigration legislation. It compares unfavorably not only with Catherine's initial invitations but also with Alexander's own proposals at the beginning of his reign. The new ukase laid special emphasis on strict adherence to passport regulations. Its demand for property qualifications to the extent of 600 imperial guilders contrasts with Catherine's assurances of subsidies for travel and the first year of sojourn and with the 1805 requirement of 300 guilders.[33] Exemption from taxes was limited to six years instead of fifteen and ten respectively, and even this concession was made subject to the settler's remaining at the same place for at least twice that time and paying dues for the second half. Whether for his benefit or supervision, he was put "under the special protection of the Commission *de l'intérieur et de la police*," and only exemption from military service for himself and his children was maintained.[34]

Despite adverse conditions in Switzerland, this latest Russian edict failed to attract settlers and consequently made necessary a more generous, and more successful, offer promulgated three years later. Alexander's tutor Laharpe himself took a hand in sponsoring it, and Louis V. Tardent from Vevey put it into practice. Freedom of religion, exemption from military service, exemption from taxes for ten years, free gifts of 60 dessiatines of land and 6 dessiatines of vineyards were promised, and free return after payment of all debts and three years of taxes was guaranteed. Colonists, whether agriculturists, vineyard workers, or craftsmen, were allowed to establish factories and engage in trade. In spirit and content, the new offer thus resembled earlier invitations; a property requirement of 300 rubles was, however, maintained.[35]

The place chosen for the colony was Chabag in Bessarabia, near the mouth of the Dniester. Since it seemed particularly well suited for vineyards, the invitation was addressed primarily to the fellow citizens of Laharpe in the Swiss canton of Vaud, famous for its wines. Tardent himself inspected the region before engaging in the recruiting work.[36]

As it turned out, this colony was no more successful than earlier ones. In July, 1822, some twenty-eight men left Switzerland and after a four months' trip reached Chabag. Hard times were ahead; many died of fever, lack of care, or intemperance.[37] In the years 1826 to 1830 additional colonists came, and gradually the settlement was put on an economically sound basis. But it remained insignificant and the Russian government reneged on its promises. Land was not turned over to the individual settler as his personal property but was surrendered to the colony as a whole, with collective property rights and providing solely for the *usus fructi*. An oath of allegiance to the Russian tsar was demanded, while the settler was required to renounce his Swiss nationality.[38] In 1871, the colony came under the laws of the Russian empire and in 1874 lost its privilege of exemption from military service. This blow was all the harder since many members belonged to religious sects, such as the Mennonites, who conscientiously objected to army training.[39]

After 1822, no new project for Swiss immigration into Russia was developed for some time. The lure of southern Russia was somewhat lost because of the disappointing experiences at Chabag, and attention was gradually directed to other parts of the empire. Among them was Poland, which offered both agricultural and industrial opportunities. In view of the unsettled political situation there, the Russian government at first was not at all anxious to complicate matters by permitting the immigration of people from central and western Europe. In 1832 it flatly stated that Poland was in no need of manpower, that the Russian government did not at all look for colonists, and that if people came despite warnings travel costs would not be refunded.[40] But later, after the Polish rebellion of 1833 had been suppressed, a change of policy occurred, and in May rules were published according to which foreigners were to be received who intended to settle in Poland.[41]

In line with the general policies of Nicholas I, political reliability became the foremost consideration. Prospective immigrants were therefore required to present themselves first to Russia's agents abroad who would examine them, and if finding them acceptable, give them the necessary permits. With special speed for agriculturists, passports were thereupon issued. Nevertheless, upon arrival in Warsaw and before proceeding to his place of destination the immigrant had to present himself again to the authorities.

As to the conditions under which he could settle, he was warned that he should not expect special privileges, nor believe assurances of recruiting agents except in so far as they referred to exemption from import duties on personal belongings brought along. Neither would refund of traveling costs be granted nor land be made available unless all costs were defrayed by the settler. Yet, certain advantages were still to be gained. They included exemption from military service for the immigrant himself and his children and the issuance of passports for his return journey, provided he fulfilled all his public and private obligations. Exemption from taxation was fixed at six years, or at twelve years if the cultivated soil needed improvement. The property requirements for those who wanted peasant estates were fixed at 400 Rhenish guilders. Jews remained subject to the restrictions according to the fundamental law of March 2, 1816.

A few years later, another edict regarding immigration into Poland was published, this one referring to industrial workers in the mines.[42] The provisions were surprisingly enlightened. The immigrant laborer was exempted from military service and personal taxes. He received a house built for him and land for a garden which he could amortize at a low rate. Upon leaving he could sell his home, but only to other workers in the same factory. His working hours were fixed beforehand (although they still amounted to twelve), and so was his salary. He received health insurance to the extent of one half of his wages and free care in the mine sanitarium for himself and also for the members of his family. Both life and accident insurance were provided for, paying when due from one sixth to one half of his wages; in case of death one half of his salary was to paid to his widow. After ten years of service he was entitled to a pension. His children were guaranteed free education in elementary schools. Return to his fatherland at any time was promised, provided that he lived up to his obligations, and advances for the costs of traveling were granted.

The edict is of unusual interest as it reveals an awareness and understanding of social problems generally associated by historians only with a much later period, and even then rather with Germany, England, and the Scandinavian countries than with Russia. Few, if any, textbooks, either in economic or in Russian history, mention the remarkable modernism of its stipulations.

Inasmuch as the offer came at a time when industrialization all over Europe, including Switzerland, created grave economic distress for part of the population and when the United States, with her wider opportunities and liberal political institutions, beckoned to the destitute, the Swiss authorities felt compelled to review their stand with regard to emigration. Their conclusions differed with each separate canton and were probably consciously or unconsciously determined by economic forces dependent upon local factors. Yet, by 1840 the need for a general directive was clearly recognized,[43] and after careful studies in various parts, thirteen cantons sent delegates to a conference on emigration in October, 1846. As the minutes of this conference—concerned with emigration in general, but thinking in terms of America rather than of Russia[44]—surprisingly show, the view still prevailed that emigration was neither to be supported nor to be facilitated. It was argued that if a prospective emigrant possessed financial or spiritual resources, his country stood to lose a valuable man; and if he did not possess these qualities, he was likely not to prosper abroad either. The majority insisted that the diligent worker could make a living at home as well as abroad; and no money should be spent on those who left their country and thus avoided fulfilling their duties as citizens.

The shortsighted position taken at the conference could not prevail for long. The most vigorous protest came some years later from the canton of Aargau, which, because of the particular economic stress under which its population suffered, was generally inclined to more liberal views. It was stated that the support and protection of emigration was one of the definite tasks of a state, whether it was poverty or wanderlust that induced a man to seek a new home. True to the liberal tradition of the day, it was added that it was not within the competence of a state to interfere in the "free will of the independent citizen, whose decision is not bound by any lawful cause."[45]

The controversy affected emigration to Russia to a small degree only, for on the one hand, the eyes of the Swiss desirous of improving their lot were generally turned toward America, and on the other hand, Russia under Nicholas I continued its reluctance to admit western immigrants with their dangerous social ideas. The number of Swiss colonies in Russia thus remained unchanged, and the total of the settlers in the various regions amounted at each of the larger places to several hundred and seldom reached the thousand mark.[46] Those colonists who had arrived in the early period and had overcome the initial hardships had mostly prospered, but at least up to 1861 their example offered little inducement for others to imitate them. Only the radical changes which occurred in the tsarist empire after 1861, following the emancipation of the serfs, renewed interest in emigration to Russia. But by then state domains were no longer available and private enterprises now filled the place of state sponsorship.

An example of adaptation to the new conditions is furnished by an enterprise directed by a Captain Johann Michel from Böningen, who in 1862 promoted the establishment of a new Swiss colony.[47] Michel made arrangements with a private landowner, who offered to put land on the banks of the river Chadagosh in the government of Novgorod, about 400 kilometers from St. Petersburg, at the disposal of the colonists. The settlement was to start with ten families of eight to ten persons each, of which at least three had to be male and capable of work. Probably because of the recommendation of Michel, preference was given to people from the canton of Bern.

The terms offered were remarkably generous. The colonists were to receive as free gifts a church, a cemetery, forty dessiatines of forest, a bath house, a bakery, and a well. In addition, each family could get sixteen dessiatines of tillable land and ten dessiatines of forest, for a period of six years free of all fees. A house in Bernese chalet style and a barn were to be erected for each and could be rented for 99 years. Hunting and fishing were permitted, state taxes were paid by the owner, and cash advances up to 200 rubles could be secured. In exchange, the newcomers had to make interest and amortization payments on the investments of the owner; from the sixth year on a certain rent was added, which up to the twentieth year could be annually increased. However, beginning with the fourteenth year, the colonist had the right to purchase his land.

On the basis of private arrangements, other offers followed. One of them was that of Fieldmarshal Prince Bariatinsky, who offered in 1878 to put his estate of 40,000 dessiatines at the disposal of immigrants, to let them rent it for 99 years and to charge for the first ten years one franc per dessiatine yearly, and more thereafter in proportion to actual returns from the land.[48]

After the hundred years of Swiss colonization in Russia we thus find the basis of the whole emigration movement to Russia completely reversed. At the beginning, Russia had been desirous of receiving colonists and Switzerland adverse to letting them depart; at the end, the Swiss would have been happy to see as many as possible leave for more promising lands, if only Russia had still been as anxious to open her gates. In 1765, the most attractive offers were made to scientists, educators, artisans, and peasants; in 1878, aside from individual immigration, essentially only agriculturists could settle in Russia, and even then, only if they fulfilled passport regulations designed for keeping them out rather than for admitting them.[49] When Catherine came to the throne, concentrated, state-directed efforts sought through generous offers to turn deserts into prosperous habitable lands; under Alexander II laissez-faire ideology envisioned the same objectives, subject, though, to the economic aims of private enterprise and in proportion to its narrower scope.

In its various stages this development has been traced here with the help of two types of documents, one embodying the ever-varying conditions offered by Russia to prospective immigrants, the other showing reactions to the Russian appeals in the country to which they were addressed. Once the material has been assembled, studies, evaluations, and comparisons become possible which add to our knowledge of an important phase in the building of the Russian nation and throw light on general problems involved in all large migration movements.

Chapter X

EMIGRATION: SOME EIGHTEENTH-CENTURY CONSIDERATIONS*

Few subjects lend themselves so well to comparative historical study as the subject of migration. Of its three components —emigration, immigration, and remigration (*Aus-*, *Ein-* *und* *Rückwanderung*), only the second has been at all widely investigated. Nothing to equal the research done concerning immigrants exists for the emigrant and the effect of emigration on the home country,[1] and still less is known about the problems of remigration. Yet, even on remigration, documentary evidence is not scarce: Switzerland, whose particular policy allowed those leaving the country a possibility of returning without losing their cantonal citizenship rights, harbors large amounts of historical material on the subject, which has hardly been explored. Lack of investigation is true not only for Switzerland but also for other countries, including Italy which has seen the return of so many emigrants. Alfred Vagts recently published a book on German remigration,[2] and Theodore Saloutos, one on Greek remigration;[3] both, however, leave many important questions unanswered.

What gives a rather particular fascination to the study of emigration, immigration and remigration is that it must be undertaken as a part of history as a whole. An isolated treatment would be impossible. As one deals with the subject, he

---

*Reprinted with permission from *Comparative Studies in Society and History*, Vol. 5, (1963).

automatically speaks of political, economic and social questions; nor have those who held the political, economic or social power in a country ever failed to take an interest and a hand in the emigration movement. They have consistently sought to direct it—often on the basis of preconceived and generally ill-founded notions about economic as well as demographic consequences.

A distinction has to be made between migrations to colonies and those to foreign lands. In many regards migrations to foreign lands offer a more complex picture. This is true for emigration to the New World after it gained its independence, but it is particularly noticeable also for emigration to Russia, which in the eighteenth century assumed a very prominent place among the destinations of Europeans leaving their homelands. For, compared to the New World, which from its opening to immigrants onward has constituted a part of Western civilization, Russia has presented to the Western immigrant a society rather different in character. As against the West with its "dynamism," the East appeared "static" to the Westerner. Rightly or wrongly, originality and entrepreneurial spirit were deemed somewhat lacking in Russia, and this assumption led, in addition to agricultural settlers, to many adventurous individuals from Europe seeking their fortunes there —speculators who for the sake of social position and quick gains were willing to forsake such personal freedoms as they might have found in Australia, America or other countries.[4] All, however, had to realize that in going to Russia they were not setting out to build a new nation, but that they were to join, and be assimilated by, a well established society.

For this reason, as well as because of the proximity of Russia with its threatening power potential, Western European nations have generally looked with special misgivings upon plans for emigration there. For the sake of preserving an at least assumed superiority, they have again and again put obstacles in the path of the traffic in goods and men to Eastern Europe. As early as the Carolingian period sales of arms to the Slavs were prohibited; and in the fifteenth and sixteenth centuries emigration of artisans in particular was hindered. A well-known incident is that of the Goslar burgher Hans Schlitte, who in 1548-49 started with some hundred companions for Russia, but most of them were arrested on their way to enter the service of the Tsar.[5]

In the eighteenth century the problem of emigration to Russia took on new significance. At the very time when new economic and social theories, in contrast with the mercantilistic theories of the preceding period, were to change prevailing views on emigration, and when humanitarian elements formerly lacking came to the fore as a result of the acceptance of the world-view of the Englightenment, Russia, in line with her simultaneous "Westernization," renewed her appeals to the dissatisfied peoples of the West.[6] Addressing herself to the many Europeans suffering under economic, political or religious restrictions, she offered work to impoverished artisans, positions to scientists and artists, and virgin lands and help to settle on them to agriculturists. As a result, the governments of the various European states found themselves compelled to pay new attention to the issue of emigration. Conservative and somewhat behind the times, the governments failed to consider, though, the changes in the general mood; and their measures—with exceptions—collided with the new entrepreneurial drive of the individual.

Soon the steps taken by the governments demonstrated that many of them sought to meet the problem by traditional types of legislation rather than by remedying ills which caused emigration. In their customary restrictive policies they were confirmed by a great variety of theorists, who came by their views through the most diverse, and often contradictory, methods of reasoning and who, for the most part, opposed emigration on principle. There was the mercantilist who, out of fear of losing a share of the nation's industry, wanted to prevent the departure of any worker; the industrialist who, less concerned with the loss to the nation than with the gain to a competitor, tried to hinder the transfer of skills abroad; the physiocrat who, not so much interested in industry as in agriculture, wished to check the outflow of the rural population, which actually furnished the greatest number of emigrants; the military forces which objected to the departure of men who could be impressed into navy or army; the churches which argued dogmatically that an emigrant, trusting his own abilities, was likely to forget that man does not shape his own fate and might then turn into an enemy of Christianity; the demographer who felt capable of proving that "a population cannot be large enough since a surplus in population would always produce a surplus of nourishment;"[7] and the humanitarian who, aware of generally adverse conditions awaiting the immigrant abroad, sought to save him from a worse fate than he could possibly meet in familiar home surroundings. Fewer were those on the other side. They included humanitarians—insisting this time, however, that if conditions at home seemed intolerable, it would be unethical to try to retain people who might be able to improve their condition abroad; there were also laissez-faire idealists who simply advocated abstention from interference.

Diversity of opinion and argument manifested itself in still other ways. For while there were some who felt that rich people specifically should be prohibited from leaving a country since they were depriving it not only of the most valuable human element but also of funds, others, in contrast, argued against the emigration of the poor—of the average worker who possessed no more than the skill of his hands. Even the most wretched, who were a burden to Church and community, were to be forbidden to leave inasmuch as just these made up perhaps the best prospects for army and navy.[8] Prohibitions were also proposed for specific categories of an entirely different kind, exempting, for example, female persons or Jews or beggars.

An indirect approach to the problem of how to face the pressure of those desirous of emigrating was taken by some who wanted to avoid outright prohibitions yet sought to achieve the same end by other deterrent measures, such as depriving the emigrant of all hope of ever being able to return. They wished to see the Rückwanderer threatened with many kinds of punishment. Some such measures had been taken by Colbert in 1672, who sought to prevent French Canadian settlers from retarding France's colonial expansion by quitting in the face of the hardships confronting them in the colonies. But it was an entirely different matter if in the eighteenth century punishments were imposed for emigrants returning from foreign lands. For they were not designed to keep colonists on their jobs but were aimed at preventing people from emigrating in the first place. Interestingly, the same aim was sought also by diametrically opposed measures, namely, instead of by punishing the Rückwanderer, by trying to persuade or force the emigrant to return. To be sure, in the eighteenth century governments were reluctant to resort to measures such as employed by Venice earlier, which was said to have sent out murderers to kill those artisans abroad who refused to obey summons to return. But numerous efforts were made to recover emigrants. Mercantilists in France favored appeals even to expelled Huguenots.[9]

Besieged on all sides, yet unable to judge the merits of the case, the statesmen felt compelled to act. Pressure of circumstances increased further when Catherine II of Russia (1762-1796) made a determined effort to lure enterprising settlers to the undeveloped southern areas of her empire. For this purpose, the Tsarina sent out, or appointed abroad, a number of recruiting officers (Werber). Notwithstanding the spreading concept that a contractual link existed between state and individual and the growing humanitarian attitude that espoused "the principle of personal freedom," including the right of emigration,[10] their activities aroused the ire of the various governments and led to the establishment of new regulations. These merit far broader comparative study than they have so far received. For they reflect not only different aspects of the problem and different humanitarian ideas, but also different stages in the development of societies and institutions.

Within the confines of the German empire, in Bavaria, in 1764 the death penalty was decreed for all who undertook the work of recruiting; those who listened to such agents were threatened with prison and confiscation of their goods. In Saxony, an older ordinance stipulating death on the wheel or by hanging was revived and remained in force until 1772. In Mecklenburg, strict punishments were imposed for both recruiting officer and emigrant—especially if the latter were a serf or a servant.[11] In Hannover, where emigration to America played a greater role than that to Russia, a sequence of two steps was introduced: first, a warning was issued; then, prison and forced labor were imposed. Prospective emigrants, if needed, were to be retained by force.[12] In the Palatinate, in view of a severe shortage of domestic servants, emigration was prohibited in 1764; and restrictive laws were promulgated also in Frankfurt, in the Rhineland, etc. The Dutch stadholder, the Prince of Orange, gave the order to use the utmost persuasion if "capable and well-to-do" subjects of his Nassau possessions expressed the desire to leave; and finally, the problem induced the Emperor Joseph II to publish a rescript under the date of July 7, 1768, which prohibited emigration wherever permission was not granted by local authorities.[13]

In comparison with the measures taken in various states of the Empire, those taken in several other states of Europe were, if anything, still more vigorous. The authorities of the various Swiss cantons, holding views very similar to those of the German princes, acted without compunction.[14] The Spanish king prohibited emigration from his Luxemburg and Netherlands possessions. It is surprising, however, that of all nations, France took particularly extreme steps. We are not accustomed to connect French history with the problem of emigration, except for the two short periods of violence at the time of the persecution of the Huguenots and during the great French revolution; and the history of French colonizing ventures demonstrates no urge on the part of France's inhabitants to leave their country, such as we witness in England, Ireland, Germany, or, later on, Italy. Yet if we are to believe Gonnard, in the eighteenth century the belief prevailed that, of all people, the French were especially inclined to seek foreign lands;[15] and it is a fact that the French government was particularly aroused when, in 1764, two Frenchmen, Meunier de Précourt and Le Roy, were put in charge of Catherine's recruiting agencies and, operating from Hamburg,[16] began with their work.

As it turned out, only small numbers of French subjects listened to their enticements. Those immigrants seem to have been primarily Germans from Alsace and Lorraine and, later, inhabitants of Corsica. In addition, there were a few enterprising French merchants from Atlantic coast regions and some military people who hoped to attain quickly and easily high rank and pay in the Russian service.[17] Nevertheless, the sharpest measures were immediately prescribed. As early as 1749, the government of Strassburg had prohibited emigration, threatening to send to the galleys those who were caught in the attempt;[18] soon hanging was prescribed. As time went on, such brutal punishments were confirmed by general edicts, despite the fact that the vigor with which the French government proposed to proceed was hardly warranted by objective considerations. Nor was it in keeping with a policy that envisaged the establishment of closer ties with Russia. Indeed, it cannot have escaped the attention of the French government that for the sake of the desired expansion of economic relations a certain amount of emigration, even of skilled workers was bound to be of advantage to France. Yet, the government ignored all advice in this direction by bankers, merchants economists, and officials and instead lent its ears to those shortsighted enough to propose restrictive policies.* Only in the wake of the great revolution did a radical change take place.

This change brought about a new, but not a satisfactory and lasting situation. Not long after the revolutionary period, in 1818, the Grandduke of Baden gave expression to the tenets of the liberal age when he voiced the view that "the state cannot be a prison, and that the citizen who wishes to make no longer use of his rights should also, as a rule, no longer be held to the performance of his duties."[19] But the nationalist and communist state of the late nineteenth and the twentieth centuries has once more rejected the idea of freedom implied in the uncurtailed right of an individual to emigrate and therewith to abrogate his duties at the same time he is renouncing his rights. Indeed, in recent times the death penalty, which the *ancien régime* of France was inhumane and unintelligent enough to impose, has been revived in some areas of the world. Studies carrying the investigation through the most recent period and coordinating this reversal of policy with the economic, social and ideological changes of the last hundred years would seem, therefore, to promise rewarding results.

---

*Two documents appended to the original version of this chapter, in *Comparative Studies in Society and History*, are of considerable interest, especially if their tenor is compared with that of the Hannoverian documents published above. (Letter of M. de Lesseps, consul general of France in St. Petersburg, January 26, 1780. *MSS.*, Archives nationales, Paris, AE. B I-988; and Rescript of March 21, 1787, *MSS.*, Archives nationales, Paris, F 12-644.) While throwing light on emigration in general, they throw into relief also the conditions and spirit, so much debated, of the *ancien régime*.

Chapter XI

SAMUEL BENTHAM AND SIBERIA*

Jeremy Bentham's younger brother Samuel is little known in history.[1] He seems to have made few contributions to the "greatest happiness of the greatest number." Even the *Dictionary of National Biography* speaks of him as "troublesome." Constantly suspicious of "intrigues," he got on badly with others; as a rule, his associates disliked him and were anxious to rid themselves of him. He quarrelled with his father, whose desire to see him associating with men of "sobriety" he spurned. In Russia he became entangled in a love affair in which, according to his own testimony, he behaved like a gentleman; but this view was not shared by others, and the affair brought heartbreak to the lady and condemnation from many sides. As a member of the Navy Board in England during Napoleonic times he became involved in acrimonious controversies with the Admiralty. No doubt he was justified in his demands for reform and in his struggle against the prevailing nepotism and corruption, but his methods were inappropriate, and he was dismissed, although eventually he received his full pension. As soon as peace was made, he left for France and did not return to his country for many years. He was a man of energy and ideas, and most of his difficulties derived from a tireless, driving will, seeking improvements through ever-renewed plans and schemes.

---

* Reprinted with permission from *The Slavonic and East European Review*, Volume XXXVI, No. 87, June 1958.

Several years of his life Samuel Bentham spent in Siberia,[2] and he was in Russia for twelve. A brief article recently published about this phase of his life tells us virtually nothing about his observations abroad.[3] Yet valuable information can be gathered from his letters, notes and journals; for although they fail to give answers to many questions of fact which we should like to see answered, they allow us through their sharp criticism of prevailing practices to draw a number of conclusions which correct existing views on the technical and economic conditions of eighteenth-century Siberia.

Samuel Bentham no longer represents the high-minded, enthusiastic, utopian age of Enlightenment in which he was born. He was a child of the technical age, offspring of the Enlightenment. Less concerned with the moral progress of mankind through reason toward liberty, this age demanded the practical application of reason to immediate material problems and to technical improvements. With a certain scorn Bentham looked on his enlightened predecessors in Siberia who, as he wrote to Prince Potemkin in January, 1783, after his return, made excellent reports, but no suggestions for improvement. His sojourn did not permit him "de regarder avec l'oeil indifférent de la simple curiosité"[4] the institutions and installations of the country. He felt that his approach had to be practical, and essentially he shared in this the general attitude of Russia toward Europe. Alien to the inquisitive spirit of the West and to Faustian aspirations, Russia had always sought to grasp only the practical aspects of European inventions, and while doing so had, even under the westernizing tsars, Ivan the Terrible and Peter the Great, rejected the theoretical, intellectual basis on which Europe had built. Instead of seeking the enlightenment of man and the satisfaction of his thirst for knowledge of nature and its workings, Russia had been concerned with tasks which Lee, an adviser of Peter the Great and a compatriot of Bentham, had wanted to assign almost a century earlier to an institution which he had significantly called a College for the Improvement of Nature.

Bentham's journey to Siberia began in January, 1781, when he had received the necessary permission from Catherine II to proceed there. He left St. Petersburg on February 6. Being twenty-four and having so far made no place for himself in the world, he set out to mend his fortunes—an interesting fact in itself, for not one of the other early Western travelers in Siberia seems ever to have conceived of his trip in a similar way. At the most, it was through service in the Russian bureaucracy that they hoped to secure advancement indirectly, if they volunteered for work in Siberia. In April, 1781, he arrived in "Nigni Taghil" (Nizhne-Tagil'sk on the Tagul river), 140 versts north of Ekaterinburg on the Asiatic side of the Urals, where he stayed for almost six months on an estate of the Demidov family and interested himself in mines and iron-works.[5] He then went to Perm', but spent Christmas, 1781, in Ekaterinburg. On January 11, 1782, he set out for Tobol'sk, where he arrived on the thirteenth. From there, he traveled via Tara (January 17), Tomsk (January 21), Krasnoyarsk (January 26), Irkutsk (January 31), Kyakhta (February 4), and Selenginsk (February 18) to Nerchinsk (February 23). He remained there for a month and made his return journey by approximately the same route. But he used the month of May for a prolonged sojourn in Irkutsk and in August made a trip to Barnaul, to visit the large production centers of that area. On October 9 he returned to St. Petersburg.

The objective of his long journey was, more or less, achieved. For after due application he was offered employment by Catherine the Great. Perhaps the positions he successively received were not particularly distinguished, but he did rise quickly to high army rank and eventually stayed for a number of years; and even after he had left for England in 1791, he contemplated a return to Russia. As to financial rewards from his Siberian journey, they seem to have been neither large nor insignificant. With an eye to profit, inherited perhaps from his grandfather and father, he started to collect, while still in the Urals, minerals of various kinds. Indeed, as he wrote to Jeremy in October, 1781, he hoped "to make a little money . . . on the side," chiefly with loadstone and furs.[6] By the end of August, 1781, he had gathered some 8 to 10 cwt. of different kinds of minerals and was looking for magnets. Later he reported that he had packed 40 to 50 cwt. of copper and iron ore of considerable value, including loadstones.[7] A part of his "collection" was dispatched to England from Nerchinsk; and when on his return trip he visited Barnaul, he collected additional minerals there. From Kyakhta he sent home some parcels of tea, rhubarb and India ink,[8] and plants and seeds followed later. His ability to do so contrasts with the experiences of the Swiss traveler Jacob Fries in 1776, who also mentions the possibility of making profit from the purchase of tea and India ink, but who found no transport facilities.[9] Altogether it seems that Samuel Bentham derived some financial gain from his journey.

Within three months of his return Bentham prepared a report, which he submitted to Catherine through the good offices of Prince Potemkin.[10] This report, which gained him the employment in Russia we have mentioned, and thus a second financial return on his Siberian undertaking, is interesting in many ways. It reflects late eighteenth-century technical conditions in Russia in comparison with economic developments in England. It contains counsels for improvement of the economy of mines and salt-works in Siberia. Essentially, it deals with machinery designed by Bentham to save manpower. Intimating that the mine-owners blamed insufficient production on lack of available manpower, he justly points out that one should not complain of lack of labor if one has everything done "à force de bras." On the other hand, one should not be deterred from mechanization by fear of unemployment, for plenty of jobs were available. Nor should one put forward the argument that the value of the mined materials was so high that a small saving in manufacture was not worth while. Rather the vast resources of steam and wind power in Siberia should be utilized, and horses employed as motive power for machinery should be replaced by oxen, whereby costs could, as he claims, be reduced by approximately 80 per cent. Moreover, he insisted that more attention should be paid to local conditions, and that machinery should be adapted to local resources and needs, varying from region to region and being, particularly in the field of combustion, on a level with the latest Western developments.

With such thoughts in mind, Bentham proposed and partly designed specific installations. With regard to the salt-mines his thoughts centered around processes by which (1) with the help of pistons arranged in series, the speed could be doubled for pumping brine out of the mines, (2) fresh air and sunshine could be used rather than artificial heating in order to evaporate the water, (3) escaping heat could be conserved so as to serve the secondary purpose of preheating new water, and (4) the purity of the salt could be improved.[11] Of iron, copper, silver and gold mines, Bentham occupied himself chiefly with the second; gold mines he considered of less importance than these,[12] for obviously he recognized the potential for increasing profits to be derived from copper in an age of rapidly growing industrialization. He relates that one copper mine alone, belonging to Mr. Pogodashin, produced "upward of 50.000 pood of copper in a year."[13] He proposed machinery which would better serve to pulverize the rock and replace the powder generally used in blasting. This would also cut up the wood for fuel and thus prevent waste of useful, exploitable material, of which at that time 46 1/2 per cent was lost. He demonstrated again his concern with waste by insisting that in the copper mines, as in the salt-works, the heat generated should be better utilized.[14]

To these technical suggestions Bentham added several others of significance which deal with administrative problems. For not only in the scientific but also in the administrative management of the mines he recognized some of the causes for the slow industrial development of Siberia. He advocated that measures should be taken by the government to reduce taxation, so as to encourage investments and improvements,[15] and he proposed, with the same purpose of creating incentives, that bonuses should be paid to the inventors of new machinery; for unlike their colleagues in England, inventors in Russia seem to have been offered no share in the profits derived from their original work. According to Bentham, the failure to do so had led to stagnation and backwardness.[16] His proposals included even such details as printed forms for purchasing-contracts in Siberia, which he drafted in order to enable the government to exercise control over and to verify expenditure. Many contracts, he insisted, were disadvantageous for the crown owing to the negligence of the officers who were under the influence of alcohol when concluding them.[17]

On the whole Bentham's suggestions seem to have been far ahead of his time. His concern with costs in an age and area where manpower was ample and cheap; his efforts to avoid waste of materials; his interest in dividing the manufacturing process into various components; and his insight into the technical problem of heat and heat-transfer, expressed in his proposal to re-harness escaping heat—all this points to a fertile mind anticipating future developments. The same holds true of his suggestions regarding the need for bureaucratic control in order to avoid corruption. Also his understanding of the economic issues of his day in the creation of industries becomes evident when we observe that by proposing such modern devices as staggered taxes and incentive bonuses he sought, on the basis of self-interest, to lay a new foundation for a society which had been accustomed to collectivism and state-ownership in various sectors of its economy, and which still saw the management of a large part of the productive apparatus in the hands of the government and the hereditary nobility.[18]

Moreover, Bentham is well aware of the human shortcomings engendered by the Russian system itself. He complains of a lack of co-ordination which caused some of the factories to close down until the beginning of winter, because the supply of charcoal had failed. He condemns the miserable pay offered to the manual workers, many of whom preferred the life of "robbers and assassins" to that of industrial laborers. And he comes to the interesting conclusion that many of the higher employees accepted their positions in the imperial service in the mines not because of qualification and interest, but in order to acquire military rank. For military rank was necessary to win consideration. "This circumstance and this alone is the spring of all their actions. The servility in their character . . . is the effect of hope, not of fear," he continues[19] —a shrewd statement indeed, for in tsarist as well as in Soviet times it has been by holding out hope, and not by a system of fear and terror, that generally the Russian government has driven the average Russian to action, even if it has been the terror system which, because of its more spectacular character, has chiefly engaged the attention of foreign observers.

In spite of his criticism of production methods in Siberia and his passion for "improvements," Bentham gives an essentially favorable picture of the country he saw. From Demidov's estate he writes that he found on the Siberian side of the Urals rather more than the necessities of life. At Pogodashin's, he was able to find a copy of the Encyclopaedia and read some of its articles. He was served at meals with Parmesan cheese. He saw a plantation of some 500 orange and lemon trees; and on his way he was, as his secretary and companion reports, treated to a dinner "in the English taste . . . very clean . . . with Oranges, Lemons, Apples, etc."[20] Bitterly he rejects the "infamous, malicious, and lying work" of the French astronomer, the Abbé Chappe d'Auteroche, which was justly refuted in the anonymous Antidote, whose authorship Bentham assigns to Princess Dashkova.[21] He also insists that punishment by exile to Siberia was not so hard as it may have appeared abroad. He met some exiles who cultivated their land in freedom and gained more than they would have done in their native place. Few acts of crime were committed by them.[22]

Although most of Bentham's descriptions concerned, in line with his general attitude, what he did rather than what he saw, he too could not help leaving in his writings some indications of conditions which caught his eye, not for practical purposes, but for no other reason than simple curiosity. In his journal, kept by a secretary, he describes—although without adding much that is new—marriage ceremonies and church affairs, gives some geographical information, and comments on the prevailing drunkenness.[23] He also reports a case of arrest for slovo i delo,[24] notwithstanding that at the time of his travels this arbitrary way of dealing with crimes of lèse-majesté was, on the order of Peter III, no longer in use. He speaks of the beauty of the countryside in the eastern Urals and of the life of the people there, of their way of cutting wood, building boats, and burning coal, and of their agriculture and flour mills. He mentions that in some regions tanneries flourished until merchants in the towns succeeded in having an ukaz issued by which the undesirable competition was suppressed. He also left some remarks about working conditions and about recruiting for military service.[25]

Samuel Bentham was, according to P. S. Pallas, the "first" of his nation who, driven by "Wissbegierde," or intellectual curiosity, went far into the interior of the country.[26] The statement is interesting, for even if not quite correct, it indicates that at a time when numerous foreigners reached Siberia, not many Englishmen were among them. In any case, Pallas must have forgotten John Bell, who had visited Siberia 60 years earlier,[27] and with whose account—Bell's Travels, published in a two-volume edition in Glasgow in 1763—Bentham was acquainted. Bentham had also studied William Coxe's Account of the Russian Discoveries. Yet, whether they came for the sake of satisfying intellectual curiosity, or for the sake of promotion or financial gain, Englishmen rarely traveled to Siberia. Germans had been numerous; some, like Pallas himself, were distinguished scientists who led great expeditions or participated in explorations; others were officials in the Russian service. Bentham met some of these in Nerchinsk, where one of them was commandant. Like others, this man seems to have received very little reward for his labors, and to the observant eye of Samuel Bentham, the Nerchinsk mines stood as much in need of improvement as did those in the Urals.[28] As to Frenchmen, Bentham mentions four in Siberia: at Solikamsk, a surgeon, the only foreigner, " and an impertinent one he was"; on the Demidov estate, a Francis Migard, who visited there in order to see the copper and nearby "gold" mines; at Kyakhta, another Frenchman, who had studied in Germany and had become tutor in the house of one of the "directors," and a Commander Villeneuve, who was probably the man whom Fries had met. He was born in Montpellier, and Bentham relates that he pretended to be a son of the Duke of Orlèans and of a royal princess. His mother had expected to become queen of Spain; but as she was found pregnant, these hopes were dashed, and ever afterwards she hated her child, which was therefore "put out of the way."[29] Villeneuve accordingly ended up in Siberia. As to English people, Bentham mentions, besides a man who worked at Petrovsky Zavod, where he had introduced the "English method of casting and boring of cannons," which were manufactured there for the use of the navy in Archangel, the daughter of a Captain Webb, who had married a major and commandant of one of the forts on the main Siberian highway.[30]

When full of impressions, plans, projects, and designs, Samuel Bentham returned from Siberia, he was anxious to secure a personal interview with the empress. His connections served him well in attaining this aim. At the time of his first coming to Russia he had been furnished with introductions to Count Orlov, General Shuvalov, the British ambassador Sir James Harris, the famous mathematician Euler, and various other prominent persons. Afterwards he had made the acquaintance of Pallas and finally of Catherine's favorite Potemkin. It was through him that Bentham was admitted in April, 1783, to an audience with Catherine. Two topics seem to have been of prime interest to the empress, viz. the state of the mines and that of the Chinese frontier. Her knowledge of either does not seem to have been especially profound; for, as Bentham writes, "her questions were very general."[31] The technical data could, of course, be dealt with by Bentham in accordance with his report of January; those about China were outside his field of competence. Yet it seems that, apart from technical installations and their improvement, it was primarily the information about China that left an impression on him and that he considered worth repeating. Perhaps his remarks about Russo-Chinese relations, his note on the inhumanity of one Chinese towards another, and his description of a visit to the Sarguchey in Maimatchin, of the temples and of a theatrical performance there do not add to our knowledge. But a few points are of interest. He states that the customs house, which was originally established at Kyakhta, was removed from there to several other places. The purpose of this was to conceal from the Chinese the exorbitant prices charged in Russia for

Chinese goods because of excessive dues levied at the frontier. Actually, the Chinese did find out about it and protested, and Russia had to make at least a temporary adjustment to prevent China from discontinuing the trade.[32] Another item of interest refers to the rhubarb trade. Although it was still to be kept secret, permission was given in 1781, as Bentham reports, for private persons to trade in rhubarb, which so far had constituted a monopoly of the crown. The reason here was that, since the furs given in exchange for rhubarb were undervalued by the crown and thus the price paid for rhubarb rose very high, the monopoly proved unprofitable.[33]

A rather long passage deals with conditions in the Russian Church in Peking of which Bentham learned on his journey. He gives a brief historical review, going back to about 1658, when, as he says, the church was established in Peking by some Russian prisoners, who had been so well treated by the Chinese emperor that they had refused to return, provided they were allowed to keep their religion. By the Treaty of Nerchinsk of 1689 the status of the church was regulated anew, and in 1718 it was stipulated that every year an archimandrite, two new priests, four students and a sacristan could be sent to Peking. Such an exchange was made in 1781, and Bentham gives a long description of the journey of these men. On arrival in Peking, they were received "comme des Anges déliberateurs," for the members of the previous group had already been there for ten years and had despaired of ever seeing their homeland again. No more than five of them were left, for the others had all died of drink. Indeed, the archimandrite himself was a man of little merit, his chief characteristic being drunkenness. Owing to the good offices of the Jesuits, who had forwarded messages from them to St. Petersburg via Canton, they were now delivered. However, it seems that the new group remained no longer than a few months, being back in Kyakhta by August, 1782.[34]

What effect did Sir Samuel Bentham's report have upon the development of Siberia? Being a man of action and not a scholar, his significance must be considered from the standpoint of practical results. Certainly, great scholars, like Gmelin, Steller and Pallas, have left a permanent and deep impression. Their writings opened up new avenues of understanding, spread knowledge, and contributed to the culture of their age. It is an irony of fate that what contribution Bentham has made may ultimately be construed as belonging also to the theoretical field and as being an enrichment of our historical knowledge. It certainly had little effect in the practical field of material progress. Perhaps Bentham misjudged the character of his Russian hosts. Various historians have emphasized the "entrepreneurial" spirit of the West as having existed also in Siberia in the time of Catherine II, but, according to Bentham, such drive did not animate Russia's industrial enterprises there. No doubt, Bentham was an acute critic, but his testimony may add to other evidence showing that the reign of Catherine "the Great," in contrast to that of Peter the Great, lacked, except in external policy, the necessary element of greatness. It is in her time, especially crucial because of the incipient industrialization of the West, that the roots of subsequent stagnation have to be sought. Not only in the nineteenth century, but already in the second half of the eighteenth, when rapid scientific and technological development occurred, especially in England, we witness in Russia, and particularly in the Urals, an "unwillingness to utilize proven technological improvements."[35] When Bentham was in Siberia, Russia was still, owing to the drive developed in the age of Peter the Great, the largest iron producer in the world, having almost twice the output of England. In the Barnaul area a steam-engine, anticipating features "discovered" by Watt, had been put into use by Polzunov. And all over Siberia men were to be found who were conscious of the significance of contemporary science and technology and eager to introduce new methods. Yet they found hardly any support.[36] Within little more than half a century Russia, in spite of her abundant resources, was to have less than one-tenth of British iron production. New engines and devices were still lacking, and little inventive work was carried on. Siberia, and the Urals in particular, "were provincial, and stubbornly resisted change,"[37] and the imaginative thinking of a foreigner could not alter a pattern which native society had established. More than 100 years were to elapse before a change occurred and initiative was again displayed, and it could again be said of Siberian industrial development that, even if it was "backward," it was at least "not stagnant."

Chapter XII

WESTERN BUSINESSMEN IN RUSSIA: PRACTICES AND PROBLEMS*

The responses of the West to the challenges of the East are of fundamental interest to politician and historian alike. The reaction of the Western businessman to the opportunities and difficulties which all connections with Russia offered can serve to illustrate the wider problem; and its study can help to clarify such important and debated issues as "differences" between East and West or the "backwardness" of the East. As a matter of fact, in his _Deutsch-russische Handelsgeschichte des Mittelalters_, Professor Leopold Karl Goetz once wrote that the Han-

* Reprinted with permission from _The Business History Review_, Volume XXXVIII, Number 3, Autumn 1964. The following analysis, a condensed version of a paper presented at a meeting of the Friends of Economic and Business History in Cambridge, Massachusetts, is based on studies in the archives of Copenhagen, Stockholm, Göttingen, Paris, Venice, Zürich, and in various other depositories. Printed sources and accounts include: Goetz, _Handelsverträge_ and _Handelsgeschichte_; _Hanserezesse_; Hakluyt, vol. I-III; Thomas Stuart Willan, _The Early History of the Russia Company_ and _The Muscovy Merchants of 1555_, Manchester, 1953; R. W. K. Hinton, _The Eastland Trade_; Adam Olearius, _Moscowitische Reisebeschreibung_, Schleswig, 1656; Johann Philipp Kilburger, _Kurzer Unterricht von dem russischen Handel 1674_, in: _Büschings Magazin für die neue Historie und Geographie_, Hamburg, 1769; Marbault, _Essai sur le commerce de Russie_; Heinrich Storch, _Historisch-statistisches Gemälde des russischen Reichs_; Scherer, _Histoire raisonnée du commerce de la Russie_; Anthoine, _Essai historique sur le commerce et la navigation de la mer noire_; Hans Halm, _Habsburgischer Osthandel_; Kulischer, _Russische Wirtschaftsgeschichte_; Lyashchenko, _History of the National Economy of Russia_.

seatic businessman of the fourteenth century who went to Russia found himself in a "strange land." Christoffer Larleil, an English merchant of the sixteenth century, wrote in 1583 of the "fickle nature" of the estates of Russia and of the dealings of the tsar. Reporting on conditions another 200 years later, the Frenchman Marbault commented on the fact that commerce with Russia "did not at all resemble that with other states"; and today, after yet another 200 years, we still witness business procedures in Russia which, in view of the Soviet organization of trade, bear a stamp rather different from that most familiar to the Western world.[1]

It is not necessary here to discuss East-West trade itself. For more than 600 years it has flourished to the benefit of both sides. It was, however, not Russian but Western entrepreneurship, Western enterprise, which through centuries contributed most to providing the carriers and maintaining the connections with Russia. For the active trade overseas with the West carried on by Russians was—and still is—extremely limited. Seldom did Russians visit Western countries; generally it was the Western businessman who had to travel East—to Novgorod, Archangel, Moscow, Caffa, later to St. Petersburg, Leningrad, Cherson or Odessa. As he was far from home and moving in a foreign atmosphere, he had to adapt himself to unfamiliar surroundings and to alien ways. Again and again, an underestimation of the special character of the conduct of business in Russia has led—aside from financial losses and, upon occasion, personal injury to the merchant himself—to an incorrect historical picture.

An incorrect estimate of the Russian market is exemplified by a scheme of some Braunschweig and Leipzig merchants who, in the times of Ivan the Terrible, tried to sell false jewelry to the tsar.[2] Another occasion showing lack of understanding was the attempt of the Willeshoven Company two centuries later to sell cheap porcelain in Russia to a society which had expensive tastes and could afford the luxury of buying only the finest quality. But these are only indications of minor errors in judgment. Far more important are the fundamental issues which presented themselves to Western businessmen and which show that only those who possessed rare skill and ingenuity succeeded in adjusting to the circumstances confronting them.

Among the difficulties we find, in the first place, the fact that Western businessmen have essentially only in nineteenth-century Russia dealt with businessmen of their own kind and type. Direct contact between businessman and businessman has, as a rule, constituted the basis for successful business connections; and in the Western world, such contact has been the normal *modus operandi*. But in medieval Muscovy, even in Novgorod, and increasingly in seventeenth- and eighteenth-century tsarist Russia, the Western merchant encountered as his business partner an official or a bureaucrat who was not as free as he himself in making decisions. With the possible exception of the age of *laissez faire* in the nineteenth century, there consistently prevailed in Russia a significant combination of business and official interests. The Russian importers and exporters were only too often representatives or servants of state or tsar, both of which not only controlled a large share of all foreign business carried on by Russia but actually owned much of it and transacted it on their own account and for their own profit. They were not animated as exclusively by strict business considerations as the Westerner was, and were not accustomed to the same "rules of the game." Even those Russian foreign traders who would carry on a business on their own personal account would often be connected, as a side line, with some sector of Russian officialdom. They may have belonged to the court or to the diplomatic service or they may have had connections with a customs' office, a state monopoly, or even the police. Some of them bore proud old names, like

Stroganov, Demidov, Shuvalov, Potocki; others were insignificant subjects of the tsar chosen fortuitously.

Since in so many instances they had some official place, some rank or station that tied them to the service of official authorities, these Russian traders held a position which distinguished them in yet another way from the Western visitor. Not only were they to a certain extent deprived of that freedom of action which the Westerner enjoyed; they also had access to those who had influence on national policy. The result was that the Westerner found them frequently dependent upon considerations bearing but little upon the immediate business at hand. He had to approach them with special caution lest a false step bring political repercussions or personal danger, and it was difficult for him not to feel a barrier between them and himself.

This barrier was enhanced by additional factors. The ordinary Russian businessman, even when engaged in foreign trade, lacked not only the esteem and standing of his Western counterpart but, as Professor Gerschenkron has pointed out, certain "independent standards of value." When, on the other hand, he belonged, as he often did, to the nobility, which imitated the tsar and sought to monopolize trade as well as land, he developed—despite his mercenary undertakings—to cite the same authority, "nothing but contempt for entrepreneurial activity except [his] own."[3]

Perhaps this did not distinguish the Russian entirely from the Western nobility. In the West, too, disdain for mercantile undertakings and money grubbing did not stop the nobleman from indulging in entrepreneurial pursuits.[4] But there was a wide difference insofar as there existed in the West a large number of non-noble independent businessmen with standards of value of their own, and they had their well established place in society. The town and trading patricians and large-scale merchants were proud of their status, and by numbers as well as financial resources possessed power and influence superior often to that of the aristocracy. In Russia, with a large share of the financial resources in the hands of a nobility which led in commercial enterprises as well as public administration and which, moreover, possessed military rank, almost all power was combined in the hands of a single group. Its existence contributed to a more monolithic structure of the whole country; and unless it was with a businessman of little standing, it was with this haughty and uncongenial group that the Western businessman had to deal and to whose habits, prejudices, and pretensions he had to cater.

To be sure, there existed during the Middle Ages also the merchant patrician in Novgorod, Smolensk, Pskov and a few other trading towns, especially of Western Russia.[5] But the merchant-patrician class was small, rather dependent upon princely, municipal, or even church authority, and it diminished rather than increased as modern times approached. Soon it became indistinguishable from the landholding nobility. In 1649, there existed in Muscovy no more than thirteen important export merchants or gosti. Later in the century, there were perhaps thirty.

Yet, in the eighteenth century, the term gosti in its earlier meaning, and with it the group of foreign traders known as gosti, disappeared. Altogether, in the time of Catherine II the situation had considerably changed from that of preceding centuries. Toward the end of her reign, we thus find more Russian businessmen of the kind familiar to Westerners. However, they often went into partnership with a nobleman whose name was to lend not only distinction and standing but also the connections needed at court for sustaining their enterprises. Moreover, they still adhered to past patterns at least insofar as, unlike the Western entrepreneur with his driving spirit, they contented themselves with a rather passive attitude, approaching business in accustomed ways and within the limits of established markets, and reluctant to search for broad new outlets.

Neither Peter the Great's introduction of ranks nor Catherine the Great's charter for the merchants changed the situation. To be sure, the merchant could wear a uniform with insignia of rank, and this was especially profitable in crude new centers of the type of Cherson on the Black Sea toward the end of the eighteenth century.[6] Yet every indignity could be heaped upon him. Arbitrarily merchants could be deprived of rights; they could be flogged, thrown into jail and threatened with death. Such conditions necessarily affected their Western business connections, who feared like exposure to disrespect and punishment.

It may be suggested, though proof can hardly be adduced, that this lowered standing of the Russian merchants may have been in part responsible, despite changes in the nineteenth and early twentieth centuries, for the receptivity of some of them to revolutionary thought. Unlike the Western businessman whose well-established place in society made him averse to revolution, the Russian businessman, having less to lose, was less reluctant to support an overthrow of existing institutions. (An example is furnished by the millionaire businessman Savva Morozov, who gave enormous sums to support the revolutionary cause.)

Next to the absence of normal business partners for Western visitors in Russia, a second factor demonstrating difficulties for Western business activities in Russia existed in the extent and type of regulations limiting the scope of the visitor's operations. Far beyond anything known in the Western world, restrictions on the foreigner abounded in Russia, and most incisive were those limiting his freedom of movement. Upon reaching the border of the country, the foreigner was subjected to close inspection and passport controls. In early as in recent times, only a few roads by which to proceed to his point of destination were generally allowed him. Upon arrival there he was limited in his choice of quarters, or was, by being assigned to a specific place, entirely deprived of choice. During the Middle Ages he lived in Novgorod within the confines of the Hanseatic factory, the Peterhof; later, in Moscow, he stayed in the Nemetskaia sloboda; elsewhere, he resided in the houses of Russian hosts who often had to keep an eye on him. Frequently, he was locked up in his quarters during the night.

Lest his whereabouts or identity be concealed during his stay, he was at various times prohibited from wearing Russian dress. Actually, also in certain periods of modern times, clothing has tended to mark the foreigner.

Of grave importance for the development of business connections was the issue of religion. Matters of faith, whether in Orthodox or in Communist times, consistently set the foreign merchant apart. If during the Middle Ages the Westerner would find wherever he went in Catholic Europe a Christian community familiar to him, and among that community not only customs and rituals to which he was accustomed at home but also all the consolations which such familiarity would offer to the stranger abroad, he would be excluded in Russia from a similar comfort. Pathetic paragraphs in the writings of the famous Russian merchant Afanasii Nikitin, who went to India in 1466,[7] give us an insight into the feelings of the traveler in foreign lands. Of course, the Catholic or Protestant coming to Russia did not suffer as much as a Russian in India; he was likely to meet others of his faith and, as a rule, was able to attend services in a church of his own creed. However, he could not share with the society with which his business connected him those associations which frequenting the same church meant for him in his Western business relations.

Also of great weight was the language issue. As early as the fourteenth or fifteenth century, the language problem appeared, according to Hanseatic sources, as an important consideration and the Western businessman was conscious of it. Hanseats who came to Novgorod endeavored to learn some

Russian. Knowing what advantage linguistic knowledge would give them, they took pains to prohibit its acquisition by foreign competitors by passing regulations designed to hinder Dutch apprentices from going to Novgorod for the purpose of learning Russian.[8] Yet it seems that even among the Hanseats knowledge of Russian was very limited. In the eighteenth, nineteenth, and twentieth centuries most of the business negotiations and correspondence were carried on in German and French. The Russians were well versed in both of the languages, but by thus accommodating the foreigner they perhaps inadvertently deprived him indirectly of yet another approach to an understanding of the country which he visited and with which he tried to do business.

Business activities of Westerners were also hindered in the Middle Ages by objections to travel beyond Smolensk or Novgorod to Moscow, Tver, Riazan, Nizhni-Novgorod or other major centers unless specific permission was given by treaties such as were concluded with the North German merchants. In early modern times, the right of crossing Muscovite territory in order to reach Persia or other Oriental markets was limited to those who secured, as did the English, this special privilege, but even then difficulties were made. Later, Siberia was virtually closed to the Western trader. And even in the nineteenth century, restrictions as to travel in the interior of Russia made the development of the full potential of the Western entrepreneur impossible. A merchant of the "first category," who as a foreigner did business in St. Petersburg, could not, as late as the middle of this age of *laissez faire*, travel freely to Moscow to conduct his business there.[9] Moreover, secrecy was often demanded of him. As early as 1585, the Englishman John Cappell complained that silence was imposed on him. The Russians obviously feared that his knowledge might serve foreign governments, and imposing silence—also on scientists and explorers[10]—continued to constitute one of the major defensive weapons of Russia, serving political, military and economic purposes.

It might furthermore be mentioned that adjustments to the daily habits of the Russians made considerable demands on the Western visitor. Since it was he who moved on Russian soil and not the other way around, the adjustment was rather one-sidedly demanded of him and this rendered his work more difficult. In Cherson in the eighteenth century, for example, no business deal could be negotiated in the afternoons. In many instances Russians insisted on negotiating during late night hours when the spirits of the Westerners were at a low ebb.

A third major problem for the Western businessman, closely related to the lack of partners of his own kind, existed in the role which the Russian state assumed in business matters and by which it raised obstacles preventing normal business connections. Professor Gerschenkron has described as a "curious mechanism of economic backwardness" the role of the state, which was "moved by military interests . . . [to propel] economic progress." Indeed, there was hardly an area touching the interests of foreign businessmen upon which the Russian state did not bring to bear—and only too often for military reasons—its direct influence. The chief means of doing so was through the establishment of monopolies which were reserved for the state or for the tsar personally.

Monopolies were sometimes delimited geographically: the White Sea trade, the Black Sea trade, the inland markets, Siberia; or they referred to specific commodities: masts, wax, rhubarb, trane oil, furs, potash, iron, tobacco, tar, hemp, roses, gold. Monopolies were as likely to be conferred upon foreigners as upon <u>gosti</u>, landed aristocracy, or court officials; or they were retained by the tsar for himself. They were given "at the caprice of the tsar." But in addition to the granting or keeping of monopolies, the tsar reserved for himself also the right of first refusal, and this right was used even when a monopoly had been accorded. Therefore, even the well-established and favored Western businessman found himself exposed to an element of uncertainty practically unknown to him elsewhere. At any time, an arbitrary act could deprive him of the fruits of his privileges as well as of his labor. When St. Petersburg was founded, though it was not yet ready to take care of all the Western traffic, the Archangel trade was either forbidden or restricted, and laboriously built-up business establishments were ruined.

In yet other respects was the Westerner at the mercy of government action irrespective of guarantees given him. The British Tobacco Company, which held the monopoly for tobacco imports into Russia, ran into trouble around 1700 when, for lack of sufficient demand, it did not bring in its full share allowed by the monopoly. The tsar insisted that it thereby deprived him of an income which he had expected from customs dues, and the Company risked losing its privileges in addition to being held liable for the deficit in customs dues. Within a short time, it had to close its doors. Likewise, when sudden needs for certain commodities arose within Russia, their export was limited notwithstanding existing monopolies, and the foreign merchant might then be unable to live up to his commitments abroad.

Interference by tsar, state, treasury or other authorities in Western business occurred also in numerous ways which at least in extent distinguished the management of affairs in Russia from that elsewhere. Prescriptions as to whom one might sell and to whom one might not were perhaps not unknown to businessmen in the West, but the way in which they were handled in Russia thwarted the accustomed conduct of business. Often the Russian government fixed prices, and particularly in the age of mercantilism, payments had to be accepted in debased currency. The impact of the many regulations is reflected in

Western writings and especially in the numerous mémoires sent by eighteenth-century French bankers and merchants to their government.[11] Rates of exchange were pegged, and during the eighteenth century foreign exchange had to be brought in for the payment of customs dues, just as for a tourist's needs in recent times; yet, it was not accepted except at the low pegged rate. Different customs rates were levied in the different ports of Russia. This, too, was not unfamiliar to the Westerner; in France, for instance, dues on Russian goods were by no means always the same at Le Havre and other Atlantic ports, as at Marseilles and other Mediterranean ports. But this led to immediate objections and adjustments, while in Russia it had to be accepted.

There is still a fourth point which illustrates the hardships Western entrepreneurs experienced in their dealings with Russia: the issue of business morality. Gerschenkron writes that standards of honesty in business in the late nineteenth century were "disastrously low." Johann Philipp Weber, at the end of the eighteenth century, found "not a single honest man in Cherson." In the middle of that century, the French were outraged by the dishonesty of Count Shuvalov and his agents and of their other business contacts. Travelers and merchants in the sixteenth and seventeenth centuries often reported the sharp dealing of the Russians.[12] Goetz enumerates the various tricks employed during the Middle Ages. Russian honey or wax were sold with sand inside—just as recently, foreigners have bought butter on the markets of small Russian towns with square pieces of turnip in the center—and good and bad hemp were mixed and sold as first quality. Debts went unpaid, and redress was hardly possible. The Russian customer could return goods after years if he could not resell them. Russian exporters asked prices utterly unrelated to values—only to turn around unexpectedly if found out and without blushing adjust their demands. Of course, business morality, especially during the Middle Ages, was also low in Europe. In the Russian market German casks of herring contained false bottoms; the quality of the outer layers of English cloth on bolts differed from that on the inner layers; wine from France was sold as Spanish wine to be admitted at lower customs rates. Yet the ordinary Western businessman was quite at a loss about the ways to cope with the business morality he found prevailing in the Russian trade.

A special feature adding to the Westerner's troubles was the existing practice of bribery. "Mit Schmieren muss man oben anfangen," wrote Weber. Raimbert, French consul in St. Petersburg in the second half of the eighteenth century, insisted that of every twenty rubles which the law demanded as customs dues hardly more than one reached its official destination. To be sure, had the full customs dues been collected, most foreign trade might have been wrecked; yet the necessity for circumventing what was legally prescribed led to a general disregard of the law which reacted upon all phases of business activities. Among the Western merchants who came to Russia stealing became so common that a regulation had to be passed according to which the discovery of stolen goods in the house of a Western businessman could be held only against him personally and not against the firm to which he belonged.

Owing to the weakness of Russian legal institutions, recourse for the injured party was so complicated and so unpromising as to render appeals to the courts virtually useless unless accompanied by excessive bribes. Arbitrariness prevailed; and it was answered by the Western (as well as the native) merchant with disloyalty. The Dutchman Marselis, in the seventeenth century, committed so many dishonest acts despite the fact that he enjoyed many monopolies that his goods were confiscated and his privileges revoked.[13] Around 1700, the Englishman Whitworth, official representative of his country, had the premises of an English firm operating under tsarist license in Moscow invaded by night and its machinery broken up.[14] The Frenchman Raimbert violated the customs laws, incurring the danger of capital punishment. Actually, all of them ultimately escaped the prescribed penalties.

Sometimes the state itself encouraged means for getting around the law. In the sixteenth century, the tsar helped English interlopers who violated the monopolies which he himself had given to the English Muscovy Company. In the twentieth century, a "black marketeer" could likewise find official sanction. The Russians' mistrust of business and its rules of conduct was, as George Foster commented in 1784, behind the fact that the law did so little to protect legitimate enterprise.

The question thus arises: What was the effect of these conditions on the Western businessman and what were his responses? An examination of business records in various centuries indicates that except for the Hanseatic merchant, who understood how to build up permanently lucrative connections, the Western entrepreneur was, as a rule, induced to engage in business with Russia by expectation of profit rather than by records of profit. In view of the uncertainties facing him, he then tried to get rich quickly—if possible within a few years—rather than build up solid lasting contacts. He shunned long-term investments and long-term dispositions. Few Western firms dealing exclusively with or in Russia stayed in operation for more than one generation; no such firm is on record for the eighteenth century. The English Muscovy Company or, later, the English Tobacco Company were anything but successful in the long run.[15] The same was true for the French tobacco ventures.

If, nevertheless, the English, Dutch, French and other enterprises were carried on over extended periods, the explanation must be sought in the fact that at least someone must have benefited. This was actually the case, for while the majority of the stockholders may have suffered, individual partners of the firms profited. They managed to stake out for themselves very useful sectors of the transactions with Russia by concentrating on profitable subsidiary ventures. Some of them were members of firms which imported from the colonies the goods which were sold to the company for re-export to Russia; others belonged to banks which furnished capital to the corporation and drew high interest; or they were partners in shipping companies which earned substantial freight rates on their Russia run. In many of their undertakings, they were encouraged by mercantilistically inclined governments which sought political and military advantage. Yet, even the subsidiary ventures included grave risks. Shipping, owing to piracy in the Baltic at least up to the eighteenth century, and credit, owning to the unreliability of the debtors and the courts, deterred the ordinary businessman.[16] Actually, during the fourteenth and fifteenth centuries, the Hanse had issued strict prohibitions against the extension of credit to Russians.

Since the risk was high and pertained to a business which, in the long run, was likely to yield rather low profits, a strong speculative element was introduced. This meant that only a special type of entrepreneur was attracted to the Russian market. If he was not an outright gambler, he was often at least an adventurer. He generally had the advantage of finding comparatively little serious competition, but this advantage was offset by drawbacks resulting from the interruptions which either threatened or actually caused the cessation of trade and reduced the chances for successful speculation. Of course, manifold "flexibilities and adjustabilities are inherent in the process of economic development," and this held as true for the evolution of Western-Russian trade as for any industrial development.

Yet, under such circumstances cautious entrepreneurs were reluctant to invest their capital. They knew that the original outlay had to be very high, that constant additional expenditures were needed to get contracts, bribe officials, advance payments to suppliers, secure new privileges such as freedom from taxation, and maintain monopolies beyond an initially stipulated term against the tricks and bids of well-placed competitors. Again and again we find in the *mémoires* of Frenchmen to their government or to other bankers and businessmen exhortations first to study carefully the market for its special features. And wisely did the Dutch concentrate more on the carrying trade than on selling and purchasing goods. As to the English, impressed with Russia's insistence on the mercantilistic policy of exporting more than importing, they did not attempt to build up their own exports so much as to increase their imports from Russia. These imports they then re-exported—to the disadvantage of the French, Spanish, or other countries' balance of trade with Russia.

Considering the atmosphere which permeated Russian-Western trade under such conditions, it is no surprise to see a Russian historian like Kliuchevsky apply the term *igra*—meaning thereby "virtuosity inciting admiration"—to the conduct of business in Russia. The element of play may be inherent in all business transactions, as historians like Huizinga have pointed out and as it is obvious to all acquainted with Oriental business ways. Yet, it differed in intensity from area to area, and in Russia it was particularly marked in comparison to Western countries. A game it was that attracted those Westerners who might have failed under conditions customary in European enterprises. In 1674, the Swede Kilburger warned them lest they be outdone by the Russians. "*Pour prendre un renard*," he wrote, "*il faut un renard et demi*." Križanić, living about the same time, looked at conditions in rather the same way; and Marbault, a hundred years later, put a parallel idea into other words: "[The Russians] know a lot about trade but nothing about commerce."

It is obvious that the observations made here, based

though they are on evidence given by the most varied sources, cannot serve as more than suggestions. Naturally, conditions changed with time and place. Continuity has been strong within Russian society which, despite revolutionary tendencies, has again and again affirmed its special character and mission, distinguished from those of the West. Yet change has also been very evident, especially in the second half of the nineteenth and the first decades of the twentieth centuries. Only studies in detail can answer questions which refer to specific stages of the Russian-Western business partnership.

Still another point needs consideration. Soviet historians have often emphasized parallel developments in Russia and the West, even if they did not necessarily coincide in time. There is much justification for this point of view, but for a discussion of Western business in Russia, this general conclusion is of less significance. For it is just the fact that the developments on both sides did not coincide in time which caused the Western businessman so many difficulties. He was not aware of, or concerned with, historical events or historical laws; he operated at a given time and was faced by concrete problems. He had to battle with a given situation, and this situation meant that he often found himself, as cited in the initial paragraph of this paper, in a "strange land." His adjustment to it, his successes and failures, and those of his Russian partner stand in need of much further investigation. Sources for the Middle Ages are fairly exhausted. For modern times, they are plentiful though by no means completely available, and beckon the economic and cultural historian to further work.

NOTES

BIBLIOGRAPHICAL INDEX

NAME INDEX

NOTES

Introduction

1. By "Russia" is meant, in this and all following essays, the areas which are comprised, up to the twelfth century, by Kievan Rus; from the twelfth to the seventeenth centuries by Muscovy, Novgorod and the other principalities, first under Tatar, later under Moscow's domination, exclusive of those western parts which seceded and became either independent or subject to neighboring states; and from the eighteenth century on by the Russian empire. By "West" is meant the Romano-Germano-Christian parts of Europe which in America are generally considered to comprise "Western Civilization." The Finnish, Slavic and Magyar areas lying between "Russia" and "the West" have also, in any case at certain times, formed part of the West. But their relationship with Russia bears a special character owing to geographic proximity; their problems were not the same as those which the Germanic and Romance countries faced. Their special role merits a separate treatment which is not attempted in this book.

The above definition implies that no sharp boundary lines for "Russia" or for "the West" existed. Independently from political arrangements, they changed from century to century with the progress of religion, with the movements of peoples, with the expansion of agriculture, etc.

2. K. Schiffmann, "Die Zollurkunde von Raffelstetten," Mitteilungen des Instituts für österreichische Geschichtsforschung, v. 37, 1917, p. 488. Erich Zöllner, "Russen in der Raffelstettener Zollurkunde," Mitteilungen des Inst. für österreichische

Geschichtsforschung, v. 60, 1952. W. G. Wasiliewski, "Kiews Handel mit Regensburg," Verhandlungen des historischen Vereines der Oberpfalz und von Regensburg, v. 57, 1905. Julius Brutzkus, "Der Handel der westeuropäischen Juden mit dem alten Kiew," Zeitschrift für die Geschichte der Juden in Deutschland, v. 3, 1931, p. 99.

3. František Dvornik, Les Slaves, Byzance et Rome au IXe siècle, Paris, 1926, p. 108; and The Slavs, their Early History and Civilization, Boston, 1956, p. 218. Wasiliewski, see note 2 above. Soviet historians have only recently begun again to occupy themselves seriously with questions of Western relations and influences. Their archaeological studies can be expected to contribute to needed clarifications. For the problems here mentioned, cf. Boris Dmitrievich Grekov, Kievskaia Rus, 4th ed., Moscow, 1944, pp. 285 ff., and the versions in Istoriia kul'tury drevnei Rusi, Akad. Nauk (Moscow, 1948-51) v. 1, pp. 341 ff., by Boris Aleksandrovich Rybakov (German ed., Berlin, 1959, v. 1, pp. 315 ff.), or in Ocherki istorii SSSR, period feodalizma, konets XV v. —nachalo XVII v., Moscow, 1955.

4. G. F. Korzukhina, Russkie klady, IX-XIII vv., Moscow, 1954, pp. 64, 85, 87, 95, 101. Stanislas Baron de Chaudoir, Aperçu sur les monnaies russes . . ., 2 vols., St. Pbg. and Paris, 1936-37, v. 1, pp. 9, 12. Vera Jammer, Die Anfänge der Münzprägung im Herzogtum Sachsen (10. und 11. Jahrhundert), Hamburg, Museum für Hamburgische Geschichte, Abt. Münzkabinett, Numismatische Studien, Heft 3-4, 1952. Franz Bastian, Das Runtingerbuch 1383-1407 und verwandtes Material zum Regensburger südostdeutschen Handel und Münzwesen, Regensburg, Deutsche Handelsakten des Mittelalters und der Neuzeit, 1944, v. 1, p. 88.

5. Cf. George Ioan Bratianu, Recherches sur le commerce génois dans la mer Noire au XIIIe siècle, Paris, 1929. Wilhelm Heyd, Geschichte des Levantehandels im Mittelalter,

2 vols., Stuttgart, 1879. Michele Guiseppe Canale, *Della Crimea, del suo commercio* . . , 3 vols., Genoa, 1855-56.

6. Vladimir Leont'evich Snegirev, *Moskovskie slobody; ocherki po istorii Moskovskogo posada XIV-XVIII vv.* Moscow, 1956; Mikhail Nikolaevich Tikhomirov, *Srednevekovaia Moskva v XIV-XV vekakh.*, Moscow, 1957, p. 131.

7. Fundamental for the study of Russian-Western economic relations in Hanseatic times is Leopold Karl Goetz, *Deutsch-russische Handelsverträge des Mittelalters*, Hamburg, 1916 (Abhandlungen des Hamburgischen Kolonialinstituts, v. 37); and his *Deutsch-russische Handelsgeschichte des Mittelalters*, Lübeck, 1922 (Hansische Geschichtsquellen, N. F. 5). Among the foremost contemporary historians was Paul Johansen (1903-1965). Cf. a bibliography of his writings (to 1961) in *Rossica Externa. Studien zum 15. bis 17. Jahrhundert*, Marburg, 1963, pp. 179-188 (Festgabe für Paul Johansen zum 60. Geburtstag). See Anna Leonidovna Khoroshkevich, *Torgovlia Velikogo Novgoroda s Pribaltikoi i Zapadnoi Evropoi v XIV-XV vv.*, Moscow, 1963, which contains an extensive bibliography. N. A. Kazakova, "Iz istorii torgovoi politiki russkogo tsentralizovannogo gosudarstva XV v.," *Istoricheskie Zapiski*, v. 47, 1954, pp. 259-290. American contributions in the field are lacking, a circumstance which has unfavorably affected the presentation of the medieval economy in textbooks and general works.

8. See, e.g., *Sverges traktater med främmande magter*, ed. Olof Simon Rydberg, 15 vols., Stockholm, 1877-1934, v. 1, pp. 311 f.; v. 2, pp. 130 f., *passim*.

9. A clear distinction must be made between, on the one hand, an active trade in the sense of achieving an active balance of trade and, on the other, an active (foreign carrying) trade in the sense of active participation in ventures abroad instead of merely passively opening one's own ports to foreign entrepreneurs. Cf. Paul Johansen, "Der hansische Russland-

handel, insbesondere nach Novgorod, in kritischer Betrachtung," Arbeitsgemeinschaft für Forschung des Landes Nordrhein-Westfalen, Wissensch. Abtlg., v. 27, 1963, pp. 52-55.

10. Michael Lesnikov, "Der hansische Pelzhandel zu Beginn des 15. Jahrhunderts," in: Hansische Studien, Berlin (-Ost), 1961, "Forschungen zur mittelalterlichen Geschichte," ed. Gerhard Heitz, v. 8, pp. 258 ff, 272 (Heinrich Sproemberg zum 70. Geburtstag). However, Khoroshkevich, p. 203, ventures doubts as to Lesnikov's views regarding prices and the conclusions Lesnikov draws from his investigation.

11. Reimar Kock, MS., Rigsbibliotek Copenhagen, Thott 674, fol. 378 f, and Ny Kgl. Saml. 307.

12. We owe the remarkable record of ships and goods traveling from West to East and vice versa to the fact that dues were levied in the Sound. The Sound dues have been published by Nina Ellinger Bang et al., eds.: Tabeller øver Skibsfart og Varetransport gennem Øresund, 1497-1660, 2 vols., Copenhagen and Leipzig, 1906-1933.

13. The exaggerations are partly due to exclusive reliance on the accounts, to be sure unmatched, of the English enterprises by Richard Hakluyt, The Principal Navigations, Voyages, Traffiques and Discoveries . . ., 12 vols., Glasgow and New York, 1903-1905. For a balanced view of the opportunities for the English, cf. Thomas Stuart Willan, The Early History of the Russia Company, 1553-1603, Manchester, 1956. Cf. also Heinrich von Staden, "Eine unbekannte Version der Beschreibung Nordrusslands durch Heinrich von Staden," ed. Fritz T. Epstein, Walther Kirchner, and Walther Niekerken, in: Jahrbücher für Geschichte Osteuropas, N. F., v. 8, 1960, pp. 131-148; and Staden, Aufzeichnungen über den Moskauer Staat, ed. Fritz T. Epstein, 2nd ed., Universitaet Hamburg, 1964, (Abhandlungen aus dem Gebiet der Auslandskunde, v. 34), pp. 261-280.

14. Walther Kirchner, "England and Denmark, 1558-1588," Journal of Modern History, v. 17, 1945, pp. 1-15.

15. For lack of equivalents to port books and in the absence of business records relating to the Russian trade, the overland traffic cannot be ascertained even with that measure of approximation which may be possible for overseas ventures.

16. Regarding forms of trade in the eighteenth century, see also Bruno Lammel, "Der Russlandhandel der Franckeschen Stiftungen im ersten Viertel des 18. Jahrhunderts," in: Deutsch-slawische Wechselseitigkeit in sieben Jahrhunderten, Berlin (-Ost), Deutsche Akademie der Wissenschaften zu Berlin, Institut für Slawistik, 1956 (Veröffentlichungen No. 8), pp. 183-84.

17. K.-G. Hildebrand, "Foreign Markets for Swedish Iron in the 18th Century," Scandinavian Economic History Review, v. 6, 1958, pp. 3-52. Cf. also Arne Öhberg, "Russia and the World Market in the Seventeenth Century. A Discussion of the Connection between Prices and Trade Routes," Ibid., v. 3, 1955, pp. 123-62.

18. See L. V. Cherepnin, "Russian 17th Century Baltic Trade in Soviet Historiography," The Slavonic and East European Review, v. 43, no. 100, 1964, pp. 1-22.

19. Johann Philipp Balthasar Weber, Die Russen oder Versuch einer Reisebeschreibung nach Russland und durch das russische Reich in Europa, ed. Hans Halm, Innsbruck, 1960, "Innsbrucker Beiträge zur Kulturwissenschaft," Sonderheft 9; and Hans Halm, Habsburgischer Osthandel im 18. Jahrhundert . . . Donauhandel und -schiffahrt 1781-1787. (Österreich und Neurussland, Bd. 2) München, 1954 (Veröffentlichungen des Osteuropa-Instituts München, v. 7).

20. Erik Amburger, Die Familie Marselis, Giessen, 1957 (Giessener Abhandlungen zur Agrar- und Wirtschaftsforschung des europäischen Ostens, Ser. I, vol. 4).

21. Sven Erik Åström, From Cloth to Iron. The Anglo-

Baltic Trade in the late 17th Century, in: Societas Scientiarum Fennica (Finska Vetenkaps-societeten), "Commentationes Humanarum litterarum," Helsingfors, 1963, v. 33, pt. 1.

22. Peter Ivanovich Rychkov (1712-1777) was "one of the first Russians to master the theory and practice of double entry and the balance sheet." A. J. Pashkov, ed., *A History of Russian Economic Thought: Ninth through Eighteenth Centuries*, trans. and ed. John M. Letiche *et al.*, Berkeley, 1964, p. 442.

23. For Russia's commercial policies in the second half of the seventeenth century under A. L. Ordyn-Nashchokin, cf. Pashkov-Letiche, pp. 215-222. For the eighteenth century, *ibid*, pp. 285 ff., *passim*.

24. Henri Chambre, "Posoškov et le mercantilisme," *Cahiers du monde russe et soviétique*, v. 4, 1963, pp. 335-365. Ivan Tikhonovich Pososhkov's writings in *Kniga o skudosti i bogatstve i drugie sochineniia*, ed. B. B. Kafengauz, Moscow, 1951; Pashkov-Letiche, pp. 295-334.

25. Bertrand Gille, *Histoire économique et sociale de la Russie du moyen âge au XXe siècle*, Paris, 1949, pp. 83 f.

26. Pashkov-Letiche, pp. 259 ff. Perhaps the first influential Russian to emancipate himself from the mercantilistic idea was M. D. Chulkov in: *Istoricheskoe opisanie rossiiskoi kommertsii* St. Pbg., 1875; cf. Pashkov-Letiche, p. 463.

27. Hermann Kellenbenz, "Der russische Transithandel mit dem Orient im 17. und zu Beginn des 18. Jahrhunderts," *Jahrbücher für Geschichte Osteuropas*, N. F., v. 12, 1964, p. 493.

28. However, for the years around 1847, Patricia Herlihy writes, "The cycles of prosperity in West Europe and South Russia tended to be out of phase with one another." "Russian Grain and Mediterranean Markets, 1774-1861" (Ph. D. thesis, University of Pennsylvania, 1963).

29. The oldest Russian decree concerning joint stock companies dates from 1836. It provided, though, that the government could refuse incorporation, and a number of specific prohibitions unknown in Western Europe were made. Per Schybergson, "Joint Stock Companies in Finland in the Nineteenth Century," The Scandinavian Economic History Review, v. 12, 1964, pp. 61-78, and ibid., note 1. Cf. also Olga Crisp, "Some Problems of French Investment in Russian Joint Stock Companies, 1894-1914," The Slavonic and East European Review, v. 35, no. 84, 1956, pp. 223-240.

30. For the complications resulting from interacting difficulties of trade policies, finance, and politics, cf. Theodore Hermann Von Laue, Sergei Witte and the Industrialization of Russia, New York, 1963.

Chapter I

1. Danmark-Norges Traktater, 1523-1750, ed. L. Laursen, 7 vols., Copenhagen, 1907-1926, v. 2, pp. 20-50.

2. Cf. Appendix No. 3.

3. Cf. Appendix Nos. 5 and 6.

4. Cf. Appendix No. 10.

5. Only once, in Huitfeld's declaration of September 6, 1568, the ship is clearly designated as a "Russian ship." Cf. Appendix 9. In general, mention is made only of "Russian goods." However, there were no protests put forward by any other nation, nor do we have any indication that non-Russians had been on the ship or were in any way whatsoever connected with the incident. It was the Russian interpreter who functioned as plaintiff protesting against the attack.

6. The Kiev State and its Relations with Western Europe, Royal Historical Society, Transactions, 4th ser., v. 29, 1947, p. 42.

7. Heyd, v. 1.

8. Boris Aleksandrovich Rybakov, *Remeslo drevnei Rusi*, Moscow, 1948, p. 229.

9. Das Diedenhofener Kapitular von 805: *Monumenta Germaniae Historica*. Cap. 1, Nr. 44.

10. M. Slavianskii, *Istoricheskoe obozrienie torgovykh snoshenii Novgoroda s Gotlandom i Liubekom*, St. Pbg., 1847. Although this work is somewhat dated, it remains useful as a guide to the sources and as a good compendium of the information given by the sources.

11. This privilege, which was issued in favor of Lübeck by Henry the Lion and renewed thirty years later by Frederick Barbarossa, may not be authentic in various respects; it is reliable, however, insofar as the stipulations in favor of Russian merchants are concerned.

12. Goetz, *Handelsgeschichte*, pp. 50, 72, 96. In the treaty of 1229, for instance, the right of the Russians to visit the Trave is clearly confirmed.

13. *Ibid.*, p. 59.

14. Alexandre Eck, *Le moyen âge russe*, Paris, 1933, p. 33. The burning and pillaging of the town of Åbo by the Russians in 1317 and again in 1353 permit us to conclude that the Russians must have had some war ships.

15. *Das Rigische Schuldbuch (1286-1352)*, ed. Hermann Hildebrand, St. Pbg, 1872, No. 1511. Cf., however, his introduction (p. xxxii), where the author points out the difficulties which terms such as "de Lubeck, de Anglia, de Suecia" cause to him who wants to identify the nationality of a person. This difficulty is enhanced when there is a question of the term "Ruthenus."

16. Goetz, *Handelsgeschichte*, pp. 221 ff.

17. All these types of fraud and tricks are later (in 1514) specifically enumerated by the grandduke. *Hanserezesse*, ed.

by Verein für hansische Geschichte, Lübeck, 3rd ser.: 1477-1530, v. 6, p. 356.

18. Very derogatory reports are given about them by the somewhat cynical and prejudiced representative of Poland, John Dantiscus. He writes that they sold "ocreas, sellas, flagella, pelles, vestes pelliceas, dentes et quidquid habebant usque ad cultellos." Acta Tomiciana. Posnaniae, 1852—, (i. e., Epistolae. Legationes. Responsa. Actiones. Res geste . . . Sigismundi . . . primi, Regis Polonia [1506-1548], containing documents of Piotr Tomicki, Vice-Chancellor of Poland [1464-1536]. v. 9, p. 25.

19. Afanasii Nikitin, Khozhdenie za tri moria Afanasiia Nikitina, 1466-1472 gg., ed. Boris D. Grekov and Varvara P. Adrianova-Peretts, Moscow and Leningrad, 1948. German version: Die Fahrt des Athanasius Nikitin über die drei Meere, ed. Karl H. Meyer, Leipzig, 1920 (Quellen und Aufsätze zur russischen Geschichte, v. 2).

20. Hansisches Urkundenbuch, IX, No. 716.

21. For instance, Gunnar Mickwitz, Aus Revaler Handelsbüchern. Zur Technik des Ostseehandels in der ersten Hälfte des 16. Jahrhunderts., Helsingfors, 1938 (Societas Scientiarum Fennica, "Commentationes humanarum litterarum," v. 9, no. 8). Since writing this article, some such investigations have been carried out, but conclusive evidence for the actual level of prices has not yet been adduced.

22. Such complaints were put forward on both sides. The English, for instance, were later known in Russia for their bad manners, their drunkenness, their arrogance, their keeping of wild animals in their houses, etc.

23. Goetz Frh. von Pölnitz, Fugger und Hanse; ein hundertjähriges Ringen um Ostsee und Nordsee, Tübingen, 1953, passim (Studien zur Fuggergeschichte, v. 11).

24. MS. Kongl. Bibliothek, Copenhagen, Gl. kongl. S., No. 2546. Cf. Hanserezesse, 3. Ser., VII, 54.

25. Danmarks Riges Krønicke, Copenhagen, 1650-55, pp. 1109-1114.

26. MS. Kongl. Bibliothek, Copenhagen, (Thott), III, 378, 379. Cf. Gottfried Heinrich Handelmann, Die letzten Zeiten hansischer Übermacht im skandinavischen Norden, Kiel, 1853, pp. 20, 41, 45, 263 N. 10.

27. Cf. Pölnitz, Fugger und Hanse, p. 139 N. 20.

28. Cf. Stockholms Stadt Tänkeböger, 4 December 1520, pp. 311 ff.; N. J. Ekdahl, Bihang till Christiern IIs Arkiv, Stockholm, 1842, pp. 1336, 1349; Carl Ferdinand Allen, De tre nordiske rigers historie, v. 2, (Christiern den Anden, I), Copenhagen, 1865, pp. 270ff. It seems to me that Erik Arup's remark (Danmarks Historie, Copenhagen, 1932, v. 2, pp. 356 f.), when he speaks, in connection with such a Trading Company, of a "figment of the imagination" and a "fraud," is too sweeping in its formulation. Christian was certainly aware of the trends, and his councillor, Mikkelsen, anticipated ideas which were later realized by the English joint stock companies. But perhaps Christian misjudged the potential of his country.

29. Cf. Appendices 1 and 2. To be sure, Centurione was the illegitimate offspring of one of the most important Genoese merchant and banker families. His activity is connected, however, not with Genoa, but with Rome and the papal curia.

30. Staden, Aufzeichnungen, pp. 126 N., ff.

31. A good survey of Russian-Dutch relations in Benjamin Cordt (V. A. Kordt), "Ocherk snoshenii Moskovskago gosudarstva s Respublikoiu Soedinennykh Niderlandov po 1631 g." (Sbornik imp. russkago istor. obschestva, v. 116, St. Pbg., 1902).

32. Cf. note 1 to this chapter; also, chapter 4 of this book.

33. MS. Rigsarkiv, Copenhagen, Tegnelser over alle Lande, VI, 364. Regarding the offer of sale: Ibid., Cancl. Brevbøger, 29 July 1577; dto. 1578.

34. Linus Artur Attman, Den ryska marknaden i 1500-talets baltiska politik, 1558-1595, Lund, 1944, p. 225. Again and again the Russians had tried to build up a merchant fleet. When around 1519 they had attempted to engage in an active foreign trade, they had addressed themselves to Sweden (that is, to Christian II) for support. Thereupon, the Livonian towns demanded that Sweden should under no circumstances be permitted to help Russia build ships. Akten und Recesse der livländischen Ständetage, ed. Leonid Arbusow, v. 3, Riga, 1910, p. 276.

35. Cordt, v. 17. Appendix 10 shows that there were occasional instances of Russian merchants who were able to do business abroad on their own account.

36. Taeke S. Jansma, "Oliver Brunel te Dordrecht: De Noord-Oostelijke doorvaart en het West-Europeesch-Russische contact in de 16de eeuw," Tijdschrift voor Geschiedenis, v. 59, Groningen, 1946, pp. 337-362. Cf. Samuel Muller Fz., Geschiedenis der Noordsche Compagnie, Utrecht, 1874, p. 27.

37. Norske rigs-registranter, 12 vols., Christiania, 1861-69, v. 2: 1572-1588 (1863), pp. 183 f.

38. Inna L(i)ubimenko, Les relations commerciales et politiques de l'Angleterre avec la Russie avnt Pierre le Grand, Paris, 1933, p. 33.

39. Hanserezesse, 1436 (2nd ser.: 1431-1476), v. 1 (1922), Lübeck, p. 513.

40. Hans Uebersberger, Österreich und Russland seit dem Ende des 15. Jahrhunderts., v. 1: 1488-1605, Wien and Leipzig, 1906, p. 562.

Chapter II

1. Nikolai Mikhailovich de Karamsin, Histoire de l'Empire de Russie, 11 vols., Paris, 1819-26, v. 6, p. 448.

2. Luther himself took a special interest in this eastward movement. No fewer than seventeen letters edited and

published by the Gesellschaft für Geschichte und Altertumskunde der Ostsee-Provinzen and referring to Livonia alone bear witness to his activity and concern. *Luther an die Christen in Livland*, Riga, 1866.

Erik Amburger treats, but only very briefly, the beginnings of Protestantism in Muscovy in *Geschichte des Protestantismus in Russland*, Stuttgart, 1961, pp. 13-21. He adds a good bibliography. Cf. also Wilhelm Kahle, *Aufsätze zur Entwicklung der evangelischen Gemeinden in Russland*, Leiden and Köln, 1962 (Ökumenische Studien, v. 4).

3. Vasilii Osipovich Kliuchevsky, *A History of Russia*, 5 vols., New York, 1911-31, v. 2, p. 11.

4. Karamsin, v. 7, p. 333.

5. Robert Georgievich Wipper, *Ivan Grozny*, trans. J. Fineberg, Moscow, 1947, pp. 40ff. Joseph Kulischer correctly points out that the fall of Novgorod was a natural consequence of the "machtpolitische Ziele des Grossstaates," and that economic considerations necessarily had to make room for them. Iosif Mikhailovich Kulischer, *Russische Wirtschaftsgeschichte*, Jena, 1925, v. 1, p. 155.

6. Joseph Ehret, "Tessiner Künstler in Moskau," in *Die Garbe*, 1947, nos. 4-5, p. 2.

7. Eck, p. 437, N.

8. Karl Staehlin, *Geschichte Russlands von den Anfängen bis zur Gegenwart*, 4 vols. and Personenverzeichnis, Stuttgart, 1923-1939, v. 1, p. 233.

9. Uebersberger, *Österreich und Russland.*

10. Paul Pierling, *Papes et tsars; 1547-1597*, Paris, 1890; also his *La Russie et le Saint-Siège, Etudes diplomatiques*, 5 vols., Paris, 1896-1912.

11. Papal Legate Gattinara as reported by Uebersberger, p. 190.

12. Karamsin, v. 7, p. 126. The Russians paid subsidies to the Knights to help them in their war against Poland.

13. Danmark-Norges Traktater, vols. 1 and 2.

14. Sverges Traktater, v., 3, pt. 4, and v. 4.

15. Cf. Quellen zur Geschichte des Untergangs livländischer Selbständigkeit aus dem schwedischen Reichsarchive zu Stockholm, ed. Carl Schirren, 8 vols., Reval, 1861-1881; and Neue Quellen zur Geschichte des Untergangs livländischer Selbständigkeit aus dem dänischen geheimen Archive zu Kopenhagen, 3 vols., Reval, 1883-1885 (Archiv für die Geschichte Liv-, Esth- und Curlands N.F., vols. 1-11). Arthur Winckler, Die deutsche Hansa in Russland, Berlin, 1886.

16. Cf., Bang, Tabeller øver skibsfart.

17. Cf. Hakluyt, vols. 1-2. Also Great Britain, Public Record Office: Calendar of State Papers and Manuscripts relating to English Affairs existing in the archives and collections of Venice, and in other libraries of Northern Italy, (London, 1864—.

18. Eck, p. 361.

19. Kliuchevsky, v. 2, p. 342.

20. Igor Emmanuilovich Grabar, Istoriia russkago iskusstva, Moscow, 1910-1915, vols. 1-3; 4, p. 1; 5; 6. Cf. also Cyril G. E. Bunt, Russian Art from Scyths to Soviets, London and New York, 1946, p. 95.

21. Elie Denissoff, Maxime le Grec et l'Occident, Paris and Louvain, 1943.

Cf. the excellent discussion of the question of humanism in Russia at the time of the Renaissance and the Reformation by Günther Stökl, "Das Echo von Renaissance und Reformation im Moskauer Russland," Jahrbücher für Geschichte Osteuropas, N. F. 7, 1959, pp. 413-430. Soviet historians have for many years shunned this topic. Since the publication of the present article in the Archiv für Reformationsgeschichte, a number of interesting stories have appeared: N. A. Kazakova and Ia. S. Lur'e, Antifeodal'nye ereticheskie dvizhenija na Rusi XVI veka,

M. -L., 1955; Aleksandr Aleksandrovich Zimin, "Matvei Bashkin— vol'nodumets XVI v.," in: Voprosy istorii religii i ateizma, v. 4, 1956, pp. 230-245, and on the "heretic" Artemija, ibid., v. 5, 1958, pp. 213 ff., as cited in Stökl, p. 425; and most recently Aleksandr Il'ich Klibanov, Reformatsionnye dvizheniia v Rossii v XIV-pervoi polovine XVI v.v., Moscow, 1960, pp. 265-301, 305-332.

22. Geschichte der Völker der Union der Sozialist. Sowjet-Republiken, ed. Akademiia Nauk SSSR, Institut Istorii, 4 vols., Basel, 1945-46, v. 1, pt. 2 (Von Iwan III. bis zum Ende des 18. Jahrhunderts), p. 98.

23. Siegmund Baron von Herberstein, Notes upon Russia: being a translation of Rerum Moscoviticarum Commentarii, ed. Hakluyt Society, Nos. 10 and 12, London, 1851-52. Fletcher in: Hakluyt, v. 2, pp. 287 ff.

24. Eck, pp. 369f.

25. Friedrich von Adelung, Kritisch-literärische Übersicht der Reisenden in Russland bis 1700, deren Berichte bekannt sind, 2 vols., St. Pbg. and Leipzig, 1846. (Facsimile ed., Amsterdam, 1960).

26. Fletcher, in Hakluyt, v. 2, p. 306.

27. Eck, p. 291.

28. Sergei Fedorovich Platonov, Boris Godounov, tsar de Russie, 1598-1605, Paris, 1929.

29. Ibid., p. 104.

Chapter III

1. The following essay is based on a paper presented by the author on August 29, 1950, in Paris before the Ninth International Historical Congress.

2. The finding of the route past the North Cape by the Englishmen Chancellor and Willoughby does not represent a "discovery" properly speaking. As much as thirty years earlier, the Austrian Envoy Sigismund von Herber-

stein had already mentioned in a report a circumnavigation of the Cape in the year 1496 by a Russian interpreter who had reached Trondjhem. Another such trip was made around 1520. Moreover, a number of well known Danish and Lapp settlements existed along the Northern coast.

3. Robin George Collingwood speaks of "human self-knowledge." _The Idea of History_, Oxford, 1946, p. 10.

4. Wipper, p. 40.

5. E. g., in 1521, 1542, 1545, 1553. Cf. Georg Sartorius, _Geschichte des Hanseatischen Bundes_, 3 vols., Göttingen, 1802-1808, v. 3, p. 218. Also _Kölner Inventar_, . . . _1531-1559_, ed. Konstantin Höhlbaum, 2 vols., Leipzig, 1896-1903 (Inventare hansischer Archive), _passim_.

6. Sartorius, v. 3, p. 199. According to other sources, trade "von Gast zu Gast" was prohibited as early as 1521. Cf. Alfred Dreyer, _Die lübisch-livländischen Beziehungen zur Zeit des Unterganges livländischer Selbständigkeit, 1551-1563_, Lübeck, 1912 (Veröffentlichungen zur Geschichte der Freien und Hansestadt Lübeck I, 2), _passim_.

7. Cf. similar prescriptions for Russians in seventeenth-century Pskov, Pashkov-Letiche, p. 218.

8. _Briefe und Urkunden zur Geschichte Livlands in den Jahren 1558-1562_, ed. Friedrich Bienemann, 5 vols., Riga, 1865-1876, v. 3, p. 227.

9. Among other concessions, Narva demanded that the Russian merchants from Pskov and Novgorod pay an extra fee for the permission to trade in Narva. Cf. Aleksandr Vasil'evich Petrov, _Gorod Narva . . . 1223-1900_, St. Pbg., 1901, p. 91. Also in Narva itself, such extra fees were levied. Bienemann, v. 3, p. 229.

10. Cf. _Sverges Traktater_, v. 2, p. 311.

11. Nikolai Aleksandrovich Dobroliubov, _Selected Philosophical Essays_, trans. J. Fineberg, Moscow, 1948, pp. 105, 107, 135 (in English).

12. Monumenta Livoniae Antiquae, G. F. v. Bunge *et al.*, eds., 5 vols., Riga, Dorpat, Leipzig, 1835-1847, v. 5, p. 191.

13. Bienemann, v. 3, p. 112. There is no agreement in contemporary reports as to the treatment which Narva received after its surrender. A pardon was accorded to the town by Alexei Danilovich Basmanov in his letter of May 15, 1558; but reports which date from July, 1558, do not confirm this. They assert that not a single German was then still living in Narva and that the tsar had ordered the dead to be disintered and the churches to be handed over to the Orthodox. Bienemann, v. 1, p. 258. It is an established fact that many burghers were seized and sent to Russia in 1560; but they were allowed to return that same year.

14. All the reports of the Livonian chroniclers Russow, Henning, and Nyenstädt speak of the difficult situation of Reval. Reval merchants lost up to one half of their wealth as a result of the new paths which trade took. Under such circumstances, it is perhaps no wonder that they shipped even war materials to the Russians in Narva. They are supposed to have delivered so much lead, arms and sulphur that the Russians could not even use it all but resold it on the market at Dorpat. Dreyer, S. 85f. Karamsin reports that when the tsar of Kazan, who himself was a Russian prisoner, saw the German prisoners in Moscow, he spit into their faces and shouted: "Now that you have made your bed you must sleep in it. It was you who have taught the Russians how to use new weapons. You are responsible for your own fate, just as you are responsible for ours." (v. 9, p. 31). Regarding the possibility for Ivan to use Narva as a military bastion in his struggle with Reval, cf. Bienemann, v. 1, p. 255.

15. As to the difficulties confronting all trade with Narva, as well as with regard to prohibitions and their non-observance, cf. Bienemann, v. 3, pp. 46f., 208f.; v. 4,

pp. 36, 266, 413, *passim*. Also *Colección de documentos inéditos para la Historia de España*, v. 98, Madrid, 1891, pp. 71, 95, 158; Schirren, *Quellen* . . . and *Neue Quellen* . . ., *passim*; *Akty i pis'ma k istorii baltiiskago voprosa v XVI i XVII stolietiiakh*, ed. G. V. Forsten, 2 vols., (Vol. 1: Zapiski istoriko-filol. fakul'teta imp. S.-Peterburgskago universiteta, v. 21, 1889; Vol. 2: Zapiski v. 31, 1893), v. 1, p. 9; and Balthasar Russow, *Chronica der Prouintz Lyfflandt*, in: *Scriptores Rerum Livonicarum. Sammlung der wichtigsten Chroniken und Geschichtsdenkmale von Liv-, Ehst- und Kurland*, 2 vols., Riga and Leipzig, 1846-1853 (vol. 2). Regarding the special difficulties which arose between Lübeck and Reval and subsequent international repercussions, cf. Dreyer, p. 54, 74; Bienemann, v. 3, p. 114; v. 4, p. 274.

16. Winckler, p. 95.

17. To be sure, salt was gained in Russia especially in the provinces of Perm and Astrakhan. But production did not suffice to satisfy the demands in the country, and therefore large quantities had to be imported from the West. Both France and Spain furnished salt; yet, the major part of the imports came from Germany. No other commodity contributed so much to trade rivalries with Russia as salt did. Lübeck particularly felt threatened, for Lübeck merchants had held first place as suppliers of salt. Embargoes were bound to hurt them; yet, it was by no means sure that they were necessary or useful for the common welfare. For, whenever embargoes were imposed, the Germans sold their salt to the English. Thereupon, these would ignore all prohibitions and resell the salt to the Russians. The importance of salt in Baltic trade is also illustrated by an edict which King Erik of Sweden published in the midst of the Northern War. It permitted the French to ship as much goods to Narva as they delivered, in salt, to Sweden. Cf. chapter 5 of this book.

18. Sir Nich. Bacon to Dudley, April 6, 1564, *Calendar*

of State Papers, Domestic Series, of the reigns of Edward VI, Mary, Elizabeth, 1547-1580, ed. R. Lemon, London, 1856, p. 237. At that time, English trade in Narva was no more than four years old. Hakluyt, v. 3, p. 35.

19. Franz Nyenstädt, Livländische Chronik . . ., in: Monumenta Livoniae Antiquae, v. 2, p. 34; (Christoph Melchior Alexander von Richter, Geschichte der dem russischen Kaisertum einverleibten deutschen Ostseeprovinzen bis zur Zeit ihrer Vereinigung mit demselben, 5. vols., Riga, 1857-58, v. 2, p. 416; and Wipper, p. 109. The low level of prices was in part connected with internal English strife. Up to 1566 it had not been decided whether or not Narva was to be included in the trade monopoly which had been granted for the Russia trade to the Muscovy Company. In the meantime bitter competition had arisen among the English merchants in Narva. Eventually, the question was decided in favor of Anthony Jenkinson and Thomas Randolph (1566-68) of the Muscovy Company, who were allowed to import their goods without paying dues. In order to receive this grant from Ivan, the English had to make many concessions.

20. Bang, Tabeller øver Skibsfart.

21. Petrov, p. 96.

22. Forsten, p. 109.

23. In making this estimate I have considered that, according to Eck (p. 358), seventy English ships had been in Narva, i.e., far more than are entered in the Tabeller. According to Petrov, p. 100, the Englishman Hudson alone sold in Narva goods worth approximately Ł 11,000.-.-.

24. Walther Kirchner, "England and Denmark," pp. 3f. Regarding the special difficulties which Denmark encountered, notwithstanding the favorable treaty she had concluded with Russia in 1562, cf. Danmark-Norges Traktater, v. 2, p. 77; Forsten, v. 1, pp. 51ff.; Nyenstädt, p. 34; Friedrich Konrad Gadebusch, Livländische Jahrbücher von 1030-1761, 4 vols., Riga, 1780-83, v. 2, pt. 1, p. 73.

25. The consequences were of fundamental importance for the fate of Sweden. Swedish historians have investigated them from various points of view (among them are Eric Geijer, G. O. Fr. Westling, Claes Annerstedt, Thure Annerstedt, Harald Hjärne). But also Danish and Hanseatic scholars have discussed the issue. Suffice it here to refer to the important part which the Narva question played in the decision by Reval to submit to Sweden. Never would Reval have done this and never would the tsar have tolerated it, had Russia not been in possession of Narva.

The fall of Narva was of importance also for the development of the Swedish-Finnish port of Viborg, which became the center for smuggling of forbidden war materials. It affected the interrelations of Sweden, Livonia and Lübeck, for, owing to it, economic competition and political strife increased. Last not least, it contributed to the outbreak of the Northern Seven Years War, since Lübeck was unwilling to renounce the Narva trade while Sweden, in order to promote the role of Reval and to retain control over Russian imports, refused to permit it. Poland agreed in principle with Sweden, but she herself laid claim to Livonia. She therefore allied herself with Denmark, and thus came to oppose Swedish policy. In the course of the Seven Years War, Sweden succeeded in dominating the eastern half of the Baltic Sea. This made it possible for her, despite the threat posed by Narva, to derive also numerous advantages from Narva. For Narva was a neutral port and Sweden could buy there needed salt and war materials which her own enemies were shipping there. The role of Sweden during the war and her influence on the Narva trade contributed also to the decline of the prominent position which the Hanseatic towns and the Danes had held in Baltic trade. Dutch and English merchants were to take over. This change, in turn, led to a radical shift of the European economic and political balance of power. Cf. also Pamjatniki diplomaticheskikh snoshenii Moskovskago gosudarstva s Shvedskim gosudarstvom 1556-1586 gg. (*Sbornik imp. Russkago istoricheskago obshchestva*, vol. 129, 1910), pp. 72 f., *passim*. Also *Sverges Traktater*, *passim*; Dreyer, pp. 83, 85, 127-129; Jacques Auguste de Thou (1553-1617), *Histoire universelle . . . depuis 1543 jusqu'en 1607*, 16 vols., London [Paris], 1734, v. 4, pp. 612-617. As to effects on Sweden's internal affairs, it may suffice to mention that the Narva issue contributed to undermining the position of King Erik XIV.

26. Cf., among others, *Akta podkanclerskie Franciszka Krasińskiego, 1569-1573*, Warsaw, 1869-71, v. 1, pp. 21ff.; Staden, *Aufzeichnungen*, Anlage 6 (Zur Narvafahrt), pp. 250-252.

27. Jean Jacques Altmeyer, *Histoire des relations commerciales et diplomatiques des Pays-Bas avec le Nord de l'Europe pendant le XVIe siècle*, Bruxelles, 1840, p. 375. Altmeyer is an unreliable source, and as critics, such as Walter Leitsch, Günther Stökl, and others, have justly pointed out, the words of Alva as reported by Altmeyer must be apocryphal. It would be interesting, though, to know which sayings of Alva Altmeyer had in mind—the more so as they reflect a mood which is well in accord with Spanish Habsburg policy, which is warranted by the special situation of Spain in the Netherlands and which mirrors diplomatic uneasiness about the Russian position gained at Narva.

28. Russow, p. 85, reports about the actions of the Oprichnina in Narva. Concerning other outrages committed there, cf. Armand J. Gerson, "The Organization and Early History of the Muscovy Company," in: *Studies in the History of English Commerce in the Tudor Period*, Philadelphia, 1912, p. 83. Regarding Novgorod, cf. Karamsin, v. 9, p. 184.

29. *Sverges Traktater*, v. 4, pp. 402 ff. Trade was free "mit unvordechtigen, unvorpottenen, redlichen Kauffmanswahren wie von alters," *Ibid.*, p. 420.

30. *Ibid.*, v. 4, p. 443.

31. *Ibid.*, v. 4, pp. 442 ff.; Wipper, p. 183; Kasimir Waliszewski, *Ivan the Terrible*, Philadelphia, 1904, p. 204. Among all the merchants, it seems that those of Danzig were the only ones who actually gave up the Narva trade. Denmark, too, may have been ready to observe the prohibition of the trade—the more so as during the sixties she had generally suffered losses in her dealings with the Russians. But up to 1576, at least, she did not risk to prohibit the Russia trade to either her own subjects or to those of other countries because of the existing treaty of 1562. *Danmark-Norges Traktater*, v. 2, p. 501. Other powers, however, openly refused any concession whatsoever. The elector of Saxony even demanded that unrestricted trade be officially permitted (Forsten, v. 1, p. 150), and Jenkinson admitted frankly as to his English enterprises that war material was shipped from England to Narva (Winckler, p. 102). Perhaps it would have been best if the embargo, which was disregarded by so many sides (cf., for instance, *Kölner Inventar*, v. 2, p. 16), had been repealed. Certainly, the Hanse would have profited from such a repeal inasmuch as it needed support rather than suppression at a time when the Atlantic sea ways were increasing in importance and new nations powerful on the seas emerged. But permitting the Narva trade proved to be no less difficult than prohibiting it—the more so as in the course of time Sweden gradually came to join the ranks of those opposed to it. The cause of this change in Swedish policy may be found in the demands of Reval, which sought to regain, under Swedish leadership, its former predominance. In part, however, internal Swedish conditions were responsible for the change, since the possession of Narva led to a struggle between King John and his brother Charles (Erik Gustaf Geijer, *Svenska folkets historia*, 3 vols., Stockholm, 1876, v. 2, p. 272). Thus, instead of lifting the ban on the Narva trade, the stipulations of the Peace of Stettin (according to which the German emperor had the right to order

embargoes) were repeatedly and expressly confirmed. As time went on Sweden became altogether a vigorous defender of the treaty which, against all expectations, turned out to be a useful means for King John to pursue undisturbed his Livonian policy of conquest. In 1574, he threatened to render the entry into Narva's harbor a physical impossibility by sinking a few ships at its entrance. Alexander von Richter, Geschichte der dem russischen Kaisertum einverleibten Ostseeprovinzen bis zur Zeit ihrer Vereinigung mit demselben, 5 vols., Riga 1857-58, vol. 3, p. 249. In the following year, Sweden made the useless proposal to permit trade with Narva. This was, however, to apply only to the three northern kingdoms. Of course, Denmark would have been forced to refuse participation because of her treaty obligations to others. Danmark-Norges Traktater, v. 2, p. 356.

32. Kölner Inventar, v. 2, p. 361; cf. Charles Dançay (ca. 1510-1589), Indberetninger fra Charles de Dançay til det franske hof om forholden i Norden 1567-1573, ed. Carl Frederik Bricka, Copenhagen, 1901.

33. Thou, v. 4, p. 615.

34. "Lübeck und Narwa," Das Inland (Dorpat) v. 26, No. 12 [p. 176-180], p. 178.

35. Calendar of State Papers, Foreign Series, of the reign of Elizabeth, 1577-1578, v. 12 (1901), No. 171.

36. A. von Richter, v. 3, p. 243.

37. In 1577, the Swedes attempted the capture by sea power alone. But Admiral Gyllenanker succeeded only in putting fire to the wooden fortifications of the town and in taking a number of prisoners. Karamzin, v. 9, p. 356. In 1579, the Swedes made another attempt. Having seized a number of Danish ships during the summer, they began in the fall to invest the fortress by land. Again they failed.

38. Early in 1579, the Poles under Stephan Bathory had once more decided upon war against Russia. Consequently,

they requested the Hanse to stop all trade to Narva and finally passed an official resolution in this sense. The Hanse agreed to suspend the Narva trade for one year provided France, England, Portugal, the Netherlands and Sweden did likewise. Kölner Inventar, v. 2, p. 172. In 1582, the Emperor Rudolph decided that shipping to Narva should be handled as provided for in the treaty of Stettin; but in November, Archduke Ferdinand altogether prohibited it.

39. Helge Almquist, "Johan III och Stefan Batori år 1582," Historisk Tidskrift, v. 29, Stockholm, 1910 (Tjugunionde Årgången 1909), pp. 69-123. As late as 1583, the Poles still tried to purchase from the Swedes the fortress which they could not gain by force. Domenico Alamanni, "Legatio Domini Alemani," ed. K. I. Karttunen, Rome, 1910 (Suomalaisen Tiedeakatemian Toimituksia ser. B, v. 2, no. 8). As a matter of fact, in 1582, the Swedes returned to the Russians the fortress of Ivangorod which they had likewise conquered. Nyenstädt, p. 77.

40. Cf. Kölner Inventar, v. 2, p. 259.

41. It should be pointed out, as Professor Paul Johansen, Hamburg, once indicated in a letter to me, that in the seventeenth century a great revival of Narva occurred. It was only then, when the Swedes ruled Livonia and when the English had built up their trade in the Baltic, that the peak of Narva's development was reached.

Chapter IV

1. Winckler, pp. 35 f.

2. Gadebusch, v. 1, pt. 2, p. 388. Cf. Kölner Inventar, v. 1, p. 343. Cf. Winckler, p. 85.

3. Bartholomaeus Grefenthal, "Lifflendische Chronica": Monumenta Livoniae antiquae, v. 5, p. 115. Cf. Franz Bernhard von Bucholtz, Geschichte der Regierung Ferdinand des

Ersten 8 vols., Vienna, 1831-1838, v. 7, p. 496 N. Also MS., Rigsarkivet Stockholm, Livonia före 1600, bl. 063. (The paging indicates the number under which the manuscript is to be found among the photostat copies in the private collection of Professor Waldemar Westergaard at Los Angeles. The documents contained therein [now in the library of the University of California, Los Angeles] have been used for the present study.)

4. Most historians of the period dwell in extenso on this Russian claim of the "ancient inheritance." Cf. Bienemann, v. 1, pp. 221 ff., passim. Staden, Aufzeichnungen, Anlage 5, pp. 244-250. Also Ivan to Riga, MS., Riga Äusseres Ratsarchiv.

5. Hakluyt, v. 2, p. 352.

6. For a full discussion of the Swedish-Russian relationship, see Waldemar Westergaard, "Gustavus Vasa and Russia, 1555-1557," Pacific Historical Review, v. 2, 1933, pp. 158-169. Recent Soviet historians have occupied themselves much less with Russian-Danish relations than with Russian-Swedish, Russian-English, or Russian-Dutch connections. Cf. Ia. S. Lur'e, "Russko-angliiskie otnosheniia i mezhdunarodnaia politika vtoroi poloviny XVI v.," Mezhdunarodnye sviazi Rossii do XVII v. Sbornik statei, Moscow, 1961, pp. 419-443; N. T. Nakashidze, "Russko-angliiskie otnosheniia vo vtoroi polovine XVI v.," Tiflis, 1955; M. M. Gromyko, "Russko-niderlandskaia torgovlia na Murmanskom beregu v XVI v.," in: Srednie veka, v. 17, 1960, pp. 225-258; G. A. Novitskii, "Voprosy torgovli v russko- shvedskikh otnosheniiakh XVI v.," in: Skandinavskii Sbornik, v. 2, Tallin, 1957, pp. 38-46. See also Erich Donnert, Der livländische Ordensritterstaat und Russland. Der livländische Krieg und die baltische Frage in der europäischen Politik 1558-1583. Berlin (-Ost), 1963, pp. 185 ff.

7. MSS., Copenhagen, Rigsarkiv, Tyske Kancelliets Udenrigske Afdeling [T.K.U.A] Rusland B, vol. 47, 1558-1642, Gesandskabs-Relationer fra forskaellige Afsendinger, 93, 30 and 95, 22.

8. "In quo nihil est hominis, praeter corporis figuram." Krasiński's speech, Akta poselskie i korrespondencye Franciska Krasińskiego, 1558-1576, ed. W. H. Krasiński et al., Cracow, 1872, p. 283. Cf. the descriptions in the contemporary chronicles of Balthasar Russow, Salomon Henning, and Dionysius Fabricius in Scriptores Rerum Livonicarum.

9. Schirren, Neue Quellen, v. 1, p. 161.

10. MS., Copenhagen, Rigsarkiv, T.K.U.A., 93, 30 f.

11. MS., Copenhagen, Rigsarkiv, T.K.U.A., 93, 28-34.

12. Danmark-Norges Traktater, v. 2, pp. 21-22. Cited hereafter in this chapter as D. N. Tr.

13. D. N. Tr., II, 22. Cf. K. H. von Busse, Herzog Magnus, König von Livland, Leipzig, 1871, pp. 38 ff. Also William Mollerup, Danmarks Forhold til Lifland fra Salget af Estland Til Ordensstatens Opløsning, 1346-1561, Copenhagen, 1880, p. 124.

14. D. N. Tr., II, 22.

15. D. N. Tr., II, 23.

16. D. N. Tr., II, 24 ff. The Russian version has been used.

17. It was said in Article VIII, however, that Denmark received these lands out of Ivan's inheritance.

18. Iu. Shcherbachev, "Dva posol'stva pri Ioanne IV Vasilieviche," Russkii Vestnik, v. 190, 1887, pp. 98 ff.

19. Shcherbachev, pp. 105 ff.

20. Shcherbachev, pp. 105-118.

21. MSS., Copenhagen, Rigsarkiv, T.K.U.A., 94, 10 ff.

22. MSS., Copenhagen, Rigsarkiv, T.K.U.A., 94, 23.

23. MSS., Copenhagen, Rigsarkiv, T.K.U.A., 94, 22, 25, passim, 95, 4.; Forsten published two of Vheling's letters: Akty i pis'ma k istorii baltiiskago voprosa.

24. MSS. Copenhagen, Rigsarkiv, T.K.U.A., 95, 20-37 and 96, 5-12. Eysenberg's instructions published by Forsten, No. 60. Cf. D. N. Tr., II, 389.

25. "Jacobi Ulfeldi Legatio Moscovitica, sive Hodoeporicon Ruthenicum," in: Historiae Ruthenicae Scriptores Exteri Saeculi XVI, ed. Adal'bert Vikentievich Starczewski (de Starchevsky), 2 vols., Berlin and St. Pbg., 1841-42.

26. The treaty is printed in D. N. Tr., II, 403, 410. An account of the negotiations is given by Shcherbachev, pp. 125 ff.

Chapter V

1. Recueil des instructions données aux ambassadeurs et ministres de France, Vols. 8 and 9 (Russie), ed. Alfred Rambaud, Paris, 1890 (quoted hereafter as Rambaud, Recueil, vols. 1 and 2); F. Tastevin, Histoire de la colonie française de Moscou depuis les origines jusqu'à 1812, Paris, 1908; Léonce Pingaud, Les Français en Russie et les Russes en France: l'ancien régime, l'émigration, les invasions, Paris, 1886; P. M-yev, Diplomaticheskiia snosheniia Rossii s Frantsiei v XVII viekie, in: Istoricheskii Viestnik, v. 44, St. Pbg., 1891.

2. De Carle's mission was preceded, in 1585, by the arrival at the court of Henry III of France of a certain Pierre de Ragouse from Russia. He had been charged with announcing Tsar Feodor's accession to the throne, and he returned to Moscow with de Carle. Perhaps a Dalmatian who had come to Russia via Venice, Pierre had stayed, or visited, in the house of André Thevet, who, in his Cosmographie universelle, 2 vols., Paris, 1575 (see also, Thevet, Cosmographie Moscovite, ed. Avgustin Galitzin, Paris, 1858), dedicated to Henry III, had devoted some forty pages to Russia. Thevet's sources seem to have been partly Polish; his information is not too reliable. He even still speaks of the "hyperborean mountains." His contemporaries, Nicolas Vignier in his Bibliothèque historiale, vols. 1-3 (Paris, 1587), 4 (1650), and de Thou, Histoire uni-

verselle, availed themselves of better sources, such as Herberstein, Heidenstamm, Jesuit reports, etc. In a second work, Le Grand Insulaire, Thevet inserts a Russian dictionary (see, "Un vocabulaire français-russe de la fin du XVIe siècle," ed. Paul Boyer, in: Recueil de Mémoires orientaux [Congrès de 1905] Textes et traductions publiés par les professeurs de l'Ecole spéciale des langues orientales vivantes, Paris, 1905, p. 10) which may have been based on an account brought back by the Dieppe merchant Jean Sauvage (see page 104). Cf. Alexandra Kalmykow, "A Sixteenth Century Russian Envoy to France," Slavic Review, v. 23, 1964, pp. 701-705. Miss Kalmykow notes that Le Grand Insulaire is mentioned as early as 1584, but since Pierre de Ragouse did not get to France until 1585 and Sauvage did not make his trip until 1586, the latter year appears to be the earliest possible date for the completion of the work.

3. Rambaud, Recueil, pp. 13-15; Recueil des traités et conventions conclus par la Russie avec les puissances étrangères, ed. Fedor Fedorovich de Martens, v. 13, St. Pbg., 1902, pp. x f.

4. "Bytnost' v gorod Bordo Rossiiskago Poslannika dvorianina Ivana Gavrilovicha Kondireva i podiachago Michaeli Nevirova u Frantsuskago Korolia Ludovika XIII v 1615 godu," Otechestvennyia Zapiski, n° 78, Oct., 1826, pp. 25-46.

Boris Fedorovich Porshnev, "K istorii russko-frantsuzskikh sviazei v epokhu tridtsatiletnei voiny," Frantsuzskii ezhegodnik, 1958 (Moscow 1959), pp. 56-72.

5. Rambaud, Recueil, I, pp. ix-x.

6. Emile Haumant, La culture française en Russie (1700-1900), Paris, 1910; Inna L(i)ubimenko, "Les étrangers en Russie avant Pierre le Grand: Diplomats, militaires, intellectuels," in: Revue des Etudes slaves, v. 4, 1924, pp. 84-100; A. Mikhailov, "Kak nasazhdalas frantsuzskaia kul'tura v Rossii," Istoricheskii Vestnik, v. 122, 1910.

7. Adelung, v. 2, pp. 320-322; M. Pierre de la Ville, Discours sommaire de ce qui est arrivé en Moscovie depuis le règne de Juan Vassilyvich, Empereur, iusques à Vassily Iuanouits Sousky (Bibliothèque russe et polonaise), v. 5, pt. 2, Paris, 1859. De la Ville also mentions (p. 23) other Frenchmen (soldiers and prisoners) in Russia.

8. Wilhelm Michael von Richter (Vil'gel'm Mikhailovich Rikhter), Geschichte der Medicin in Russland, 3 vols., Moscow, 1813-1817, v. 1, p. 322.

9. Hedwig Fleischhacker, Die staats-und völkerrechtlichen Grundlagen der moskauischen Aussenpolitik (14.-17. Jahrhundert), Jahrbücher für Geschichte Osteuropas, Beiheft I, Breslau, 1938, pp. 30 ff.

10. For the Church, cf. Pierling, La Russie et le Saint-Siège; for the Empire, cf. Uebersberger.

11. Goetz, Handelsgeschichte and Handelsverträge.

12. Winckler, Die Deutsche Hansa in Russland.

13. One author, who is, to be sure, not very reliable, even speaks of "draps de Flandre" as one of the articles exchanged in Novgorod and Pskov in the eleventh and twelfth centuries. Altmeyer, p. 27; two other authors, Prosper Boissonnade and P. J. Charliat, mention on the basis of good sources, which, however, they did not always use to best advantage, the interest which the King Philippe le Beau demonstrated and the agreement which he made with a group of merchants. Colbert et la Compagnie de commerce du Nord, 1661-1689, Paris, 1930, p. 25.

14. Goetz, Handelsgeschichte, pp. 425-433.

15. Ibid., p. 320.

16. As cited by Charles Woolsey Cole, French Mercantilist Doctrines before Colbert, New York, 1931, pp. 1-2.

17. Ibid., pp. 21-22.

18. Uebersberger, p. 301.

19. Bang, Tabeller øver Skibsfart. All figures here

given with regard to the traffic through the Sound are based on the Tabeller. Of course, the author is well aware of the difficulties which every careful investigator will encounter when using the Tabeller or, for that matter, any type of statistics. Re: Tabeller, cf. Aksel Erhardt Christensen, Le commerce hollandais vers la Baltique autour de 1600, Copenhagen and La Haye, 1941, pp. 34-104. While aware that the absolute figures given in the Tabeller have to be used with caution, the author feels that his particular study here is not too much influenced by these shortcomings; for the relationships can be considered reliable, and no figure has been given which has not been promptly put in relationship to another figure.

20. Martens, Recueil des traités, v. 13, p. 111.

21. Bang, cited by Walther Kirchner, "The Genesis of Franco-Russian Relations," in: Delaware Notes, 19th ser., 1946, p. 23.

22. Conclusions based on an investigation of the commodities which were shipped back to France can serve as additional proof. Furthermore, occasional references to Franco-Russian trade can also serve the investigator, as for instance mention of French merchandise in a permit which the king of Sweden, Erik XIV, gave to French merchants and which allowed them to ship as much goods to Narva, at that time besieged by the Swedes, as they were willing to send salt cargoes to Swedish harbors. Gadebusch, v. 2, pt. 1, p. 73.

23. The profits must have been very high. One document speaks of some French merchants from Narva who, by way of political retribution, were detained in Moscow for fifteen months. Nevertheless, after their release, they had returned to Narva and had purchased there goods for 2 million livres ("vingt cent mille"). To be sure, ultimately they had the misfortune of falling into the hands of the Swedes, who deprived them of their merchandise. Charles de Dançay to the Queen Mother, July 8, 1581, Handlingar rörande Skandina-

viens historia, 40 vols., Stockholm, 1816-1860, v. 11, p. 151.

24. Karamsin, v. 10, pp. 334-337; Giles Fletcher, Of the Russe Common Wealth. Russia at the Close of the Sixteenth Century, Works issued by The Hakluyt Society, v. 20, London, 1864, p. 13.

25. We have no figures for the quantities of these imports; all we know is that the French ships came from Courland, Riga, and Narva. It is not possible to say what cargoes for France the other ships carried.

26. For a more detailed description of Dançay's activities and the complications resulting from the French diplomacy in Poland, cf. Kirchner, "The Genesis . . . ," pp. 26-32.

27. Dançay to Monseigneur, December 18, 1570, Dançay, p. 74.

28. Henri Emmanuel Marquis de Noailles, Henry de Valois et Pologne en 1572, 3 vols., Paris, 1867, v. 3, p. 19.

29. Handlingar, v. 11, pp. 58-62. Cf. La Chronique de Nestor. Tr. en français . . . accompagnée de notes et d'un recueil de pièces inédites touchant les anciennes relations de la Russie avec la France . . . par Louis Paris, 2 vols., Paris, 1834, v. 1, pp. 345-366.

30. Dançay to the King, September 7, 1581. Handlingar, v. 11, pp. 160-161.

31. Actually, the success of the English was very limited. There were years when no ship at all succeeded in reaching Archangel, and others when shipwrecks consumed all the profits made on earlier successful voyages. Yet, an individual voyage, if it succeeded, brought very large profits.

32. Isaac Massa, Histoire des guerres de la Moscovie, 1601-1610, ed. Michel Obolensky and A. van der Linde, 2 vols., Bruxelles, 1866, v. 2, p. XLV. The account given by Massa is not very reliable, but it throws an interesting light on the state of affairs in Russia at the beginning of the seventeenth century.

33. Regarding the Danish king's negotiations to have his sovereign rights for the northern route recognized, cf. Kirchner, "England and Denmark," pp. 7-11.

34. Dançay to the duc de Joyeuse, November 28, 1583, Handlingar, v. 11, p. 241.

35. Georges (Iurii Vasil'evich) Tolstoy, The first forty years of intercourse between England and Russia, 1553-1593, St. Pbg., 1875, p. 261.

36. October 20, 1587: Chronique de Nestor, v. 1, pp. 385-395; Adelung, v. 1, pp. 361-365.

37. See note 2 to this chapter. The names of two other merchants who availed themselves of the privileges of Tsar Feodor are given by Pierre Bonnassieux, Les grandes compagnies de commerce, Paris, 1892, p. 469.

38. As indicated above the figures given here and in the following are derived from Bang's Tabeller. For an estimate of the value of smuggled goods, which certainly would alter the data considerably, especially during war time, cf. Pierre Jeannin, "Les comptes du Sund comme source pour la construction d'indices généraux de l'activité économique en Europe (XVIe-XVIIIe siècle)," Revue Historique, v. 231, 1964, pp. 83 f., 100, passim. Cf. also James Dow, "A Comparative Note on the Sound Toll Register, Stockholm Customs Accounts, and Dundee Shipping Lists, 1589, 1613-1622," The Scandinavian Economic History Review, v. 12, 1964, pp. 79-85.

39. The state of disorder in France was well known in Russia. Ivan the Terrible himself showed himself indignant about the massacre of the night of St. Bartholomew. In a letter to the Emperor Maximilian II, he protested against the cruelty of Charles IX. Chronique de Nestor, v. 1, p. 376; Haumant, p. 2.

40. Cf. Eli Filip Heckscher, Der Merkantilismus, 2 vols., Jena, 1932; also William Robert Scott, The Constitution and Finance of English, Scottish and Irish joint-stock Companies to 1720, 3 vols., Cambridge, England, 1910-1912.

41. Cole, p. 74.

42. Cited in Cole, p. 70. In connection with this issue, one may refer to Arnold Toynbee's discussion of "Challenge and response." A Study of History, London and Oxford, 1939, vol. 1.

43. April 5, 1595. Rambaud, Recueil, v. 1, p. 17; Chronique de Nestor, v. 1, p. 327. Cf. Karamsin, v. 10, p. 367. Also Alexander Brueckner, "Russen und Franzosen," in: Zeitschrift für allgemeine Geschichte, v. 3, 1886, p. 693.

44. Jacques Margeret, Estat de l'empire de Russie et Grand-Duché de Moscovie, ed. Henri Chevreul, Paris, 1855. Another report in French, but not written by a Frenchman, is that of Barezzo Barezzi, Discours merveilleux et véritable de la conqueste faite par le ieune Demetrius, grand duc de Moscovie . . ., ed. Prince Augustin Galitzin (Avgust Petrovich Golitsyn), Paris, 1858.

45. National Assembly.

46. Martens, Recueil des traités, v. 13, p. XII; Rambaud, Recueil, v. 1, p. 19; cf. p. 161 N. 3.

47. In connection with this embassy, Martens speaks of the lack of common political interests between the two countries. His interpretation might have been different, though, if the French government had recognized existing chances. Recueil des traités, v. 13, p. VII.

48. According to Pierre Jeannin, the figures after 1618 may not be comparable with those before that date. For, a reform of the system of collecting dues in the Sound had been carried out in Denmark which reduced the amount of smuggling and led to more realistic figures in the records. Jeannin, "Les comptes du Sund," pp. 307 ff.

49. Heckscher, v. 2, p. 28; Georg Herzog zu Mecklenburg (Graf von Carlow), Richelieu als merkantilistischer Wirtschaftspolitiker und der Begriff des Staatsmerkantilismus. Beiträge zur Geschichte der Nationalökonomie, Jena, 1929;

Franklin Charles Palm, _The Economic Policies of Richelieu,_ Urbana, 1922 (University of Illinois Studies in the Social Sciences, v. 19, no. 4).

50. Mecklenburg, p. 180; cf. p. 190.

51. Dépot des mémoires et documents, vol. III, pièce 4, Affaires étrangères, Russie, cited by Rambaud, _Recueil,_ v. 1, p. 11.

52. Cf. Boris Fedorovich Porshnev, who in particular defends the view about a significant role played by Russia on the European state, " K voprosu o meste Rossii v sisteme evropeiskikh gosudarstv v XV-XVIII vv, " _Akademiia Obshchestvennykh Nauk,_ Uchenye zapiski, v. 2, Moscow, 1948.

53. _Mémoires du Cardinal de Richelieu,_ v. 10, Paris, 1910, p. 167.

54. Cf. the report from Persia by Lawrence Chapman. He found "nothing like to such as be brought into England out of other places: & the price is so high that smal gaine will be had in buying of them." "Better it is therefore in mine opinion to continue a beggar in England during life, then to remaine a rich Merchant seven yeeres in this Countrey." Hakluyt, v. 2, 1907, pp. 111-112 (Everyman's Library).

55. Rambaud, _Recueil_, pp. 22-23. Ever since the time of Ivan III, the Poles, though laying claim to providing the eastern bulwark of Catholicism, did their utmost to hinder the Catholization of Russia, lest this country be accepted as a full member of the European family of nations. They thereby sought to hinder also any alliance between Austria and Russia and keep the Austrian Habsburgs dependent upon their own alliance. This Richelieu, however, intended to break.

56. Richelieu, _Mémoires,_ v. 10, pp. 164-165. He was under the impression that ordinarily no more than two or three French ships per year made the voyage into the Baltic and that they sailed to Danzig.

57. Doneseniia frantsuzskikh poslannikov i povierennykh

v dielakh pri Russkom dvorie . . . 1681 po 1718 god (Sbornik imp. Russkago istoricheskago obshchestva, Vol. 34, 1880, pp. II-III; Rambaud, Recueil, v. 1, pp. 23 ff.; Richelieu, Mémoires, v. 10, pp. 413 ff.

58. M-yev, passim; Martens, Recueil des traités, v. 13, pp. XIX-XXI; cf. the report of an official of the Ministry of Foreign Affairs, (Nicolas Louis) Le-Dran, Traités d'entre la France et la Moscovie, 1613-1717. -Mémoire sur les negociations entre la France et le czar . . . Pierre I . . . 1719-1722, in: Sbornik imp. russkago istor. obshchestva, vols. 34, 40, and 49 (1881, 1885). Alexander Brueckner, "Aktenstücke zur Geschichte der Beziehungen zwischen Russland und Frankreich, 1681-1718," in: Russische Revue, vols. 22 and 23, St. Pbg., 1883.

59. Henri Pigeonneau, Histoire du commerce de la France, 2 vols., Paris, 1885-1897, v. 2, p. 441.

60. J. Chailley-Bert, Les compagnies de colonisation sous l'ancien régime, Paris, 1898, pp. 22-23.

61. Haumant, p. 8.

62. Brueckner, "Aktenstücke," p. 2.

63. Haumant, p. 5.

64. Križanić, a Serb, as cited by Alexander Brueckner, Culturhistorische Studien v. II: Die Ausländer in Russland im 17. Jahrhundert, Riga, 1878, pp. 23 ff.

65. Brueckner, "Aktenstücke," p. 310.

66. Haumant, p. 5.

Chapter VI

1. Sven Svennson, Den merkantile backgrunden till Rysslands anfall på livländska ordensstaten, Lund, 1951, p. 98.

2. Goetz Frhr. v. Pölnitz, Fugger und Hanse, pp. 185

ff.; about other financial negotiations, cf. same, *Jakob Fugger: Kaiser, Kirche und Kapital in der oberdeutschen Renaissance*, 2 vols., Tübingen, 1949-52, v. 2, 282.

3. Cf. Goetz, *Handelsgeschichte*; also introduction to Otto Blümcke, *Berichte und Akten der Hansischen Gesandtschaft nach Moskau im Jahre 1603*, Halle, 1894 (Hansische Geschichtsquellen, v. 7).

4. Eck, pp. 372, 471.

5. Pierling, *La Russie et le Saint-Siège*, v. 1, p. 131.

6. Walther Kirchner, "Über den russischen Aussenhandel zu Beginn der Neuzeit," in: *Vierteljahrschrift für Sozial-und Wirtschaftsgeschichte*, v. 42 (1955).

7. Philipp Carl Strahl, *Geschichte des russischen Staates*, 2 vols., Hamburg, 1832-39, v. 1, p. 540. Also Mickwitz, p. 117.

8. Conditions in neighboring Livonia may lend themselves to enlightening comparisons. Cf. Vilho Niitemaa, *Der Binnenhandel in der Politik der livländischen Städte im Mittelalter*, Helsinki, 1952 (Academia Scientiarum Fennica, Annales, ser. B., vol. 76, pt. 2).

For the varied activities of the Stroganov, cf. Andrei Aleksandrovich Vvedenskii, *Dom Stroganovykh v XVI-XVII vekakh*, Moscow, 1962, pp. 156 ff.

9. Staden, *Aufzeichnungen*, pp. 126 ff.; Jens Andreas Friis, *Klosteret i Petschenga. Skildringer fro russisk Lapland*, *Kristiania*, 1884.

10. Eck, pp. 161 ff.

11. Mikhail Ivanovich Tugan-Baranowsky, *Geschichte der russischen Fabrik*, Berlin, 1900 (Sozialgeschichtliche Forschungen. Ergänzungshefte zur Zeitschrift für Social- und Wirtschaftsgeschichte, Nos. 5 and 6), p. 6.

12. *Acta Tomiciana*, v. 9, p. 225.

13. Piotr I. Lyashchenko (Petr Ivanovich Liashchenko), *History of the National Economy of Russia to the 1917 Revolution*, New York, 1949, pp. 224 ff. Erik Amburger, "Zur Geschichte des Grosshandels in Russland, die gosti," *Vierteljahrschrift für Sozial-und Wirtschaftsgeschichte*, v. 46, 1959, pp. 248-261.

14. Lyashchenko, pp. 207, 218 ff.

15. Hakluyt, v. 3, p. 95.

16. A. S. Muliukin, *Ocherki po istorii juridicheskago polozheniia inostrannykh kuptsov v Moskovskom gosudarstve*, Odessa, 1912 (Novoross. Universitet, Juridicheskii fakul'tet, *Zapiski*, v. 8).

17. Kulischer, pp. 355 ff., points out that all prescriptions and restrictions were regularly circumvented. Evidence confirms his view.

18. Dmitrii Vladimirovich Tsvetaev, *Protestantstvo i protestanty v Rossii do epokhi preobrazovanii*, Moscow, 1890.

19. Bang, *Tabeller øver Skibsfart*.

20. Constantin Mettig, "Die Exportwaren des russisch-hanseatischen Handels," *Gesellschaft für Geschichte und Altertum der Ostseeprovinzen Russlands*, Riga, Sitzungsberichte, 1904, pp. 93 ff.

21. Elena F. Tsereteli, *Elena Ioannovna, velikaia kniaginia litovskaia*, St. Pbg., 1898, p. 13.

22. Staden, *Aufzeichnungen*, p. 227.

23. Benjamin Cordt (V. A. Kordt), "Ocherk snoshenii Moskovskago gosudarstva . . . .".

24. Adelung, v. 1, p. 186.

25. Joseph Fiedler, "Nikolaus Poppel," *Sitzungsberichte der Wiener Akademie, Philosophisch-historische Classe*, v. 22, Wien, 1857; Ludwig Petri, *Die Popplau*, Breslau, 1935.

26. Ludmilla (Buketoff) Turkevich, *Cervantes in Russia*, Princeton, 1950, p. 3.

27. See chapter 5.

28. Thomas Stuart Willan, "Trade between England and Russia in the second half of the sixteenth Century," English Historical Review, v. 63, 1948, pp. 307-321.

Chapter VII

1. This study is based on documents found in the Archives Nationales of Paris (cited as A. N.).

2. Sergey Rodjestvensky (Rozhdestvenskii) and Inna Ivanova L(i)ubimenko, "Contributions à l'histoire des relations commerciales franco-russes au XVIIIe siècle," Revue d'histoire économique et sociale, vol. 17, 1929, pp. 362-402.

3. Paul M. Bamford, Forests and French Sea Power, 1660-1789, Toronto, 1956.

4. Bamford has used mainly the Archives de la Marine (Paris), series B I, B III, B VII, and D III. A doctoral dissertation (unpubl.) by Frank Fox at the University of Delaware, based on the series "Affaires étrangères" and "Commerce," deals with the entire and over-all problem of Franco-Russian economic relations.

5. Earlier Russian offers to the French had come to naught. In particular, the negotiations of 1668 had collapsed because the French had demanded too far-reaching privileges. Pashkov-Letiche, p. 221.

6. A. N., Af. Et., B III-474, 19 November 1705. Unless otherwise stated, all the manuscripts here cited belong to the Archives nationales. I wish to express my gratitude and thanks to the directors and aides of the archives for the kindness they have shown and the help they have given me during my work there.

7. A. N., F 12, 58, fol. 131, 153.

8. A. N. Marine, B VII-475, C 53, N[o] 22. "In general, it appears that the most potent item of economic policy was war," writes Raymond William King Hinton in his study of British

policies (The Eastland Trade and the Common Weal in the Seventeenth Century, Cambridge, England, 1959, p. 163).

9. A. N., Af. Et., B I-982 (5 September 1718), B I-984 (11 September 1730).

10. A. N., F 12, 58, fol. 153; Af. Et., B I-982 (22 August 1717); 983 (1724); 985 (28 June 1731); Marine, B VII-441 (23 August 1779).

11. Much later, in January 1786, the possibility of Franco-Spanish cooperation was investigated anew. It was proposed by the Spanish side, with the aim of combating in this way the "slavery" which Britain imposed on all others.

12. Cf. Pashkov-Letiche, p. 224, regarding the New Commercial Code of 1667 which sought "to prevent the export of precious metals . . . [by] provisions against the purchase of luxury goods."

13. A. N., F 12, 1427 (1750), "Harmonie du Commerce;" F 12, 622 (15 December 1757), Marine B VII-402, "Analise" B VII-425 (31 October 1765); B VII, 457; C 53 (N° 22), F 12-622 Traité de 1787. P. Coquelle (L'alliance franco-hollandaise contre l'Angleterre, 1735-1788, Paris, 1902) speaks of the bad faith shown by the British around 1782. He writes: "Les offres de George III étaient illusoires et ses intentions louches." (p. 266).

14. A. N., Af. Et., B I, 987 (January 1768); Marine, B VII-426 (23 October 1767).

15. Six per cent export taxes, 5 per cent commission, 12 per cent for packing and loading at the port of departure, 8 per cent insurance; 2 per cent Sound dues; 6 per cent maritime risks; 42 per cent customs dues in Russia.

16. A. N. Marine, B VII-261 (5 May 1726); Af. Et., B I-985 (25 March 1731); Marine, B VII-457 (1744); Af. Et., B I-986 (24 June 1745); Marine, B VII-414 (7 May 1760); B VII-425 (31 March 1766); Af. Et., B I-988 (15 September 1788).

17. A. N., B I-982 (years 1716-1717).

18. A. N., Af. Et., B I-983 (28 November 1723); Marine, B VII-261 (5 May 1726); B I-989 (2 October 1786).

19. A. N., F 12, 54, fol. 153 f.; Af. Et., B I-982 (30 August 1716), F 12-622 (15 December 1757) passim.

20. A. N., Af. Et., B I-986 (14 August 1745). Cf., however, the statistics given below which indicate that in many years after 1747 adverse trade balances resulted.

21. A. N., F 12-644; proposals by Lille and Dunkerque in 1703; Af. Et., B I-989, fol. 385-396; Marine, B VII-431 (29 July 1771); F 12-58, fol. 153 (1713); Af. Et., B I-983 (September 1724); F 12-63, fol. 114 (1718); F 12-80 (29 October 1733).

22. A. N., F 12-58, fol. 153 (1713); Marine, B VII-261 (5 May 1726), Af. Et., B I-982 (23 October 1716-22 August 1717); F 12-622 (15 December 1757); Af. Et., B I-988 (15 September 1778).

23. A. N., Af. Et., B I-987 (29 May 1759); Marine, B VII-425 (17 February 1766). Moreover, many categories of merchandise which had not been mentioned at all in earlier Russian customs tariffs were, beginning with 1757, subjected to rather high duties.

24. Villardeau alleged at that time that during the preceding twenty years not even a twentieth of the import duties prescribed by law had actually been paid. He considered this, however, an advantage especially for Russia because of the otherwise prohibitive character of the duties. He likewise tells in connection with the police raid that the government extended an amnesty to those merchants who paid the owed duties. But like the other members of the foreign colony in St. Petersburg (who sent a protest to the empress), he bitterly complained against the imposition of capital punishment not only on those who in the future would be found guilty of fraud, but even on those who failed to denounce those who had defrauded the government. Af. Et., B I-985 (10 May and 24 May 1732).

25. Af. Et., B I-983 (June 1724); B I-984 (29 July 1725; 21 January 1727), F 12-622 (15 December 1757); Af. Et., B I-988 (15 September 1778); Marine, B VII-427 (4 November 1760).

26. Af. Et., B I-982 (22 August 1717); B I-983 (29 October 1723).

27. Af. Et., B I-984 (August 1727).

28. Af. Et., B I-474 (7 October 1716); B I-982 (13 November 1716). No figures in the Russian statistics of the time can be relied upon because of the extent of the corruption in the customs service. Marine, B VII-402 (10 October 1758); B I-988 (27 August 1776); (15 September 1778). See above, note 2.

29. Af. Et., B I-987 (9 May 1769, 27 July 1770, 26 February 1771); B I-988 (30 September 1773); Marine, B VII-431 (29 July 1771).

30. Rodjestvensky and L(i)ubimenko, "Contributions . . ."; Rambaud, Recueil.

31. F 12-51 (1706), fol. 402; Af. Et., B III-432 (1761); B I-987 passim; K 1308 (1787).

32. Af. Et., B I-983 (1722-1723). A large number of Lavie's reports is printed in Doneseniia frantsuzskikh poslannikov . . . 1681 po 1718 god (see above Ch. V, note 57) and Diplomaticheskaia perepiska frantsuzskikh poslannikov i agentov pri Russkom dvorie 1719-1723 (Sbornik imp. Russkago istor. obshchestva, v. 34, 1880, and 40, 1884).

33. Af. Et., B I-983 passim.; Marine, B VII-175, p. 548 (2 September 1743).

34. Marine, B VII-175, p. 144; Af. Et., B I-986 (November 1743); Marine, B VII-457 ("Mémoire sommaire").

35. The Marquis de la Chétardie, who between 1740 and 1742 had supported the cause of the Tsarevna Elizabeth, was ordered to leave St. Petersburg within 24 hours on June 17, 1744, when Empress Elizabeth was informed of the disrespectful

remarks he had made about her in his official correspondence. Behind his ouster was the Vice Chancellor Bestuzhev-Riumin, whose pro-English and anti-French policy he, in concert with Prussia and Sweden, had opposed.

36. For biographies of Lavie, Villardeau, La Chétardie, d'Alion and the other French consuls and diplomats and for their political activities, cf. Rambaud, Recueil.

37. Af. Et., B I-989 (24 April 1788).

38. Jakob Fries, Eine Reise durch Sibirien im achtzehnten Jahrhundert. Die Fahrt des Schweizer Doktors Jakob Fries, ed. Walther Kirchner, München, 1955 (Veröffentlichungen des Osteuropa-Instituts München, v. 10).

39. Af. Et., B I-987, 988, 989, passim. It was Peter the Great who, as he did in connection with the establishment of Russian consulates in France, took the first steps. According to a report by Villardeau of September 1724, the tsar sent a man to France who was eventually to become Russian consul, but whose initial task consisted in studying the country and in reporting what interesting chances it might offer for Russian overseas trade. Villardeau feared, however, that if a Russian merchant marine were created, it would deprive France of the trade. He therefore gave the cunning advice that when Russian ships arrived in French ports, they should be received there as they were by the Dutch. These were supposed to extend to them a nice welcome but to make their stay so costly by delaying their departure and by offering so little merchandise for sale that the Russians were discouraged from coming again (Af. Et., B I-983). It seems that the Spaniards acted in the same way: when a Russian ship arrived in Cadiz in 1726, business for it was so poor that the whole undertaking cost the Russians half of their capital (Af. Et., B I-984). A certain "Jean Alexioff" became consul in Bordeaux on February 11, 1725 (Af. Et., B III-474). S. Rodjestvensky and I. L(i)ubimenko, "Contributions . . .", p. 474. Instructions for First

Lieutenant Alexeev in Polnoe Sobranie Zakonov, VII (1830), p. 143, No. 4341.

40. MS., Longwood Library (now Eleutherian Mills Hagley Library, Wilmington, Del.), Henry Francis Du Pont, Collection Winterthur. A copy in Paris (A. N., Af. Et., B I-988, 1780-1790). None of the copies has a date or a signature, but that in the Longwood Library shows a note "par M. Le Gendre." A handwritten note on a letter sent, together with many other enclosures, by Lesseps to Marshal de Castries on February 19, 1784, mentions an "Extrait des articles soulignés pour M. Du Pont le 25 avril 1784" (Af. Et., B I-989, fol. 89). The Du Pont in question is the well known physiocrat Samuel Du Pont de Nemours, who later moved to the United States where his family founded the Du Pont powder mills. The contents indicates that the mémoire, which is 329 pages long, must have been written between August 1782 and November 1785. It is possible that the information contained in it came from Raimbert. In that case, it is likely that Raimbert had written his report in the second half of 1783 and addressed it to a "M. Le Gendre," who in turn would have sent it in November 1783 to the minister. A copy was perhaps addressed to de Lesseps, who was not on very good terms with Raimbert. I wish to express my thanks to the Librarian of the Longwood Library, Dr. David, and to Mrs. Windell, of the same library, who have directed my attention to this mémoire and have aided me in my work.

41. F 12, 58, fol. 153 (1713); Af. Et., B I-982 (October 1713); Marine, B VII-261 (1713); Af. Et., B I-983 (September 1724); B I-989, fol. 361 (1780). However, the same author who in 1780 advocated "Liberty, Equality (and) Free Competition" asked in 1786 to be appointed sole agent for all purchases of the numerous Russian goods which could be shipped by way of the Black Sea (Marine, B VII-448, April 3, 1786). For the attacks which were made in England against all privileged

companies and in favor of free trade, beginning in the early seventeenth century, cf. Hinton, p. 56. A study of British methods is often recommended by the numerous French mémoires, as for instance in F 12-622 (15 December 1757).

42. Marine, B VII-402 (26 November 1758); Af. Et., B III-432 (April 1758); B I-989 (29 September 1786-29 March 1788); F 12-2427 "Harmonie du commerce."

43. The customary French export goods—those described by Campredon as best suited for the Russian market—were wine, champagne, brandy, indigo, alum, almonds, raisins, glassware, paper, syrup, olive oil, sweets, sugar, dresses, dress materials, silk, woven materials with gold threads. Russia's customary export goods consisted in wax, hemp, tallow, linen, potash, leather, furs, skins, iron, grain, timber. See below and appendix C.

44. See below, chapter 8.

45. F 12-622 (15 December 1757); Af. Et., B I-988 (15 September 1778); B I-987 *passim*, B II-425 and 432 *passim*, B I-985 (25 March 1731).

46. Af. Et., B I-988 (15 September 1778); F 12-622 (15 December 1757).

47. Af. Et., B I-982 (9 July 1716); B III-432 (27 August 1743), F 12-58, fol. 153; Af. Et., B I-987 (April 1758), F 12-622 (15 December 1757).

48. Marine, B VII-261 (5 May 1726), B VII-431 (29 July 1771), B VII-465, I; Af. Et., B I-989 (fol. 385-396). See the recommendation of the Chamber of Commerce of La Rochelle in favor of larger ships in Émile Garnault, *Le commerce rochelais au XVIIIe siècle*, La Rochelle, 1900, v. 5, p. 152.

49. See Chapter 8.

50. See note 40.

51. Marine, V VII-412 (8-19 April 1759), B VII-425 (28 February 1766); Af. Et., B I-988 (15 September 1778), B I-989 (1781); Marine, B VII-465-I *passim*. Regarding

negotiations with Turkey, see F. Charles Roux, "La monarchie française d'ancien régime et la question de la mer Noire," Revue de la Mediterranée, v. 23, 1948, pp. 271-276, 394-409. There existed even a "Project to permit the transit of French wines by way of the Black Sea to Russia and Poland." Dated June 18, 1745, it proposed the establishment of a system of dues in the Bosphorus so that Turkey would receive the same dues there which wine coming from Russia and other Northern countries had to pay in the Sound.

52. Besides the already cited reports, still others bear on the same subject, as for instance: Af. Et., B II-432; Marine, B VII-457; Marine, B VII-441; as well as F 12.

53. Marine, B VII-261 (5 May 1726).

54. F 12-51, fol. 37, 67 (1701); 332 (1705); F 12-54, fol. 45 (1707); Af. Et., B I-982 (October and November 1713).

55. Marine, B VII-261 (1713); Af. Et., B I-982 (22 February 1715); F 12-58, fol. 153; F 12-59, fol. 147 (1713-1716); Af. Et., B I-983 (28 November 1723). Cf. also Rambaud, Recueil, v. 2, p. 431.

56. Af. Et., B I-987 (around 1760 and 28 February 1757); B III-432 (January 1757 passim); Marine, B VII-425 (17 February 1766).

57. F 12-94, p. 211; Af. Et., B I-986 (25 February 1747).

58. Af. Et., B I-982 (22 February 1715); B I-986 (24 and 26 December 1747).

59. With regard to Michel, who from time to time was employed also for diplomatic missions, and who made a trip to France in 1758 in order to negotiate with the tax farmers about import taxes for Russian tobacco (Af. Et., B I-987, April 1758), cf. Rambaud, Recueil, v. 2, p. 28 and passim; and Rodjestvensky and L(i)ubimenko, "Contributions . . .", p. 391.

60. Raimbert's own estimate in 1767 was that in the period from 1765 on he had shipped by sea French goods to the value of about three million livres. He furthermore stated

that he employed five French apprentices so that at least a few Frenchmen would gain the necessary understanding for Russian conditions. In order to increase his purchases, he offered to buy grain to be shipped from Le Havre in the following years. But he confessed that in order to be able to carry out this operation he needed credit.

61. Af. Et., B I-988 (1778), Observations. Lesseps lists in this document the French firms which existed in St. Petersburg.

62. Af. Et., B I-987 (6 December 1765), B I-988, Observations (1778 and 17 February 1781).

63. Regarding the Compagnie des Indes, see above, note 50. Also Rodjestvensky and Lubimenko, p. 373. Regarding Anthoine, see his own writings: Baron de Saint-Joseph Anthoine (Antoine Ignace), Essai historique sur le commerce et la navigation de la Mer-Noire, Paris, 1805. See also his correspondence, Af. Et., B I-989, fol. 361-384 passim and Marine, B VII-448 (1773-1786). For a very favorable judgment of Anthoine, see Weber, Die Russen, ed. Hans Halm, pp. 164-168.

64. F 12-74, fol. 648; F 12-75, p. 738; F 12-78, p. 476 and 510-512; F 12-84, p. 491; F 12-98, p. 285; F 12-75, p. 962; Af. Et., B I-984 (16 June 1728). Roquette submitted to Villardeau also a letter in which he informed him of his discoveries and views "regarding the cosmos and place of the earth." He hoped to receive a prize from the Academy for his discoveries. (Af. Et., B I-985, 15 July 1732).

65. Af. Et., B I-474 (18 January 1718); Lavie, letter of 10 November 1718; Michel (letter 1760); Marine, B VII-414; Af. Et., B I-986 (16 November 1745).

66. See chapter 10.

67. Ibid.

68. See chapter 9.

69. F 12-51, fol. 326; F 12-54, fol. 264; Af. Et., B I-982 (3 April 1713), K 1352 (1716); B I-474 (29 August

1716 and 21 November 1718); B I-480 (15 May 1777); B I-989 (7 May 1784).

70. Bang, Tabeller øver skibsfart. The Sound Dues Tables have been subjected to ample and well founded criticism by numerous scholars, such as Astrid Friis, Axel E. Christensen, and Pierre Jeannin (see also Tabeller, Avant-propos, relevés 1661-1783, v. 1, pp. x-xv). However, Professor Jeannin seems to go much too far in his communication at the XIth International Congress of Historical Sciences (Stockholm, 1960); see its printed printed resumé in the Report of the Congress, pp. 137-139.

71. Af. Et., B I-983 (10 May 1720); Marine, B VII-261 (5 May 1726); Af. Et., B III-432 (1728). See appendix A.

72. F 12-643, "Tableau général . . . par l'arrêté du Conseil." See the commentary of Ruggiero Romano with regard to the "trade balance" of France in Studi in Onore di Armando Sapori, 2 vols., Milan, 1957, v. 2 ("Documenti e prime considerazioni intorno alla "Balance du Commerce" della Francia dal 1716 al 1780") pp. 1265-1299 (table quoted: p. 1288).

73. The Sound Dues Tables show for this period substantial figures for French ships: up to 50 ships per year coming from Riga, up to nine from Narva, and up to 43 from St. Petersburg. According to the tables, the number of English ships was from three to five times as high (see the curve in appendices A and B).

74. See note 65.

75. F 12-622; Appendix B.

76. Marine, B VII-426.

77. F 12-643; F 12-243, 244 and 245. A detailed official list for the traffic in 1775 is given in Appendix C. Cf also the export figures from Bordeaux in Theophile Malvezin, Histoire du commerce de Bordeaux, 4 vols., Bordeaux, 1872, v. 3, p. 218. According to Heinrich Storch (Historisch-statistisches Gemälde des Russischen Reichs am Ende des achtzehnten Jahrhunderts, 8 vols., Leipzig, 1797-1802, v. 4,

p. 25) the exports from the port of St. Petersburg for France amounted in 1773 to 260.000 rubles (11 ships) and in 1774 to 346.000 rubles (18 ships).

78. Af. Et., B I-988 (26 December 1773).

79. Af. Et., B I-988 (27 August 1776); the Baltic ports thus handled about 86.5 per cent of the exports and 96.25 per cent of the imports.

80. F 12-242. The customs offices of Chalons, Amiens, and Marseille likewise are mentioned, though in other years. Le Havre is mentioned by Storch, v. 6, p. 25, who calls it the most important port for the commerce with Russia.

81. F-12-251; F 12-250; F 12-1835; F 12-243, 244. The average for the years 1787 to 1789, that is for the last three years before the revolution, amounts to 6.849.000 livres for imports on 20 French, 16 Russian, 4 English, 31 Dutch, and 44 ships of other nations. Exports amounted to 6.523.000 livres, carried in 11 French, 11 Russian, 3 English, 10 Dutch, and 15 ships of other nations. The tonnage of the French ships which were engaged in the Franco-Russian trade amounted to one ninth of the corresponding tonnage of all the other nations combined. F 12-252, fol. 125. See also Benedikt Franz Johann (von) Hermann, Statistische Schilderung von Russland, St. Pbg., 1790, pp. 426 and 445.

82. F 12-243, 244; Marine, B VII-457; C 53 No 22; Af. Et., B I-485 (19 September 1780); Marine, B VII-451 (commerce via Archangel, 1784); F 12-1835.

83. Af. Et., B I-989 (29 January 1786).

84. For example, Eduard Winter, Die deutsch-russische Begegnung und Leonhard Euler (Quellen und Studien zur Geschichte Osteuropas, v. 1, Berlin, 1958).

85. Af. Et., B-982 (3 April 1713), B I-985 (13 February 1731).

86. On December 3, 1771, Prince Golitsyn charged Diderot with the purchase of these paintings. The sale was

carried out on January 4, 1772. The sales contract (L III-482 and L XXIII-935) has recently been on exhibit in Paris.

87. T 319-4 and 5 (24 May 1787).

88. Rodjestvensky and L(i)ubimenko, "Contributions . . ." (p. 385) cite, however, the opinion that "the Russians can as little forego our wines as we their raw materials."

Chapter VIII

1. The tobacco issue has recently caught the attention of two historians, but only insofar as Russian imports of American tobacco, and not the export of Ukrainian tobacco, was concerned. Cf. Jacob M. Price, _The Tobacco Adventure to Russia. Enterprise, Politics, and Diplomacy in the Quest for a Northern Market for English Colonial Tobacco, 1676-1722_, Philadelphia, 1961 (American Philosophical Society, Transactions, N.S. vol. 51, pt. 1); and Alfred W. Crosby jr., "The Beginnings of Trade between the United States and Russia," in: _The American Neptune_, v. 21, 1961, pp. 207-215.

2. Marbault, _Essai sur le Commerce de Russie avec l'histoire de ses découvertes_, Amsterdam, 1777, who coined the phrase that the Russians know something about trade and nothing about commerce, mentions Ukrainian tobacco and briefly deals (pp. 152-153) with its export during Empress Elizabeth's reign. Jean-Benoît Scherer, _Histoire raisonnée du commerce de la Russie_, 2 vols., Paris, 1788, makes (vol. 1, pp. 182-186) some remarks about Ukrainian tobacco. Anthoine, _Essai historique_ . . . , does not mention Raimbert's plans for Ukrainian tobacco, despite his extensive efforts to promote trade in the Black Sea region (cf. note 57). Paul M. Bamford likewise does not mention the trade in Ukrainian tobacco.

3. In Peter's times, tobacco plantations existed in "Circassia," in the eastern parts of the Ukraine, and in the

region of the lower Don. It had been forbidden, though, even under penalty of death, to expand the area of tobacco plantations or to ship tobacco from these to other regions of Russia, lest this interfere with the general fiscal policies of the tsar who envisaged a high revenue from the collection of customs dues on American tobacco. Price, pp. 28, 58.

4. Ibid., p. 22.

5. Peter Ivanovich Shuvalov (1711-1762), general and statesman, exercised a great, and at some times decisive, influence on the policies of Elizabeth. He never neglected his own financial interests and secured for himself various monopolies, including those of the export of timber and of fats. He died, leaving large debts. Neither the old Russian, nor the current Soviet Encyclopedia mention his tobacco interests.

6. Storch, v. 5, p. 390.

7. Re Raimbert and Michel, cf. Rambaud, Recueil, passim. Cf. Raimbert's "Mémoire" of 17/28 August 1757 in Anton Friedrich Büsching, ed., Magazin für die neue Historie und Geographie, vol. 9, Halle, 1775, pp. 131 f.

8. On January 24, 1758, the French consul in St. Petersburg, St. Sauveur, reported at length on the plans for the importation of Ukrainian tobacco into France. MSS., Paris, Archives nationales, Af. Et. B I-987.

9. The English house was that of Gomm. Gomm acted as banker of Catherine II during the early part of her reign. The firm achieved almost a monopoly in the northern timber trade and built ships for Russia. Cf. Dietrich Gerhard, England und der Aufstieg Russlands, München and Berlin, 1933, p. 67, note 108. William Gomm had paid 16.000 roubles for the export monopoly. Price, p. 94.

10. MSS., Paris, Af. Et., B III-432, 2 June 1758.

11. Ibid., Af. Et. B I-987.

12. Rodjestvensky and L(i)ubimenko, "Contributions . . .".

13. Aleksei Petrovich Bestuzhev-Riumin (1693-1766) was chancellor from 1744 to 1758 and actual director of all Russian foreign policies. He was pro-English and anti-French, and the reversal of alliances led to his downfall. His vice-chancellor, Michail Illarionovich Vorontsov, who was friendly to France, succeeded him (until 1763).

14. The amount of tobacco mentioned in the sources varies. In the previously cited mémoire of June 2, 1758, the author speaks of 300,000 poods or 10,000,000 pezant de feuilles; here, "100 Mille quintaux" are given. A third version is that of the French Consul St. Sauveur, who in his letter of October 10 speaks of only "20,000 Quintaux" for 1759 and the same quantity for 1760, at a value of 69,000 roubles. MSS. Paris, Af. Et., B VII-402, 22 April and 10 October. A "quintal" is equal to 100 lbs., a "pood" to 16,38 kg—ca. 40 Russ. lbs. — 32.76 Germ. lbs. —ca. 36 Engl. lbs.

15. MSS., Paris, F 12-622, 15 December 1757, submitted by Godin & Comp.

16. Ibid., Af. Et., B III—432, Mémoire sur les feuilles de Tabac d'Ukraine (1762).

17. Ibid., Af. Et., B III-432.

18. MSS., Paris, Af. Et., B I-987, 23 July 1758.

19. Cf. ibid., 23 August 1759; Marine B VII-402, "Annalise." Interesting plans with regard to the Black Sea route had been proferred as early as 1745. In a "Projet d'accorder le transit des vins de France par la mer noire pour Russie et Pologne" (MSS. Paris, Af. Et. B III-432, 18 June 1745), it was suggested that Turkey be paid the same dues which merchandise passing the Sound paid. It was, however, asked that the privilege of the passage of the Dardanelles be reserved for France and that ships should not be held up in Constantinople any longer than warranted for the sake of paying the dues. This proposal was intended as a blow to England, which did not ship perishable merchandise such as wine and, therefore,

should not be deemed to be entitled to equal advantages. As to tobacco, it should be noted that Turkey herself was an important producer. The quality of Turkish tobacco was far superior to that of Ukrainian tobacco.

20. MSS., Paris, Af. Et. B I—987, 5 July 1759.

21. MSS., Paris, Af. Et. B III-432, Mémoire, 1762. Early in the century, the English, in their turn, had sent men over to teach Russians—if not the methods of growing then those of manufacturing tobacco. They had even shipped over the necessary machinery. But protests against the transfer of new skills to Russia, which were bound to hurt the own trade of the English, led to the lawless destruction of the machinery in Moscow by the English diplomatic representative and his agents there. Price, p. 74, *passim*.

22. MSS., Copenhagen, Rigsarkiv, Sund Register, 1759, fols. 86, 89, 92. I wish to express my special thanks to Mr. Bro Jørgensen of the Rigsarkiv for his help and cooperation in tracing discrepancies between the original records and Bang, *Tabeller øver Skibsfart*. This publication contains no reference to any tobacco delivery at all for 1759 (cf. below, note 36); yet, there is no doubt about the shipments, for aside from their being entered in the original Sound records, the French correspondence of early 1760 (cf. MSS., Paris, Marine, B VII-414, Febr. 26, 1760) gives details which correspond to those of the original records.

23. MSS., Paris, AE. B III-432, Mémoire, October 1760. Cf. *ibid.* Marine B VII-414, 16 September 1760.

24. 8bre 1760. Mémoire sur les droits perçus au Sund sur les tabacs d'Ukraine en feuilles chargés à St. Petersbourg pour les ports de France dans les années 1759 & 1760. (Source: MSS. Paris, Archives nationales, Af. Et., B III - 432: for text see *Jahrbücher für Geschichte Osteuropas*, v. 10, 1962, pp. 510-512.)

25. "Zu Copenhagen: 1 Pfund = russ. 1 Pfund, 13 sol.,

52 Hund.; zu Paris: 1 Pfund = russ. 1 Pfund. 18 sol., 47 Hund." Hermann, p. 487.

26. Jean François Ogier d'Enonville (1702-1775) was French ambassador in Copenhagen from 1753 to 1766. He had formerly been a president of the parlement de Paris.

27. Wilhelm August von der Osten (1698-1764), son of Court Marshal Peter Christoph v. d. Osten, was director of finances 1743-1746 and director of the Øresund customs house 1738-1764. His cousin, Adolph Siegfried v. d. Osten, had been ambassador to Russia since 1755, where he had become involved in the difficulties which existed during the Seven Years War between Empress Elizabeth and Catherine, then grand-duchess. He had also had a hand in the intrigues between Catherine and Poniatowski. Although he was described in the instructions to the French ambassador to Russia, the Marquis de Bausset, as an "intrigant du premier ordre," he seems to have acted with tact in a difficult situation. Rambaud, Recueil, v. 2, pp. 240 ff.

28. E.g., 26 Febr. 1760; 29 May 1760; 9 and 29 June 1760; 15 July 1760; 22 Sept. 1760; 14, 23, 28 Oct. 1760; 27 Jan. 1761; 14 Febr. 1761; 15 Febr. 1762. MSS., Copenhagen, T.K.U.A., Alm. Afd. Realia, Litr. Ø, Øresundstolden, 1720-1770; and MSS., Paris, Marine B VII-402, 414, and B III-432.

29. Johan Hartvig Ernst Bernstorff (1712-1772) was born in Hanover, but from 1732 was in the Danish service. In 1751, he became foreign minister. A mercantilist, he took an active interest in trade affairs. His career was brought to an end by the famous Struensee in 1770.

30. MSS., Paris, Af. Et., B I-987; MSS. Copenhagen, T.K.U.A., Realia, Lit. Ø. The French argued that treaties made with Holland did by no means automatically apply to Russia. Raimbert had suggested that Russia complain directly to Denmark about the dues levied in the Sound. But nothing appears in the Copenhagen archives among the documents in

the Øresunds Toldkammerets Arkiv, 1729-1829, Russiske Varers, No. 22.

31. The printed Tabeller list a quantity of 900,584 lbs., shipped on Dutch ships from St. Petersburg to France. This figure is, however, not repeated, as is customary in this publication, under the total for St. Petersburg. In the original manuscript of the records of the Sound dues, we find, e.g., on fol. 81 a Vriesland skipper, Rein Goshes, who passed the Sound on August 3 on his way from St. Petersburg to Le Havre with a cargo of 321,007 lbs. of tobacco, for which he paid 58 1/2. 18 rigsdaler. In the same year, Polish tobacco was shipped from Danzig to Dieppe.

32. MSS., Copenhagen, T.K.U.A., Realia Ø. Øresundstollen, 1720-1770.

33. Ibid., 14 October 1760.

34. Cf. enclosure to mémoire of October, MSS. Paris, Af. Et., B III-432.

35. This was in line with a suggestion to the cultivators that the lower leaves of the plants should be cut off to improve the upper ones, and that these should not be cut off too early.

36. MSS., Paris, Af. Et., B III-432.

37. Zollkämmerer of Helsingfors to Count Bernstorff, January 4, 1768. (Source: MSS., Copenhagen, Rigsarkiv, Øresunds Toldkammerets Arkiv, 1729-1829. Russiske Varers. 5 Bind, No. 22: for text see Ibid., p. 512.)

38. MSS., Paris, Af. Et., B III-432, "sur les droits du Sund."

39. The mémoire confirms, in a subsequent paragraph, the figures here given by indicating that in the course of three years a total of 3 million pezant was furnished to the tax farmers. On the other hand, the Tabeller by Nina Bang et al. shows no entry whatsoever for Russian tobacco shipments to France in 1761. We thus are once more confronted with the problem of the validity of the Sound Dues Tables, both the Tabeller as

published and the original records preserved in Copenhagen. They differ considerably (cf. also above, note 22 and below, notes 47 and 48).

As to the year 1761, while the Tabeller show no tobacco shipments from St. Petersburg to French harbors, the original records (Øresundstold Regnskaber 1761—Bluhme and Puttscher) show four (Dutch) ships which sailed from St. Petersburg to France. Two are entered under Nos. 449 and 450 (p. 104) of October 6, both being destined for Bordeaux, carrying a total of 475,120 lbs. of tobacco, and paying 890 Rdl. in dues; two others can be found under entries 367 (p. 101) and 388 (p. 104) of September 28 and October 11 respectively, destined for "Morlaix" and Bordeaux and carrying 668,320 lbs. of tobacco and paying 1,253 Rdl. in dues. The total agrees well with the indications about shipments made in the French mémoire here mentioned. (I owe the information about these figures to Professor Heinz Ellersieck of the California Institute of Technology, to whom I herewith extend my special thanks.)

Unfortunately, the figures known to us from the records of St. Petersburg cannot serve well as a check for those to be found in the Sound records. Contemporary observers are unanimous in exposing the incorrectness of all customs declarations in Russia. French merchants have gone so far as to state that out of twenty roubles due to the Russian authorities, up to nineteen were never collected because of fraudulent declarations (MSS., Paris, Af. Et., B I-985, 1732. Cf. B I-988 for 1776 and 1778). See chapter 7.

40. MSS., Paris, Marine, B VII-424, 13 Jan. 1766. Grigorii Nikolaevich Teplov (1711-1779), who was also a musician and a writer, was an official who became assistant to Empress Elizabeth's brother-in-law, K. G. Razumovskii. Cf. above p. 183. In 1763, together with V. A. Gudovich he secured a tobacco monopoly for the Ukraine. He contributed to the improvement of the culture of tobacco there and in 1765 even published a book on the planting of tobacco.

41. Storch, v. 2, p. 338. William Tooke (A View of the Russian Empire during the Reign of Catherine II and to the Close of the Present Century, 3 vols., London, 1799), however, gives for the ukase the date of December 11, 1763.

42. MSS., Paris, Marine B VII-425.

43. Ibid., Marine B VII-427, 29 May 1768. According to Pavel Vladimirovich Bezobrazov, O snosheniiakh Rossii s Frantsiei (Moscow, 1892, p. 337) a Russian ship, Nadezhda Blagopoluchiia, sailed on August 11, 1764, from Kronstadt to Livorno, her cargo including tobacco.

44. Büsching, v. 9, p. 165.

45. Storch, v. 6, p. 119.

46. MSS., Copenhagen, Øresunds Toldkammerets Arkiv, Russ. Varers, Nos. 31-33 (1780-1781), February 25, 1780.

47. Ibid, Øresundstold Regnskaber 1779, vol. II. The two ships paid a total of 1,173 Rdl. in dues. (I owe also these figures to the kindness of Professor Ellersieck.) Bang's Tabeller for the years 1777 to 1779 contain not a single tobacco shipment from Russia.

48. MSS., Copenhagen, Statement prepared for Bernstorff, February 25, 1780, Øresunds Toldkammerets Arkiv, Russ. Varers, Nos. 31-33 (1780-1781). Out of the total for the three years 1777-1779 of 17,360,692 lbs., cargoes amounting to 14,074,778 were destined for Holland (as against the above mentioned 2,657,298 lbs. for France). Of course, the shipments refer not by any means only to Ukrainian tobacco but also to other tobacco, such as that from Turkey. Shipments, in addition to those from St. Petersburg, came from German ports and especially from Danzig, and also from Courland, Riga, Narva; a few came from Sweden.

49. Ibid., Ukr. Tobaksbl., Dept. f. u. A., Alm. Korr. Ø 15, Forhandlg. med Russland, 8 Febr. 1780. Cf. inquiries of government from customs office, ibid., 8 March, 14 March, 12 April 1780.

50. Ibid., 15 July 1780.

51. Ibid., 15 July 1780. According to the Tabeller, 1,499 Skpd. of tobacco were sent from St. Petersburg to France; another 1,070.4 Skpd. were shipped to the Netherlands and of these assuredly a substantial part had ultimately also reached France. In addition, there had been a number of small shipments. The original records include for the same year, besides some small shipments, those of August 9 (34,358 lbs.) and of August 11 (206,127 lbs.) and one as late as December 16 (17,160 lbs.). The dues levied on these amounted to 45 1/2.9, 368 1/2 and 32.9 Rdl. respectively.

52. Karl Magnus von Sacken (1733-1811), Count since 1797; tutor of Alexander I's brother, Konstantin.

53. Marcus Gerhard Rosencrone (1738-1811) succeeded Bernstorff in 1780 as head of the Department of Foreign Affairs (until 1784). The policy followed in his time was one of cooperation with Russia.

54. Ibid., Ukr. Tobaksbl., 1781. Cf. the internal Danish correspondence of 17 August 1781, 22 August 1781, and the note of the Danish minister in St. Petersburg, 12 September 1781.

55. Ibid., Despatch to Schuhmacher, Danish resident in St. Petersburg, of 27 October 1781.

56. Article 6, 1: "Que le tabac en feuilles de Russie, connu en Europe sous le nom de tabac d'Ukraine, au passage du Sund ne payera à l'avenir que huit Stuvers pour dix pouds du poids de Russie." Danske Traktater, 1751-1800, Copenhagen, 1882, pp. 391-412, as quoted to me by Denmark's Rigsarkivar Svend Aakjaer. I herewith express my thanks to him. Cf. Storch, v. 6, p. 44 and v. 8, p. 19. Eight Stuvers were worth approximately one fifth of a silver rouble. Ibid., vol. 5, p. 402.

57. MSS., Paris, Af. Et., B I-989 (1780), fol. 370. For a rather positive estimate of Anthoine's role, which is often adversely judged by historians, cf. Halm, Habsburgischer

Osthandel, and J. P. B. Weber: Die Russen, ed. Halm, Anhang IV, pp. 164-168. Cf. above, p. 293 (note 63).

Chapter IX

1. Oct. 14, 1762. A. Jenny, "Leistungen und Schicksale der Russland-Schweizer," Glarner Geschichte in Daten, v. 3, Glarus, 1936, p. 219.

2. MSS., Bailiff of Lausanne to the Council of Geneva, Aug. 26, 1765, Geneva, Staatsarchiv (Archives cantonales), P. H. 4888, vol. 237 (1765).

3. They were first under the impression that they were to teach young ladies. Ibid. Later it developed that they were to be governesses of the young nobility of Imperial House of the Cadet Corps. MSS., Bern, Staatsarchiv, Russlandbuch A. Cf. Ernst Wagner, "Bern vereitelt Russlandgängerei," Berner Zeitschrift für Geschichte und Heimatkunde (1943).

4. The servants were to be hired at the wages of three rubles per month, one dress per year, and free board. If they behaved well, they received free return to their home in Switzerland after the expiration of their contract; otherwise they had to pay for the return trip themselves. If male lackeys, they were guaranteed four rubles per month, free board, and a suit per year.

5. Bülow had engaged no more than four ladies and eight servants. Bern, Staatsarchiv, Russlandbuch A.

6. Mayor of Bern to the Council of Geneva, Sept. 13, 1765, Geneva, Staatsarchiv, P. H. 4888, vol. 237.

7. Bülow to Councillors of Bern, Oct. 20, 1765, Bern, Staatsarchiv, Russlandbuch A.

8. Georges Morel, Les rapports économiques de la Suisse avec la Russie, Geneva, 1934, p. 87.

9. Bern, Staatsarchiv, Russlandbuch B.

10. Geneva, Staatsarchiv. Copies also in Bern, Aarau, and various cantonal archives.

11. Likewise a copy in the Geneva Staatsarchiv and in several others.

12. A dessiatine being about 2.7 acres, this meant from 25 to 200 acres.

13. MSS., Zurich, Staatsarchiv, Auswanderung nach Neu Russland, 1765-66. According to Morel (p. 20), the agents who brought colonists to Russia were promised by Catherine three per cent of the territories allotted to the colonists, provided they also recruited a contingent of voluntary soldiers and formed regiments.

14. Jacob Etterlin, Russland-Schweizer und das Ende ihrer Wirksamkeit, 2nd. ed., Leipzig and Zurich, 1938, p. 90.

15. E. Zeugin, Prattler Auswanderer im Osten Europas, Pratteln, 1938, p. 12.

16. The documentary evidence in Swiss archives is abundant. In 1495, for example, in the midst of an era when foreign mercenary service—a result of economic pressure—drained the manpower resources of the country, a law was passed prohibiting emigration from the country. Zurich, Staatsarchiv, Abschieds-Register 1494-98, B VIII, 82. At the beginning of the seventeenth century, when great poverty again prompted many to leave their homes, another law was passed. This time it was persuasive rather than prohibitive; special warnings were voiced against settling in Catholic lands, lest souls—persuaded to give up their Protestant faith—fall in damnation. Significantly, the authorities emphasized the need for definite practical steps for economic relief as the best measures to retain prospective emigrants. Zurich, Staatsarchiv, E I, 2, 1 and 2. As time went on, material considerations such as loss of feudal dues in case of emigration conflicted more and more with growing humanitarian views, and often the prohibitions and warnings were not enforced by local organs. This, combined with frequent bad experiences of many emigrants partly due to untrustworthy agents, led to an

increasingly vacillating attitude on the part of authorities. MSS., Basel, Staatsarchiv, Auswanderung A, passim.

Aside from emigration by whole groups, there occurred, of course, the emigration of numerous individuals who left for private motives. Cf., e.g., Fries.

17. A family meant husband, wife, and small children, or two adult men, or four adult women.

18. Bregenz, July 25, 1803, signed by G. v. Escher, Zurich, Staatsarchiv, K III, 338, 1, St. 1. Th. 1, No. 1.

19. Fribourg, Oct. 2, 1803, Rundschreiben des Landammann, Basel, Staatsarchiv, Auswanderung A, Allgemeines und Einzelnes, 1801-18.

20. Zurich, Staatsarchiv, Auswanderung, June, 1804.

21. MSS., Aarau, Staatsarchiv, Auswanderungen, I A, No. 5, Mar. 19, 1804. The right to citizenship implies—and still does imply—that even after generations of life abroad Swiss citizens or their descendants could return to their home canton, take up residence there, and claim benefits to which other citizens of the canton were entitled. This right has been of fundamental importance because it reduced the risks of emigration. It also furthered the settlement of Swiss in the United States, despite adverse reports of many who returned from there, disappointed with the opportunities, unable to make a living in the new world, and full of complaints and denunciations. This aspect has rarely been treated by American historians; in view of its sociological interest and the abundant documentary material available, it may well be worthy of consideration. In more recent times, the Bürgerrecht again played an important role when after the Soviet revolution hundreds of colonists decided to return to the homes of their ancestors.

22. Direktor von Muralt to the Justiz-und Polizei-Kommission, Zurich, Staatsarchiv, K III, 516, 1-2, fol. 93. An interesting, very modern point of view with regard to criminals was taken by the police of Basel-Land in 1883. They insisted

that America was too strict with regard to emigration and paid too much attention to the past of an immigrant instead of his physical and spiritual capacities. "Why should not a man dependent at home upon support from his canton be able in America to make his living as well as others, why not a condemned man become in a different atmosphere a useful member of human society?" MSS., Sept. 6, 1883, Liestal, Staatsarchiv Basellandschaft, Auswanderungsakten A, Allgem. u. Einzelnes.

23. Zurich, Staatsarchiv, K III, 388, 1 St. 1, Th. 1, No. 29.

24. Cf. ibid., 514, 4, 71 and 515, 3, 85.

25. Jakob Etterlin, Die ehemaligen Schweizerkolonien in Russland, Bern, 1945, p. 52. Cf. Leo Weisz, "Glarner in Russland," Neue Zürcher Zeitung, No. 1385 of July 24, 1932. In the same newspaper, Weisz published "Schweizer im Kaukasus," (No. 1681 of Aug. 31, 1930) and "Schweizer in Taurien," (No. 966 of May 21, 1931).

26. July 20, 1804, Zurich, Staatsarchiv, Auswanderung 1804.

27. Two reports (one of 1838?, the other of 1844) regarding the colony Zürichthal in Bern, Bundesarchiv, Auswärtiges, Handelskonsulate "St. Petersburg."

28. Ernest John Knapton, The Lady of the Holy Alliance. The Life of Julie de Krüdener, New York, 1939, p. 187.

29. Ibid., p. 188. Cf. Leo Weisz, "Schweizer im Kaukasus." The archives of the Basel Missionary Society contain valuable material on Russia which has so far been exploited essentially only in the field of religious history. Cf. Wilhelm Schlatter, Die Basler Mission, Basel, 1916; Anna Katterfeld, Felician von Zaremba. Ein Christuszeuge im Kaukasus, Stuttgart and Basel, 1939; Carl Friedrich Ledderhose, Leben und Wirken des Missionars Dr. Felician von Zaremba, Basel, 1882. Students of Russian social history can gather valuable material from the same sources if they use them for their specific purposes.

30. Mar. 2, 1816, Zurich, Staatsarchiv, K III, 342, 1, 23.

31. Special rules allowed Jews to secure transit visa through Poland.

32. Bezirksamt Lörrach to Kanton Basel, Jan. 2, 1817, Basel, Staatsarchiv, Auswanderung A, Allgemeines und Einzelnes, 1801-18.

33. If they had less than six hundred guilders they could get only a small estate sufficient to start a garden and have one cow. They had to make their living by hiring themselves out as day laborers. Those who had less than one hundred guilders could receive no land at all. "Bekanntmachung . . . für diejenigen die sich in Pohlen niederzulassen gedenken," Bern, Bundesarchiv, Verhandlungen auswärtiger Staaten mit den Bundesbehörden, Russland, No. 2174 (1814-24), fol. 125.

34. _Ibid._

35. Etterlin, _Russland-Schweizer_, pp. 68 ff.

36. Etterlin, _Die ehemaligen Schweizerkolonien in Russland_, p. 44.

37. Cf. Report of April, 1843, Bern, Bundesarchiv, Auswärtige Handelskonsulate, Odessa, No. 1977. According to the Swiss consul, the Germans, owing to their industry, were the most successful, and among them particularly the religious sects of Moravians and Mennonites.

38. Sept. 22, 1874, Political Department of Swiss Federation to Basel Stadt. Basel, Staatsarchiv. Cf. Zeugin, pp. 12 and 15.

39. One of the stipulations for Chabag colonists read: "Chacun des membres de la commune est tenu d'avoir un psaume et un catechisme pour chacun de ses enfants, plus une bible et une carabine pour sa famille." Zeugin, p. 30.

40. Apr. 18, 1832, Bern, Staatsarchiv, Manual des diplomats, Département No. 1, p. 268.

41. Apr. 28 to May 10, 1833, Bern, Bundesarchiv, Verhandlungen auswärtiger Staaten mit den Bundesbehörden,

No. 2176 (1833-48), fols. 4-7. The edict was communicated to the various cantons under "26 Heumonat 1834," cf. Aarau, Staatsarchiv, Russland, AA No. 1.

42. "Bekanntmachung über Vergünstigungen für ausländische Berg-und Hüttenarbeiter im Königreich Polen. 1837," Bern, Bundesarchiv, Verhandlungen auswärtiger Staaten mit den Bundesbehörden, No. 2176 (1833-48), fols. 51-53.

43. The arbitrariness in handling emigration permits is exemplified by a report of March 22, 1832, according to which the governor in Thun (canton Bern) refused to issue passports for emigrants to Russia. Bern, Staatsarchiv, Manual des diplomats, Département, No. 1, p. 222.

44. "8. Herbstmonat 1846," Basel, Staatsarchiv, Auswanderung A, 1819-47.

45. Aargau to the Grosser Rat, May 17, 1854, Basel, Staatsarchiv, Auswanderung A, 1854-63.

46. In April, 1843, the Swiss colony at Odessa, for example, numbered 150 to 200 persons, Bern, Bundesarchiv, Auswärtige Handelskonsulate, No. 1977. According to Morel (p. 15), there were about 1,670 Swiss residents in Russia in 1850, and 5,902 in 1897; between 1828 and 1915, about 7,000 Swiss emigrated to Russia. Ibid., p. 17.

47. Bern, Bundesarchiv, Auswanderung Russland, 1862. Further references to Michel's plans can be found in Bern, Staatsarchiv, Missiven-Buch, No. 43, pp. 315 and 449, under Apr. 24, 1863.

48. Oct. 1, 1878, Bern, Bundesarchiv, Auswanderung Russland, 1878.

49. Passport questions, i.e., the questions of admittance of foreigners, are in themselves worthy of more scrutiny. An entire volume dealing with them may be found in Basel, Staatsarchiv, Niederlassung R 12, Pässe nach Russland. Cf. Bern, Bundesarchiv, Auswärtiges, Handelskonsulate where an interesting description of the difficulties is given from Moscow,

under Oct. 16, 1843. Also the migration of individuals was severely hampered by regulations; but this type of migration—important for Switzerland and Russia with regard to officers, scientists, peasants, merchants, artisans, industrialists, cheese makers, etc.—calls for separate treatment in connection with the "Westernization" of Russia.

Chapter X

1. A recent valuable study of the effect of emigration on the home country is that of Warren Candler Scoville, _The Persecution of the Huguenots and French Economic Development_, Berkeley, 1960. The book shows the erroneousness of many assumptions with regard to the effects of Huguenot emigration, to which we had become accustomed. Altogether, we may be inclined to assume too much. This, in any case, has been suggested by René Gonnard, _Essai sur l'histoire de l'émigration_, Paris, 1928, who states, for instance, that contrary to general beliefs emigration does not always result in population losses; through the creation of new opportunities among those staying behind, it often serves to stimulate population growth. Likewise contrary to general assumptions, economic growth rather than decline has often resulted from the departure of even large numbers of enterprising citizens, for their absence stimulated others to develop enterprises which previously had little chance.

2. Alfred Vagts, _Deutsch-amerikanische Rückwanderung_, Heidelberg, 1960 (Jahrbuch für Amerikastudien, Beiheft No. 6).

3. Theodore Saloutos, _They Remember America: The Story of the Repatriated Greek-Americans_, Berkeley, 1956. On the basis of personal interrogation, Saloutos traces many "case histories"—a method which necessarily limits the scope of his investigation.

4. Is it possible to still find out—perhaps with the help

of surviving correspondence—what made so many emigrants prefer Russia to America? Was it chance, accident, misconception, or definite material advantages? To what extent did incidental considerations (such as fear of the dangers of the sea voyage) play a role?

5. Pierling, La Russie et le Saint-Siège, v. 1, pp. 317-359, and "Hans Schlitte," Revue des questions historiques, v. 19, 1898, pp. 202-210. It should be remembered, though, that at the same time, emigration also to colonies was restricted—even to Spaniards.

6. See chapter 9 of this book.

7. J. J. v. Justi in 1758, as cited by Renate Vowinckel, Ursachen der Auswanderung gezeigt an badischen Beispielen aus dem 18. und 19. Jahrhundert (Vierteljahrschrift für Sozial- und Wirtschaftsgeschichte, Beiheft 37, Stuttgart and Berlin, 1939), p. 32.

8. The unemployed and destitute miners in the region of the Harz mountains in Germany furnish an example of this category. MSS., Hannover, Des. 38 A., A5. Promemoria, 3 January 1756; ibid., Des. 47 II, Nr. 89. P.S. to a rescript addressed to Berghauptmann von Bülow, Hannover, 16 May 1757. To Professor Walther Mediger, Hanover, to whom I owe knowledge and transcripts of these documents, I herewith express my special thanks.

9. Vagts, p. 25. Gonnard, p. 148. It may be noted that in the 1890's, the tsarist government allowed the emigration of Jews or Dukhobors but did not allow their return.

10. Cf. Eugen von Philippovich, Auswanderung und Auswanderungspolitik in Deutschland, Leipzig, 1892 (Verein für Sozialpolitik, Schriften No. 52), p. 4.

11. Ibid., pp. 4, 56, 288.

12. MSS., Hannover, Cal. Br. Arch. Des. 23 b, Paket II, 1. Nr. 8, Auswanderung. Cf. Sammlung der Verordnungen . . . des Hannoverschen Staats, ed. Ernst Spangenberg, Han-

nover, 1819, v. 1, Nr. 893, pp. 340-41: Hannover den 1. May 1753. Signed: G. A. v. Münchhausen. Ibid., Nr. 453, p. 130, 26 September 1765. For the text of these documents, I owe special thanks to Professor Mediger.

13. Friedrich Karl Hüttig, Die pfälzische Auswanderung nach Ost-Mitteleuropa im Zeitalter der Aufklärung, Napoleons und der Restauration, Marburg, 1958 (Johann Gottfried Herder-Institut, Wissenschaftliche Beiträge zur Geschichte und Landeskunde Ost-Mitteleuropas, No. 31), pp. 50 ff. Ewald Schnitzer, Der Nationalgedanke und die deutsche Auswanderung nach den Vereinigten Staaten von Amerika in der ersten Hälfte des 19. Jahrhunderts, Dresden, 1935, p. 11. Very often, humanitarian reasons were given for the prohibitions; yet, occasionally, emigration was permitted in cases of the desperate home situation of a prospective emigrant.

For a view of Prussia's enlightened policies under Frederick the Great, so widely admired by his contemporaries and by posterity, in regard to emigration, cf. Briefe über die Auswanderung der Unterthanen besonders nach Russland, Gotha, 1770, p. 88. One of the anonymous correspondents, who gives the arbitrariness of princes as the chief reason for emigration, writes that in a well governed country no need exists for restrictive legislation. In "one such country he knows," only two people have decided to emigrate.

14. See chapter 9.

15. Gonnard, pp. 167 ff. The statement is not borne out by French reaction to the Russian appeals. Only a very small French colony ever existed in Moscow or St. Petersburg. Cf. chapter 7 of this book. K. Miller, Frantsuzskaiia emigratsiia i Rossiia v tsarstvovanii Ekateriny II, Paris, 1931, dealing exclusively with the revolutionary emigration, adds little to our investigation. On the other hand, (Joseph) Jean Hecht, in his fine study of the servants in eighteenth-century England, has indicated the large numbers of cooks, maids,

teachers, engravers who emigrated to England. The Domestic Servant Class in Eighteenth-Century England, London, 1956, pp. 44, 62, passim. (Also in: Smith College Studies in History, v. 40, Northampton, Mass., 1954.)

16. The emigration of people of the Catholic faith seems often to have been channelled via Hamburg. Cf. Hüttig, p. 37, who mentions that several thousand German Catholic families were awaiting in Hamburg embarkation to Russia.

17. Pingaud, pp. 80, 83.

18. Vowinckel, p. 68.

19. As cited by Schnitzer, p. 22.

Chapter XI

1. Samuel Bentham, born 1757, was the son of Jeremiah Bentham and his second wife. Apprenticed in 1770 to a master-shipwright of the Royal Dockyards at Woolwich, he began at the age of fifteen to submit proposals to the Navy Board for technical improvements. He studied naval sciences. In 1779 he left for Russia; in 1781-83 he was in Siberia, and in 1784-88 a lieutenant-colonel in southern Russia and the Crimea. He participated in the Turkish war, and in 1789-91 was colonel in the Ob' River region and on the Chinese frontier. He was made brigadier-general in the Russian army. In 1791 he returned to England and worked on technical inventions, helped to design his brother Jeremy's "Panopticon" for prisons, and in 1795 was appointed inspector-general of Naval Works. Bentham advocated changes in naval establishments, designed improvements for guns, machinery, and steam-dredging apparatus, and conducted chemical experiments. He was a critic of civil management of the Navy; combated corruption, abuses, waste, the system of appointments and education. In 1805-1807 he was on a futile mission to Russia, trying to organize the building of ships there for the use of the British Navy. In 1807,

after abolition of the office of inspector-general, he became a member of the Navy Board and submitted further proposals for reform. In 1812 his post on the Navy Board was abolished. Then followed a prolonged struggle over compensation or pension. In 1814-1827 he retired and lived in France, but continued to make suggestions for naval improvements. He died in 1831. His biography was published by his widow, Maria Sophia Bentham (Life of Brigadier-General Sir Samuel Bentham, London, 1862).

2. His name and work are not included in my introductory account of eighteenth-century Western travelers in Siberia, published in my edition of Fries. Not until the summer of 1956, while I was studying in the Manuscript Department of the British Museum in London, did I come across Samuel Bentham's letters.

3. Matthew S. Anderson, "Samuel Bentham in Russia, 1779-1791," in: The American Slavic and East European Review, v. 15, no. 2 (1956), 139-172.

4. MSS., British Museum, London, 33.555, p. v.

5. MSS., British Museum, 33.539, vol. 169; 33.552, fols. 113 ff. About the Demidov family, cf. Roger Portal, L'Oural au XVIIIe siècle. Etude d'histoire économique et sociale, Paris, 1950, pp. 54 ff.; Fries, p. 102, n. 73.

6. MSS., British Museum, 33.539, fol. 257.

7. Ibid., 33.561, fols. 29 ff.

8. Ibid., 33.539, fol. 285.

9. Fries, p. 95.

10. MSS., British Museum, 33.555, fol. 1.

11. MSS., British Museum, 33.555, pp. vi, viii, ff. Cf. also 33.561, fols. 55 ff.

12. Ibid., 33.539, fol. 275.

13. Ibid., fol. 228. For the mines at Nerchinsk, cf. ibid., 33.552, fols. 262 ff.

14. Ibid., 33.555, pp. xii-xvi.

15. Ibid., p. xvii.

16. Ibid., 33.539, fol. 278. It may be questioned to what extent English inventors benefited from their work. Patent rights were often not enforced, royalty payments were not punctually made, and many inventors who themselves sought to exploit their inventions went bankrupt.

17. Ibid., 33.552, fol. 291.

18. See chapter 6.

19. MSS., British Museum, 33.539, fol. 275.

20. Ibid., 33.552, fol. 161.

21. Jean Chappe d'Auteroche (1722?-1769), A Journey into Siberia . . . in 1761, London, 1770 and 1772 (French ed.: Voyage en Sibérie, St. Pbg., 1770). Antidote (The), or An enquiry into the merits of a book entitled: A journey into Siberia made in 1761, by a Lover of Truth, London, 1772; cf. Chappe d'Auteroche. Cf. Fries, p. 21.

22. Written from Barnaul, MSS., British Museum, 33.552, fol. 271.

23. Parts of the journal excerpted in M. S. Bentham, Life of . . . Samuel Bentham.

24. MSS., British Museum, 33.552, fol. 190.

25. Ibid., fols. 211-24.

26. Ibid., 33.539, fol. 135.

27. Fries, p. 14.

28. MSS., British Museum, 33.552, fols. 262 ff.

29. Ibid., fols. 136, 202, 246, 273. Cf. Fries, p. 75.

30. MSS., British Museum, 33.552, fols. 228 ff. On Bentham's second journey to Siberia in 1789 to 1791, of which no important observations about the country are reported, he was accompanied by English sailors and officers, all of whom were unsuccessfully engaged on a plan for the establishment of transportation lines in the Arctic Ocean and the Sea of Okhotsk.

31. MSS., British Museum, 33.529, fol. 336.

32. Ibid., 33.552, fol. 241.

33. *Ibid.*, fol. 247. Cf. *Fries*, p. 95, n. 65. As a matter of fact, Russian policy had long been hesitant and a strict government monopoly had not been enforced for many years.

34. *MSS.*, British Museum, 33.529, fols. 307, 309 f., Cf. *Fries*, p. 85, n. 54 d.

35. Marshall Goldman, "The Relocation and Growth of the Pre-Revolutionary Russian Ferrous Metal Industry," *Explorations in Entrepreneurial History*, v. 9, 1956, p. 19.

36. Cf. Erich Laxmann, *Sibirische Briefe*, ed. August Ludwig Schlözer, Göttingen and Gotha, 1769. Also *Fries*, p. 22, n. 52.

37. Goldman, p. 23.

Chapter XII

1. In the late nineteenth century, American manufacturers heard that "everything is about the opposite of our way and the police force is the whole thing. They regulate everything . . ." as quoted in George S. Queen, "The McCormick Harvesting Machine Company in Russia," *Russian Review*, v. 23, 1964, p. 170. And "of all civilized countries, this is certainly the queerest on earth," *ibid.*, p. 173.

2. "Heinrich von Staden, Eine unbekannte Version der Beschreibung Nordrusslands," p. 134; and *Aufzeichnungen*, p. 266.

3. Alexander Gerschenkron, *Economic Backwardness in Historical Perspective*, Cambridge, Mass., 1962, pp. 60 *et passim*.

4. Fritz Redlich, "Der fürstliche Unternehmer, eine typische Erscheinung des 16. Jahrhunderts," *Tradition*, v. 3, 1958, pp. 17-32.

5. Amburger, "Zur Geschichte des Grosshandels in Russland"; Sergei Vladimirovich Bakhrushin, *Stat'i po eko-*

nomicheskoi, sotsial'noi i politicheskoi istorii russkogo tsentralizovannogo gosudarstva XV-XVII vv., Moscow, 1954 (his Nauchnye trudy, v. II).

6. Re attractions of rank, cf. the views of Samuel Bentham cited in chapter 11.

7. Afanasii Nikitin, Khozhenie za tri moria.

8. It may be noted that the Chinese surrounded themselves not only by a wall of stone but also by a linguistic wall. In the eighteenth century, the teaching of their language to foreign merchants was strictly prohibited. This played a role in the Russian-Chinese border trade as well as in political and trade negotiations.

9. William Ropes, Sr. and William H. Ropes to Hardy Ropes, St. Petersburg, May 25 and October 5, 1833, MSS., private collection of Mrs. Cabot Ropes, Boston Mass., to whom I herewith extend my thanks for kind permission to use her collection. On membership in the three guilds, cf., Herlihy, pp. 149 ff.

10. Messerschmidt (d 1735), Pallas (d. 1811), and Alexander von Humboldt (d. 1859) were among those scientists who were allowed to undertake their explorations only if they kept silence about everything the Russian government did not authorize for publication.

11. Besides numerous memoirs in French and Russian archives, cf. also Winterthur Collection of Manuscripts, Eleutherian Mills-Hagley Library, Wilmington, Delaware; see also chapter 7 of this book.

12. Kulischer, v. 1, p. 335

13. Amburger, Die Familie Marselis, pp. 105 f., 124 f., passim.

14. Price, pp. 62 ff., 67.

15. Willan, Russia Company, p. 273; Price, pp. 68 ff.

16. "A foreigner does not stand much of a show in Russia . ... before the courts," as quoted in Queen, p. 168. "To most American manufacturers business was not particularly attractive in a country where mortgages and estates seemed inseparable, where long credit terms were universal, and yet where foreigners reportedly found it almost impossible to collect debts," as quoted *ibid.*

BIBLIOGRAPHICAL INDEX

The bibliography indicates the page where the bibliographically complete title of literature used by the author is to be found; it contains the names of the authors, and for anonymous works and for symposia, the key word under which the publication is to be found in library catalogs.

NAME INDEX